RAISING
MONEY

Ron Merrill

Rick Sichor

RAISING MONEY

Venture Funding and How to Get It

Ronald E. Merrill
and
Gaylord E. Nichols

amacom
American Management Association

Library of Congress Cataloging-in-Publication Data

Merrill, Ronald E.
     *Raising money : venture funding and how to get it / Ronald E.
Merrill and Gaylord E. Nichols.*
          p.   cm.
     ISBN 0-8144-5966-8
     1. Venture capital. I. Nichols, Gaylord E. II. Title.
HG4751.M47   1990   89-46215
658.15'224—dc20   CIP

Printing number

10 9 8 7 6 5 4 3 2 1

For

Warren Howard Merrill

Wanda Merrill-Wahus

Teedo Nichols

Mike Nichols

Melinda Langston

Vickie Shelton

Contents

Foreword:
Rosen's Ten Rules

When I was at CalTech some thirty-odd years ago, and we were assigned, say, a physics problem, there more often than not was a unique answer to that problem. Well, the answer to a business problem may not be unique. In fact, in many cases, there is no answer.

Apparently many technology-based companies are unaware of the answers also. In personal computers, for instance, out of about 150 companies that have entered this field, only about a half dozen or so are solidly and consistently profitable with major market share: IBM, Apple, Compaq, Tandy, and one or two others. Some have even said that the personal computer industry is entering a new chapter: Chapter Eleven. Or, if you look at personal computer software since Microsoft started the business in 1976, there have been something like 17,000 software companies started, and again, only a handful of major profitable companies.

Tens of thousands of software companies and hundreds of personal computer companies have failed, losing well over a billion dollars in the last five years in these endeavors. Well, it may be okay for, say, an AT&T or a Japanese multinational to lose hundreds of millions of dollars entering this field; they can weather it. But it can be hazardous to the health of a venture capitalist or a start-up or a young technology company to lose millions of dollars. Our business in venture capital is to help entrepreneurs create new technology companies, bring new technologies to market; but we cannot survive if the odds against us are a thousand to one, or even a hundred to one. We have got to figure out a way of narrowing the odds.

Looking back at my own beginning in venture capital five years ago, I teamed up with L. J. Sevin who had just left as the cofounder and CEO of Mostek Corporation, a semiconductor company. After we raised our first $25 million in 1981 for our first fund, we made our first million dollar investment in a company named Synapse Computer, a fault-tolerant computer company that some time later went bankrupt. So, we regrouped and decided to invest a little less aggressively; we put $100,000 into a second-round investment in a company called Osborne Computer. Well, Osborne Computer went bankrupt, so we were off to a not very auspicious start. Those were our investments in 1981, our first year in the business.

We decided we were doing something wrong, so we got together and we said, "Okay, no more of this. We are going to invest only in seasoned entrepreneurs who have sound business strategies."

So, in early 1982, I called L. J., who was in Dallas, and said, "L. J., I just got a call from a friend of mine, Mitch Kapor, who wants to start a company to sell a new integrated spread-sheet-database-graphics program."

L. J. said, "Well, that's great. Software is an area we are interested in, but following our new rules, what is his background?"

"Well, he's been a teacher of transcendental meditation."

L. J. said, "Well, that sure beats our new profile. What else has he done to qualify to run a major software company?"

I said, "Well, he also has on his resumé that he was a disk jockey for two years."

We nonetheless invested, and Lotus went on to become the most successful start-up in personal computer software.

Shortly after that, L. J. called me and said, "Ben, I got a call from three fellows who just left Texas Instruments in Houston, and they want to start a personal computer business."

I said, "That's okay. That is a business we are interested in, but it is pretty competitive. What is their niche?"

"Well, they are not exactly a niche company."

"What is their business strategy?"

"They want to go head-on against IBM."

I said, "Well, there have certainly been hundreds of examples of companies that have successfully done that in history. How is their business plan documented?"

"Well, they don't exactly have a business plan."

"What do they have?"

"Well, they have some drawings."

"You mean the engineering drawings that show this new computer?"

"No, there is a place mat from the House of Pies and there is a sketch on the back of it that's got this portable computer."

Anyway, we invested in Compaq and that turned out to be a successful investment. They did $111 million their first year, a half billion their third year. The god of venture capital does move in mysterious ways.

I have been asked what it takes to go into venture capital. In New York State, where I live, you have to have a license to cut someone's hair, you have to have a license to drive a car, you need a license to own a dog. Well, in venture capital you can own a whole portfolio of dogs with no license whatsoever. There is real ease of entry in this business.

We learned early that while we usually don't repeat our major mistakes, we have been very creative about finding new mistakes to invent along the way, so we continue to have failures along with our successes. But one of the things we have learned from investing in over thirty high-technology companies in a five-year period is that there are some factors for success common to all of these companies. I believe these factors also apply to existing companies as well. So here are my personal rules for how to get to market in high technology.

Number one: Segment the market. There was a G.E. study some years ago that found most companies that have more than 30 percent market share in their market segment are consistently profitable. Those with shares of their market segment under 15 percent are invariably unprofitable. So it behooves a young company to segment the market so that it can find a segment small enough from which it can get a significant market share.

Let's take the semiconductor industry as an example of how to and how not to enter the marketplace. When L. J. and I started the company (he as a former semiconductor CEO and I as a former semiconductor analyst), our first vow was that we would never invest in a semiconductor start-up. We could not see any strategy for competing against the American giants of Texas Instruments, Intel, Motorola, and National, and also the oncoming Japanese onslaught in semiconductors.

Yet we did finally invest in the semiconductor business. When T. J. Rogers came to us, he proposed to segment the market into thirty-million-dollar segments. His company, Cypress Semiconductor, set the goal of taking a large share of the very high-performance market. The company started in 1982, went public in 1989, is shipping at over a fifty-million-dollar rate, is very profitable, and grew consistently through the semiconductor slump.

The personal computer industry is replete with corporate corpses because most of the 150 companies that have entered the personal computer field did not segment the market initially; they just went broadly at the desktop market where IBM was dominant, and found it was very difficult to gain enough share to become profitable.

By contrast, despite my earlier comments, the strategy that Compaq used was indeed to segment the market. We initially went after the portable personal computer market, which at the time was under 10 percent of the total market. IBM wasn't in the business at the time and we were able to gain a dominant share of the portable market, which we still enjoy. Because we got so strong there, we were able to successfully fight off IBM's later entry into the portable. In fact, IBM even withdrew its product. Plus, dominating the portables segment at that time provided the company with a beachhead from which to attack another segment, the high-performance personal computer market. We are now successfully competing with a family of 286- and recently 386-based personal computers.

Number two: Look for an unfilled market need. Any of you who go to trade shows find thousands of products, most of which the world doesn't seem to want. Again, looking at personal computers, we have seen many variations for which there are no significant needs. Mindset was a company in personal computers that had a graphics-oriented unit that was too expensive for home use and not functional enough for business use. The company went out of business. Gavilan had a very expensive, incompatible, laptop computer. Even such splendid companies as Hewlett-Packard have stumbled. HP's initial entry featured a touch screen. But there weren't an awful lot of people who wanted to interface with their computer by touching the screen. So, that was not a successful product. T.I. tried to introduce voice recognition as their gimmick. Technology at the time wasn't far enough advanced, so there wasn't a big need for that. We started a software company called Menlo, which makes a friendly front-end for information databases. It turned out that it was "friendly" to very few people, and the company soon went out of business. So, you have got to find an unfilled market need that is significant enough to support a new company.

It is hard to discern a need and a technology one or two years in advance, that is, one that is also unlikely to be filled by a major competitor. However, I think, some of the companies in our portfolio have done this successfully. Calera Recognition Systems, a company started by some CalTech alumni three years ago, is just starting to ship an omnifont document reader using some major new technology. We think this is going to meet a tremendous market need. Convex Computer was started three years ago in the scientific computer field, and started shipping late last year. They have been very successful in that area. To be successful, companies have to anticipate customer needs several years in advance.

How do you discern a future need? Established companies typically use market research techniques. These are generally okay if you can afford them, but often small companies cannot. Also, the risk in market research is that if you ask the wrong question you get the wrong answer. Just ask Ford, whose market researchers told them that the Edsel was the car everyone wanted. Ask Coca-Cola, which found out from its market research that the world wanted New Coke. So, it is very easy to be misguided. In our companies, we rely more on the founder's intuition to discern these needs. Also, we ask ourselves when we are investing, "Is this the kind of product that *I* would like to use?" In fact, some of our most successful investments have involved products that we have fallen in love with. We represent a small sample, admittedly, but it seems to work.

One risk in technology start-ups is that companies tend to be technology driven. Usually, it is a group of engineers who get together and want to start a company. They very often are tempted to employ new technologies there simply because the technologies exist. It's the Mt. Everest theory: You put it in because it is there. Then you find products that too early employ such functions as bubble memory, touch screen, or voice recognition when the technology is really not ready yet. In our venture capital portfolio, our motto is: We will introduce no technology before its time.

Number three: Produce a significantly superior product. Now, that sounds like a given. Bill Davidow, who is ex-Intel, says that "slightly better" is dangerous. That is true; if you want to enter the marketplace, you cannot enter it with a slightly better product. It has to be a step function different.

Lotus successfully competed against VisiCalc because 1-2-3 was a step-function improvement over VisiCalc. The sixty companies that have tried subsequently to compete with 1-2-3 have not had step-function differences and have not been able to dislodge 1-2-3 from its leadership position.

IBM entered the portable personal computer market fifteen months after Compaq. Its product wasn't sufficiently different to dislodge Compaq from its leadership position.

Today, there are many personal computer companies that are trying to enter the market with products that functionally are no different (or, in fact, often subsets of what is already available), and their marketing strategy is to sell the same functionality at a lower price. That generally is a losing strategy in the long term because there is always someone out there who will sell it at an even lower price.

Why is it necessary to have a product that is so much better? Why can't you be just slightly better? It turns out that most corporations that buy products today have corporate standards, approved lists, and a lot of inertia; it is very hard to get someone to change. There are so many costs associated with change: the cost of evaluating a new product, inventorying a new product, training people in the new products, supporting a new product, and new documentation. It just is not worth the trouble for something that is only slightly better.

In addition to superiority, there are some other attributes of products you want. It is always nice to be first. If you are first, you become the corporate standard, and you acquire the shelf space either at the buyer or at the dealer level. If you are first, it is a much lower cost to enter the market than if you try to dislodge someone who is already established.

As an example, because the Compaq portable was first, we were able to get in there at low cost and protect our position. It was the same with 1-2-3. It was also the same with Convex in the affordable supercomputer field against, now, twenty competitors.

By contrast, we introduced another product with one of our companies, Ansa Software. The product is called Paradox and it is a relational database management system. The product, in my own unbiased evaluation, is clearly better, easier to use, and faster than its major competitor, dBase. A lot of independent evaluations have supported this. dBase was introduced seven years ago, six years earlier than we introduced Paradox. Well, it is much more challenging to penetrate a market when your competitor—whatever the merits of the product—has been there for six years. Paradox is doing well; we achieved in our first year $10 million in sales, which is second only to Lotus. Nonetheless, with all that success, we are still only one-tenth the size of our competitor. That just shows you how hard it is to make a penetration against someone who is established early.

Another desirable attribute of a product strategy is that you want to obsolete yourself. Don't wait for your competitor to obsolete you. VisiCalc was an example of a company that did not upgrade its product and allowed 1-2-3 to come in and displace it.

It is also desirable to have a proprietary product. Of course, we all know about Polaroid dominating instant photography, and Xerox with the Carlson patent dominating xerography for at least the life of the patent. But that kind of dominance is hard to achieve today. Technology changes too fast. By the time you get a patent and try to enforce it, the technology is two generations later. We think the best proprietary edge for a high-technology company is six months lead time, and that leads to the fourth element of success.

Number four: Follow through with good execution. You live with the thrill of meeting schedule and the agony of slippage. The ability to bring out reliable products on time as promised is critical to a new company's success. Schedule slippage can be a sure road to failure for a small company. Even for a large company it means share loss. When Hewlett-Packard was six months late with its Spectrum Computer, it cost them an estimated $200 million. That was not fatal for HP; it is a $7 billion company. When you slip in a small company, it's not just that you lose share or lose competitive advantage; it means more typically that you run out of money and you go out of business.

Number five: Have a winning selling strategy. An oft-heard sales strategy among all of our entrepreneurs is the following: "This product is so good it is going to sell itself." We have yet to find one succeed with this approach.

Selling in the technology business is a lot different from selling in the consumer business. In the consumer business, you spend a large part of your sales on advertising, on promotion, on packaging, and on creating pull. The consumer actually pulls the product from the manufacturer through the distribution channel into his or her hands. In technology, it is different. Usually you, the manufacturer, must push the product. You push it through the distribution channel, through the direct sales force or the dealer. You push it by having service, by having post-sales support, product documentation, training, customer education, and application support. Contrast this with the consumer area where there is little product documentation and little post-sales support (for example, if you were selling toothpaste).

Another contrast is that in consumer selling, just the advertising alone often sells the product. Well, while there is advertising in the technology business, it very rarely sells the product. What advertising does is create awareness, and create in the potential user a desire to learn more.

The technology sale is often multitiered. You are selling the engineer, you are selling the purchasing agent, and very important, you are selling management. So you need selling strategies that cater to all three tiers.

An impediment to the high-technology sale, as I mentioned earlier, is inertia in the system because it is so costly to change whatever you are doing. In the consumer business, it is not. The typical teenage girl changes shampoo brands four times a year, and she can do this with impunity because if she does not like a particular shampoo, she can throw it away and buy something else. Well, if you are a buyer of spreadsheets for a corporation that has 1,000 personal computers, you don't lightly change from 1-2-3 or whatever to something else. The training time and the cost of shifting is just too onerous.

Number six: Communicate information from the manufacturer to the customer. Traditionally you think of market communications as simply informing the potential customer about the nature of the product or the service. But, more important, it builds credibility for the company. You can sell the engineer with the specifications of the product, but you also want to sell top management. If you are a new company, they want to know: "Are you going to be around in five years? Are you credible? Are you well financed?" You have to communicate positive answers to these questions. Otherwise, you are just not going to make this sale because customers are aware of the statistics about how many new companies go out of business. No one wants to buy a product that shortly is going to be an orphan.

You can do this through advertising, or you can do it through public relations. For smaller companies, it is much more cost effective to use public relations than advertising. A full-blown public relations budget costs in the low six figures, while advertising is in seven figures and not always in the *low* seven figures. Also, public relations tends to be more credible: You are getting a third party to attest to the qualities of your product and your company as opposed to a paid advertisement. Articles tend to be more believable than ads. So, all of our companies actively, from day one, engage in a public relations program.

We aim to level the playing field; our much larger competitors have advertising budgets ten to one hundred times larger than ours.

By public relations, I don't mean just sending out press releases; that is probably the least effective method. It is establishing long-term relationships with whatever industry you are in with the tastemakers and the influencers, and you do this for a year or two before you introduce your product. This is the business press, the trade press, the technical press, industry luminaries, consultants, reference accounts, and financial analysts. You make speeches, you go to conferences, all of this to get the word of mouth going about your company and about your product. Word of mouth is probably the single most important factor in a successful sale by a new technology company.

When we launched Lotus 1-2-3 on October 14, 1982, that wasn't the launch of the product; it was really the end of our communications program. We started it six months earlier by seeding beta versions of 1-2-3 with analysts, with consultants, with the press, with corporate buyers, with anyone we could find to let them know about the product. The press conference was the culmination of all of this so, when the product was announced, the world knew about 1-2-3.

We also have a Big Bang method. When Compaq introduced its DeskPro 386 Computer, we did it around the world in twelve cities simultaneously, and the New York introduction was at the Palladium, the largest disco in the city. It was the first time a lot of people had ever been to a disco at ten o'clock in the morning, but it was very effective and we got tremendous press coverage worldwide for that announcement.

Marketing communications is also important in helping you position the product the way *you* want to position it. For instance, when Convex started to build the scientific computer, the outside world was positioning this as a super-mini, a product, say, at the upper end of the DEC VAX line. Well, there are about thirty companies in the super-mini area, and that really was not the way we wanted to be considered. So through various effective marketing communications, we repositioned the product as what it truly was: an "affordable" supercomputer. So, instead of being positioned with thirty-odd companies at the lower end of the scale, we positioned Convex with Cray at the upper end of the scale. And, similarly, we had repositioned Compaq from its original role as a portable computer company to a high-performance personal computer company.

In summary, it is very noisy out there; you need effective marketing communication to rise above the noise level to get your product and your corporate message heard.

Number seven: Marshal maximum financial resources to compete. You can get money for your new technology company in a variety of ways: You can get it from the bank, you can get it from relatives, you can get it from your own personal resources, you can bootstrap it. You can do it by having alliances with larger companies. Many software companies unable to get venture capital are either getting acquired or forming marketing alliances with established software companies. Another way is to go to your friendly neighborhood venture capitalist.

Venture capitalists tend to invest in the hundreds of thousands to millions of dollars. From the viewpoint of the recipient, the benefit in getting a large amount of money at the start is that you can grow more rapidly than if you try to bootstrap it. Lotus could never have gotten to $53 million its first year had it not raised $4.7 million in venture capital its first year. Compaq could never have done $111 million in its first year of operations had it not raised $30 million in venture capital, a large amount at the time.

The disadvantage, of course, is that the founder has to give up more equity than if he or she raises the money by borrowing. There are trade-offs involved, and that is something the entrepreneur has to decide himself or herself. And then, of course, there are some entrepreneurs who just don't like dealing with venture capitalists. I cannot understand why!

But maybe it is explained by the story of the rabbi, the Hindu, and the venture capitalist walking along the farm road one night looking for a night's lodging. They saw a farmhouse, knocked on the door, and said to the farmer, "We would like a place to sleep." The farmer said, "Well, I have a bedroom that sleeps two, so one of you will have to sleep in the barn." The Hindu said, "Oh, that's no problem, I'll go sleep in the barn." So the rabbi got in one bed, the venture capitalist got in the other, and the Hindu went to sleep in the barn. A few minutes later there was a knock at the bedroom door. It was the Hindu. He said, "There's a cow in the barn, and my principles and scruples do not permit me to sleep in the same place as a cow." The rabbi said, "Oh, that's all right, I'll go sleep in the barn." So, the Hindu got in the bed, and the rabbi went to sleep in the barn. A few minutes later, there was a knock on the bedroom door. It was the rabbi. He said, "There is a pig in the barn, and of course my principles and scruples do not allow me to sleep in the same place as a pig." So, the venture capitalist said, "All right, I'll sleep in the barn." So, the rabbi got in the bed, and the Hindu got in the other, and the venture capitalist went off to the barn. A few minutes later there was a knock at the bedroom door. It was the pig and the cow. Now, I don't know how stories like that get started. . . .

Venture capitalists try to offer the entrepreneur more than just money. In many cases, we are involved in incubating a starting company. Kleiner Perkins started Genentech, the most successful genetic engineering company, in its office with one of its partners as CEO. They also started Tandem Computers—the inventor of fault-tolerant computers—that same way, in their office. We started Convex Computer in our office, along with Merit Technology and Cypress Semiconductor. So we really get involved in the creation of the company very often. Plus, we are involved in recruiting and dealing with such outside agencies as law firms, investment bankers, commercial bankers, accounting firms, ad agencies, and PR agencies. We also get involved in the strategy and the planning of the companies. So, there are a lot of services that we try to provide.

A rule we have among our companies is: The companies should always raise more money than they think they should because companies always underestimate the amount of cash they take. The sales cycle is always longer, the development is more complicated, and you tend to run out of cash unless you raise enough at the start. Also, it is always worthwhile giving up more equity in order to raise more cash for the safety margin because you cannot raise money when you need to. As we all know, banks only give you money when you don't need it, and that is sometimes true of venture capitalists as well.

The cash forecasts are too optimistic, and the sales cycles

are longer than expected from the financial forecast. The financial forecast is always off; the problem is that we never know in which direction. Usually it errs in the wrong way, but Lotus's business plan, on the basis of which we funded them, called for first-year sales of $3 million, and they ended up shipping $53 million. This is a company that makes financial forecasting software! Compaq forecasted $20 million its first year, and did $111 million. But most companies go the other way.

Financial resources alone, while important, do not ensure success in any business. Certainly, the personal computer business is replete with examples of companies with tens of millions of dollars in financing that ended up as massive failures.

Number eight: Create an effective organization both managerially and structurally. Now, "managerially" means you have to start at the top with the right people. The problem, as you have seen from our people who are either disk jockeys, transcendental meditation instructors, or come from a variety of other backgrounds, is that none of them has ever run a company before. So, we have to take a chance on them to see whether or not they can run a company. There is really no uniform role model, but it is very important that you try to get the right person to run the company at the beginning. In some cases, we are successful in telling the founder that if he or she doesn't look like he or she can be or should be the CEO, to instead become the chief technical officer. We did this in the case of Convex. The founder of the company is now very successful as the vice president of technology. The founder of Ansa Software is now the vice president of software and never wanted to be CEO. On the other hand, Lotus, Cypress, Compaq, and a host of others have grown very successfully with their original technical founders as the chief executive officers.

With respect to structure, most technology companies are very small relative to their established competition. It is amazing to me that any small company can succeed at all in business today, particularly in technology, because the odds are so stacked against you. The disadvantages are enormous. You start a new company. No one has ever heard of you. You have no brand awareness. You have very little credibility because so many small companies go out of business. Your marketing costs are dwarfed by those of your competitor ten to one or a hundred to one; the competitor can put ten feet on the street for every one you can. The R&D budgets of your larger competitors are an order of magnitude higher. And worst of all, the small company is allowed just a single failure. You fail once and typically you go out of business, while a large company can fail many times with impunity.

Nonetheless, the advantages of a small company override those disadvantages. One of the most important advantages is that the decision-making speed is so much greater in a small company than in a large one. There are fewer layers of management, and there is more urgency in making the decision. Intuitive decisions are more permissible; you don't have to justify your decisions as much in a small company. You can attract creative talent easily with the financial incentives you have by offering equity. You can also offer the professional incentive that an individual in a small company can very often affect the destiny of his or her company, which is very hard to do in a large company. You can use your top management in sales in a small company. In the early days of Intel, Bob Noyce went out on sales calls. At Advanced Micro Devices, Jerry Sanders went out on sales calls. At Apple, Steve Jobs went out on sales calls. It is very effective when you are competing against a large company where the CEO rarely makes individual sales calls.

And, finally, there is a very fast design cycle. At Compaq, we can go from conception to marketing a new computer in a six- to twelve-month period. Our new DeskPro 386 was shipping in volume twelve months after we started development. That is hard to do in a larger company as evidenced by the fact that IBM's 386 machine was introduced much later than ours. It is just an infinitely great advantage for a small company to have that speed of design cycle.

The results of these advantages are that the venture-backed (and even the nonventure-backed), technology-based entrepreneurial companies are the most innovative, the most productive, the most job-creating parts of our economy today. They are also some of our great hopes in the international competitive battle in which we are engaged. This sector of the economy in the last couple of decades has been responsible for new technologies, new products, and indeed, entire new industries. This sector has created the personal computer, which is now a $20 billion a year industry, an industry in which the United States leads the world. It created the whole applications software business, the minicomputer business (Digital Equipment), the fault-tolerant computer business (Tandem), and the microprocessor (Intel). The microprocessor is the seminal product from which almost everything technological is built today. It has helped commercialize genetic engineering, one of the major new industries of the next couple of decades. So it is absolutely vital and important to the country.

Fortunately for our country, this venture-backed, technology-based entrepreneurial sector is a uniquely American phenomenon. Whenever I go visiting other countries, no one ever beats up on me by saying or implying things such as: "Boy, what a lousy steel industry you have," or, "Why is your auto industry so far behind?" They always say things such as: "How can we start another Silicon Valley? How can we get these entrepreneurs to go out and start companies?"

Well, one reason we can do it, and it is so hard to do elsewhere, has historical roots: For two hundred years we have had an entrepreneurial culture, a culture that allows people to take risks and allows people to fail without stigma. That is not true in Europe; it is not true in Japan.

We also have the most liquid and the deepest capital markets, private markets such as venture capital as well as public markets that allow these companies to raise large sums of money subsequently, and provide an exit for the original investors.

We have the broadest technology base, and something else keeps feeding this: We have so many role models now. Young engineers or programmers see a Mitch Kapor, a Bill Gates, a Steve Jobs, or a Rod Canion, and many of them knew these people when they were working on a bench next to them. So they say: "Boy, I'm as smart as he is; I can do that," and indeed many of them go out and try it.

It is important that as the entrepreneurial companies grow, they maintain this small, flexible, rapid decision-making structure, and not get hardening of the corporate arteries as they become large. Also, it is a challenge to all of us, as our companies grow large, to keep this "small is beautiful" syndrome.

It is also important, I think, for large companies to try to emulate this, and some are doing it extremely successfully. The single best example is what IBM has done. In 1980, they created an "Independent Business Unit," divorced from corporate, in Boca Raton, with twelve people. That gave birth to the IBM personal computer. This is a way in which a large company can try to emulate what small companies are doing with one exception: the ability to give significant equity ownership for that group.

As our small companies grow large, we can do things, too. Lotus, for instance, is starting to invest in people who are leaving the company instead of losing them totally. By contrast, Intel has lost many entrepreneurs as has Fairchild Semiconductor. Instead of losing them, they should just recognize that some people are always going to leave. The managements of these companies are beginning to realize this and take equity interests in their spinoff companies.

At Compaq, what we have done recently is, in effect, go into the venture capital business ourselves. We have just taken a minority interest in an innovative new disk drive company. So, there are a variety of ways that both small and large companies can preserve this unique structure, which is so innovative and productive.

Number nine: Do things at the right time. Lotus 1-2-3 was timed perfectly for the advent of the sixteen-bit personal computer. Had it been offered earlier, no computer could have done all of the wonderful things that 1-2-3 does. Had it been later, as many 1-2-3 clones are, it would have been *too* late because the leader would have been too well established.

It is also important from a timing viewpoint to recognize that timing can offer both opportunities and hazards. If technology changes, opportunities change also. As we went from the vacuum tube era to the semiconductor era, the erstwhile leaders in vacuum tubes (RCA, GE, Raytheon, Sylvania) were totally replaced by new names who saw this opportunity and had no costs sunk in tubes. Now you have names like Texas Instruments, Motorola, Intel, National Semiconductor, and others.

The same thing happened as mainframes went to minis. With the exception of IBM, such companies as Honeywell, Sperry, NCR, and Burroughs missed the mini market, which is dominated by DEC, Data General, Hewlett-Packard, Prime, and others. Again, as minis evolved into personal computers, with the exception of IBM, the mainframe and the mini companies had so much inertia, they didn't realize the technology was changing. So the micro market now is dominated (in addition to IBM) by such companies as Apple, Compaq, Tandy, and others. There have been similar transitional technology changes accompanied by leadership changes, for example, as calculators went from mechanical to electronic, as the pharmaceutical industry went to genetic engineering, and as telecommunications went from land-line to satellite.

Finally, there is a tenth factor in success.

Number ten: Be lucky. That factor is ephemeral. It is uncontrollable and hard to find, but it is always welcome. It is something that I wish all of you in your ventures.

Benjamin Rosen
Partner, Sevin Rosen Management Company

Acknowledgments

In preparing this book, we interviewed a variety of venture capitalists and other investors, as well as attorneys, accountants, and other experts on the venture financing process. We wish to thank the following people who gave generously of their time to instruct us: Tom Austin of Digital Equipment Corporation; John Baldeschwieler, professor of chemistry at the California Institute of Technology; Jim Cheney, former vice chairman of Community Bank of Pasadena, now a private investor; Chuck Cole, partner at Julian, Cole & Stein; Ken Deemer, general partner with InterVen Partners; Terry Dibble, partner at Peat Marwick Main & Co.; Anthony Hoberman, senior vice-president of Alliance Capital Management Corp.; Craig Isom, partner at Arthur Andersen & Co.; Bob Johnson, formerly partner at Southern California Ventures, now a private investor; David B. Jones, general partner at InterVen Partners and former chairman of the National Association of Small Business Investment Companies; Jim Julian, partner at Julian, Cole, & Stein; Richard Lufkin, president of Medical Marketing Specialties; Lieb Orlanski, partner in the law firm Freshman, Marantz, Orlanski, Cooper, & Klein; Thomas H. Peterson, El Dorado Ventures; Harry Sedgwick, private investor and entrepreneur; Tom Tisch of MBW Management; Thomas Turney, partner at NewCap Partners; John Wilson, principal at Touche Ross & Co.; and Thomas Winter, general partner at Burr, Egan, Deleage, & Co. Of course neither they nor anyone else should be held responsible for any possible errors in the text, which are wholly our own.

Several entrepreneurs kindly granted us permission to quote from their business plans, and we gratefully recognize Brian Berman of PAX Modular Systems, Mike Powell of CIM Software, and others who remain anonymous but not unappreciated.

We also wish to thank the members of the Executive Committee of the CalTech/MIT Enterprise Forum, as well as the many entrepreneurs and other participants in the Forum who have (sometimes unwittingly) enriched this book by providing us with the fruits of their practical experience. From their struggles, successful and unsuccessful, we have attempted to distil maxims that will assist new generations of entrepreneurs.

RAISING MONEY

Introduction

We know entrepreneurs. Lots of entrepreneurs. Over the years we've been involved with hundreds of them. They've told us about all sorts of new companies—ultrahigh-tech ventures building state-of-the-art computer hardware, a company to make stronger packing crates, an inventor with an improved type of disposable razor, another with a little gadget for making fog, bicycles, boats, biotechnology—you name it, we've seen it. Big ventures with a dozen industry experts on the team, and little ventures run by a single person off her kitchen table, and every size in between—we've encountered all sizes and shapes. The diversity is incredible. But there's one thing all these entrepreneurs seem to have in common: an intense interest in raising money for their ventures.

The American system is called capitalism for a very good reason: To nurture the myriad new companies that are the fountainhead of our economic strength requires a continuous flow of risk capital. Whatever the venture, be it an Apple Computer or a lemonade stand, a certain amount of money has to be put up to get it going. Raising that capital is the first task of the entrepreneur, and it isn't always as easy as asking Mommy to buy you some lemons and sugar and lend you a pitcher. That's why we wrote this book.

Who Can Benefit From This Book

If you are already filthy rich and starting a little company just to while away the weary hours, if you can reach into your pocket

1

and come up with all the money you need for your business, we
can't honestly say that you need this book.

Most entrepreneurs are not so fortunate. Chances are you
are going to need outside financing of some sort. Whatever kind
of company you are starting, and whatever kind of financing you
have in mind, we can help you get the necessary funding. Raising
money is a *marketing* task; you must take the initiative to *sell
financiers on investing in your company*. That's what this book
is about.

We've Got Some Good News and Some Bad News . . .

The good news is that you have more options for raising money,
and better chances of success, than ever before. The entrepreneurial explosion of the 1980s has forced the expansion of
traditional funding sources and created brand-new ones. Where
once there were only a few venture capital funds, today there
are hundreds, with new ones being formed almost weekly.
Commercial banks, which once were downright hostile to new
ventures, are now increasingly interested in tapping this vibrant
market segment. Private investor networks and venture capital
clubs continue to form. Investors of nearly all types are far more
receptive to entrepreneurial ventures and show a much greater
flexibility and willingness to do innovative deals.

Now, the bad news. All these changes have made the
financing process increasingly complex. Many of the old rules
no longer apply. It's quite possible to get lost in the bewildering
array of new financial options. Some funding sources have
become heavily regulated, and a single false step can land you
in legal trouble. Other financing routes are so wide open that
choosing the wrong person to deal with can get you taken to the
cleaners.

What's more, the competition is stronger than ever. There
are more entrepreneurs out there approaching the same funding
sources. Not only that; your competition is more savvy, more
sophisticated. Ten years ago, many would-be entrepreneurs
were so naive they didn't even understand the need for a
business plan. Today, your plan will share a venture capitalist's

desk with many other well-written plans. It takes a better plan, and a better presentation, to get funded in today's environment. You must understand the new realities and be prepared to handle the challenges involved.

What We Cover

This book provides you with a detailed road map of the entire money-raising process. From developing the business plan to negotiating the final agreement, we cover every step. Among the many specific points we'll discuss are:

- How to write an Executive Summary that will keep your business plan out of the venture capitalist's circular file.
- The Five Key Questions your business plan must answer.
- How to locate, and arrange introductions to, investors who specialize in companies like yours.
- Understanding "due diligence" and making it work for you instead of against you.
- How to spot—and how to deal with—five-percenters and flaky "investors."
- The pros and cons of approaching several investors at once.
- Grace under pressure, or how to field investor questions.
- Building a strong relationship with the investor without coming on too strong.
- How to negotiate an acceptable deal with tough venture capitalists.

We have endeavored to fill this book with practical, specific advice, not just abstract generalizations. For material, we have drawn on our extensive experience with the CalTech/MIT Enterprise Forum. More than four dozen companies have presented their plans at our sessions, and these case studies provide a rich lode of tangible, real-life lessons on the money-raising process. In addition to the formal presenters, hundreds of other entrepreneurs attend Enterprise Forum sessions, and we have learned much from their experience also.

To ensure that our subject is scrutinized from every perspective, we have also drawn on the advice of experts on the venture funding process, including the investors themselves. In the following pages you'll find comments and specific suggestions from some of the shrewdest people in the business—partners at Big Eight accounting firms, top attorneys specializing in financial deals, leading venture capitalists. They'll show you the view from the other side of the table.

We have placed a strong emphasis on venture capital funding because the process for these deals generally requires more sophisticated handling. However, we also cover many other types of financing so that you can understand and exploit different alternatives. After all, only a tiny minority of business start-ups are financed by venture capital.

At the back of the book you'll find a glossary to help you out with any unfamiliar terms you may encounter. We've also provided, in the appendixes, some typical deal documents so that you can see what they look like and learn from them.

A Journey of a Thousand Miles . . .

Getting financing for your company can be a long, difficult process. There is a lot of work involved. But if you know your way through the financial jungle, your journey will be far less frustrating—and the odds are you'll find the money you need in the end.

1

Doing Your Homework

The overarching theme of this book is the need to build a relationship with investors. But this relationship is unlikely to be successful unless it has a strong foundation—and that foundation is information. Few investors—certainly not professional investors such as venture capitalists—will put money into your business just because you are a nice person. They want to know the facts about you and your venture.

To make a rational decision on your proposal, the investor will need to know a number of crucial facts. What is your business? What makes it different? What is your plan? How good will sales be? How good will profits be? What are the risks? And wishes, guesses, or gut-feel estimates will not be good enough. The shrewd investor (and investors can be very shrewd indeed) will demand *facts*—solid, specific, quantitative facts that can be supported and backed up.

This demand for facts will be used directly to evaluate your venture, but it will also be used indirectly to evaluate *you*. Do you have your feet on the ground, or are you an impractical dreamer? Do you take the trouble to think ahead and plan, or do you try to wing it? Are you a hardworking type who does the necessary homework, or are you a basically lazy person who skimps on effort and hopes things will come out right somehow? Can you look at facts objectively and be prepared for setbacks, or has your emotional commitment to your venture blinded you to the risks?

Believe it or not, in raising money it's what you know, not whom you know, that ultimately counts. Venture capitalists often rely on referrals, it's true. A strong recommendation from a friend or colleague can get you in the door, but it won't get you the check. To get your hands on the money, you're going to have to demonstrate that you know what you're talking about.

So the very first step in the money-raising process is to *do your homework*. Taking the trouble to come up with all the necessary information in advance can make the difference between success and failure in dealing with investors. What's more, it can save you a lot of embarrassing moments. An interview with a venture capitalist is much like an oral exam; to be hit with a question you can't answer is not only frustrating, it's humiliating.

The Five Key Questions

Every business is unique. A biotechnology firm must be handled differently from a frozen fish distributor. And every financing is unique. Raising venture capital for an electronics startup requires a different approach from getting a bank loan for the expansion of its manufacturing plant eight years later. So it's not easy to come up with a general approach that can be universally applied. Yet all businesses have certain things in common: the need for sales, the existence of competition, the importance of management. From these factors we have developed a basic outline for your business homework.

The Five Key Questions

1. Who are your customers?
2. What do your customers need and want?
3. What are you selling, and why will it satisfy your customers?
4. Who are you, and why can you beat the competition?
5. How much money will it take to accomplish your business goals, and how much money will your business make?

These are broad questions with deep ramifications. To answer them properly takes a lot of digging and no small amount of thoughtful analysis. But once you've thoroughly prepared answers to these five questions, you're ready for just about anything an investor can throw at you. So let's look at them, one by one, in detail.

First, the Customer

Too often we take customers for granted. In spite of exhortations by management experts from Peter Drucker to Tom Peters, in spite of advice from dozens of best-sellers, in spite of decades of magazine articles, seminars, and workshops, very few businesspeople know exactly who their customers are, let alone what they want.

Many novice entrepreneurs have spent their entire working lives in the bowels of a big organization. Middle managers or engineers or clerks, they deal day by day with the internal operations of the corporation; actual selling is merely a vague rumble off in the distance. Like generals who have never visited the trenches, they are apt to underestimate the difficulties of the endless battle for customers. (Entrepreneurs coming from a sales background should not be too smug. A big company provides heavy marketing support for its salespeople, which they too often take for granted.)

An existing company has sales inertia. Over the years it has built up a steady clientele of customers who for one reason or another regularly buy its products or services. Whether because of good experience, brand loyalty, or simple habit, customers tend to stick with certain vendors. For the employee of a stable company a certain level of sales appears to be almost a given of the business. But a new company doesn't have this advantage. As an entrepreneur you will probably have to build up sales from scratch. If you've never done it before, you may find it a novel, shocking, even frightening experience. Your selling problems are not only greater than, but different in kind from, those of an existing company.

A company with established sales will tend to view the

market simply as all those who, by historical accident, have become customers. The company will therefore try to build on sales to this group and to extend its customer base to similar people.

The new company faces an entirely different task. You must decide what group to target for your customer base. Who are the most profitable customers? Who are the customers you can find and sell to cheaply—and quickly? Above all, who are the customers most likely to buy from your new company rather than stick with established sources?

As you can no doubt perceive, the answer to "Who is your customer?" is not so simple. Let's look at the key factors involved in answering it. Your market research should begin by investigating four key issues: market definition, market segmentation, market characterization, and market growth.

Market Definition

Too many business plans simply assert something like, "There's a strong market for pornographic stained-glass windows." This sort of vague claim is unconvincing. Worse, it can raise a red flag about the entrepreneur's basic attitude. To speak of a "market" as if it were some sort of impersonal machine that automatically devours a certain type of good or service suggests a detached, unrealistic marketing approach. Customers are central to business, and customers are people.

Who buys pornographic stained-glass windows? Pool halls? Avant-garde churches? Yuppie bachelors in Manhattan? The first task of market definition is to specify the group (or groups) of people who buy or at least might buy the product.

Market definition is the root of sales planning. Until you know *who* buys, you can't figure out *how many* customers there are, nor can you determine *how much* a typical customer buys. But once you have a market definition, you can start to develop these numbers, and from them you can calculate *market size*. That's a very important figure for investors. Later you can calculate what proportion of that market you can secure—your *market share*. That's an even more crucial figure.

Many entrepreneurs don't understand how investors look at

market share. Most business plans project that the venture will take a very small share of a very large market. The idea is that the big market will be attractive to venture capitalists because it allows room for tremendous growth and that the small market share will look conservative and easy to attain. After all, 2 percent of a $5 billion market is $100 million in sales—and getting a little tiny sliver like 2 percent will be easy, right?

Wrong. In real life, a company with 2 percent of a $5 billion market is generally a has-been on its way to bankruptcy. The big entrepreneurial successes have been companies that grabbed a dominant share of a small but fast-growing market and then grew with the market. That's what investors are looking for.

In talking to venture capitalists, we found differing rules of thumb on which they rely. One firm wants to see a projected market share in the 10 to 20 percent range. On the other hand, another venture capitalist points out that "there's research indicating that companies with over 30 percent market share are profitable, and companies with under 15 percent are unprofitable." To claim that you're going to have 90 or 100 percent of the market may be overdoing it, but certainly investors will want to see you aiming to be dominant, or at least a major player, in the market you have selected.

In general, your plan will have the most credibility, at least with venture capitalists, if you follow these rules:

1. Define and target a relatively small market.
2. Select a market that is growing rapidly.
3. Project your company taking a major share of that market.
4. Develop a convincing market strategy for becoming one of the strongest players in your market.

What if there is more than one type of customer for the goods or services you plan to sell? This is, in fact, quite commonly the case. You must then concern yourself with the next factor—market focus.

Market Segmentation

A few decades ago, market segmentation was a topic seldom considered. In the simple economy of the 1940s and 1950s, most markets were pretty homogeneous. For instance, the consumer family could reasonably be assumed to be the traditional one where Dad worked, Mom was a housewife, and the kids went to school. Today, traditional families are a much smaller fraction of the population. The consumer market is fractured into divorcés, cohabiting couples, stepfathers, retirees, and all sorts of other family types, each with its own special needs and wants for consumer items from housing to clothes cleaning.

You can't plan your marketing strategy until you understand the segmentation of your market. There are many ways to segment markets, not all of which may be relevant to your specific case. Here are some of the segmentation axes you should consider.

Obviously, you should first classify the market by type of customer. Are you selling to businesses? Or to individuals? Or, perhaps, to both?

> For instance, much low-end office equipment, such as personal computers and inexpensive copiers, is now sold to individuals for home office use. This is a rapidly expanding market. But selling to a home office user is very different from selling to a corporate purchasing agent.

If you are selling to business, the size of the customer is a crucial concern. Big businesses behave differently from medium-size or small businesses. Larger companies are generally slow and bureaucratic in their purchasing. It's necessary to penetrate thick layers of insulation to reach decision makers. Company politics and infighting may corrupt the purchasing process, and the actual user of your product or service often has little, if any, say over which vendor will be selected. Dealing with these considerations can require an entirely different selling approach from the approach you might use for small-company customers.

If you are selling to consumers, the individual's personal characteristics provide a means of classification. Consider age, sex, marital status, and family structure. Also, in our increasingly diverse society, markets tend to segment along ethnic lines for many consumer products. And don't neglect economic status. The very rich really are different from you and me.

Geography provides another important segmentation axis. For many products and services location is a key purchase factor. Californians buy lots of Japanese cars; Midwesterners mostly buy American. When it comes to fish eating, the market in Baton Rouge will take catfish; the market in Manhattan will take sashimi. Don't neglect international markets and their idiosyncrasies. Americans use utilitarian telephones; Japanese like phones with garish decorations.

The purpose of market segmentation is quite simple for a startup: to *pick one segment* to pursue. This isn't easy, by the way. When you have seventeen golden opportunities, you hate to give up any, let alone sixteen, of them. But a startup that aims at several market segments simultaneously has very poor prospects, and investors are adept at spotting such nonstarters. They don't like complicated businesses that sell into diverse markets—partly because of the very poor track record of multi-market startups and partly because such ventures are hard to understand and evaluate.

> Mee Industries provides a classic example of this error. Tom Mee invented a deceptively simple little patented gadget for making fog. (Not mist—that turns out to be something entirely different.) It had all sorts of applications—greenhouses, protecting orchards from frost, even as energy-efficient air conditioning for buildings. Serving several diverse types of customers was overloading the tiny firm's financial and management resources. The Enterprise Forum panel advised the company to pick one application and concentrate on that market. This advice was unpalatable to the founder. What? Give up all those lucrative opportunities? Turn away customers? No way!
>
> Less than a year later, Mee Industries went into Chapter 11.[1]

In our work, panelists use one concept so often that it's become a cliché with our audience: *focus*. They consistently advise presenting entrepreneurs to (1) examine potential mar-

---

1. From a public session attended by the authors.

kets, (2) pick their best shot, (3) go for it, and (4) *ignore the others*.

This advice is easy to give but hard to follow. Entrepreneurs tend to be opportunistic, quick to shift course to a new direction if it appears that there's money in it. And in fact, this flexibility is a major advantage for small companies, particularly in the startup stage. But excessive flexibility results in a limp, boneless marketing strategy that can destroy a fragile new venture.

Investors see market focus as a matter of self-discipline. They expect you, the entrepreneur, to have enough self-control to override your instincts on certain issues, and market focus is one of them.

Market Characterization

It is crucially important for you to know how your market works. Who makes the purchase decision, for instance? This is particularly important if you are selling to business. Your customer is not a business; your customer, always, is a human being. So who is it that decides to buy from you? The purchasing agent? A department head? An engineer? You may have to get three or four people to sign off on a purchase.

> A good example of shrewd market characterization is provided by Hewlett-Packard's introduction of the handheld calculator. They called it a calculator even though it had substantial computing power, and marketed it as a piece of minor office equipment so that any low-level corporate manager could authorize a purchase of one. Anything called a "computer" would have had to go through a lengthy and difficult corporate central procurement process at most big customers.
>
> Hewlett-Packard's market strategy was to appeal directly to the engineer and bypass the slow, bureaucratic, and conservative corporate data processing departments. In this way they laid the foundation for dominance in the engineering workstation market.

Another important factor in market characterization is the size of a typical sale. It costs money—often a lot of money—to make a sale. A salesperson's salary and commission, travel, samples, advertising, and many other costs may be involved. How you sell depends on how big a sale it is. If you're selling big-ticket items, you can afford to hire expensive sales help. If your product goes for a few bucks, it will practically have to sell itself.

Also critical is the length of the sales cycle. Again, we must note that selling costs money. You lay out cash for such things as advertising, soliciting prospects, trade shows, and samples and demonstration units, not to mention inventory, and these outlays occur *in advance of the sale*. That means you have to carry the selling costs until the sale is closed and you get paid. The period from the first contact with the prospect to receipt of payment is the sales cycle. A long sales cycle has a dramatic negative effect on your cash flow, so you'd better have a realistic estimate.

Market Growth

So far, we've considered your market as it is today. But you must also take into account the future. Is the market as a whole growing? Is the particular segment of the market you plan to address growing? How fast will it grow? How long will it grow? Will prices rise in the future, or drop? If you are selling something really innovative, there may not even *be* a market at present. So you'll have to project your ability to create a market and to make it grow.

The questions we've dealt with so far deal with strategic marketing factors. The answers you come up with will determine such decisions as what market segments you'll address, how fast your company can grow, and what kind of financing will be appropriate. But another set of questions deals with the tactical marketing factors, and develops out of the second Key Question.

Key Facts About Your Market

☐ What are the key customer groups that buy, or might buy, your product?

☐ What is the size of the key customer groups?
☐ How much does each group purchase?
☐ Based on the previous data, what is the size of the total market?
☐ Which market segment is most profitable? Why?
☐ Which market segment is most easily accessed?
☐ Which market segment is most receptive to new products or new suppliers?
☐ Which market segment will you address? Why?
☐ How fast is the selected market segment growing?
☐ What are your market share objectives?
☐ Who actually makes the purchase decision within the company (if you're selling business items) or family (if you're selling consumer items)?
☐ What is the average size of a sale?
☐ What will it cost you to make a sales call?
☐ How many sales calls, on average, must you make to close a sale?
☐ What is the length of the sales cycle?
☐ What is the growth rate of the market?
☐ In what segments of the market is growth fastest?
☐ What are price trends—up, down, or steady?

Second, the Customer

Once you've answered the first Key Question, you know who your customers are and the basic data about how they behave. Now comes the second Key Question, which boils down to a very gritty, practical, hands-on issue: How do you make a sale?

The major failure mode for new businesses is lack of sales. When investors evaluate your plans, their first question will be, "Will this business have sales, enough sales to succeed and grow?" Therefore, the first thing you must do is demonstrate good prospects for sales; you can worry about profits later.

So it comes back again to the customer.

There are a million or so questions about your customers that need answering. However, they can be boiled down to four basic categories.

1. *What does the customer need?* Every business ultimately begins with a need in the market. Your task as an

entrepreneur is to solve customer problems. You would like to be able to tell investors that your customers have a strong need, a compelling need, to buy your product or service. If your customers are motivated by some intense stimulus such as greed, fear, or the desire to avoid TV commercials, you're likely to be able to establish strong, stable sales.

2. *What does the customer want?* Entrepreneurs often come to grief by not considering this question. People don't always want what they need, that is, what's "good for them." Customer desires may seem irrational at times, but often there are subtle factors influencing their behavior that aren't obvious to an outsider. You have to convince investors that there is not just a need but a *felt* need for what you're peddling.

> In my first venture, I tried to sell to the big pharmaceutical companies a new type of chemical technology. It had the potential to cut their bulk manufacturing costs in half. Clearly they really needed this, right? Wrong.
>
> It turned out that chemical manufacturing represents a very small percentage of total costs for a pharmaceutical company. Marketing, distribution, R&D, and regulatory expenses are much bigger. And what's really important to them, absolutely crucial in fact, is getting FDA approval for a new drug as soon as possible. The dynamics of the regulatory process are such that using our technology would have slowed it down. Yes, they would have liked to cut manufacturing costs—but not at that price.

3. *How can you appeal to the customer?* OK, you've got a product that the customer both needs and wants. But you still haven't made the sale. You have to convince the customer that your product will satisfy. This leads to a whole host of specific questions. For instance: What is important to the customer—price, quality, convenience, service, style? What sort of ads will appeal to the customer? What media should be used for them—TV, magazines, direct mail? (And if, for instance, TV, what shows?) Where should the sale be made—at your facility, at the customer's home or office, or perhaps at a trade show? What sales tactics turn the customer on or off? How price-sensitive is

the customer? What payment methods are preferred? Knowing the answer to questions like these makes the difference between a successful and unsuccessful salesperson.

4. *How do you communicate with the customer?* All this will be wasted even yet if you can't reach the customer. You need to figure out how to identify customers; how to locate them; how to get their attention; and how to get the product to them. That's the problem of distribution.

Distribution: The Nemesis of New Products

How do you get the *opportunity* to make a sale to the customer? That is the question of *distribution*. Getting distribution has become one of the most serious obstacles to introducing a new product. Few entrepreneurs appreciate the problem, but investors do, and they are skeptical of new product introductions unless the plan clearly shows a realistic recognition of distribution questions.

How do you get your new chocolate-coated string beans to the customer? Take it to the big grocery chains? Ha. Do you know what those brown stains on the floor of your local supermarket are? Not chocolate; they're the blood of salespeople who fell in the struggle for shelf space. Outfits like General Mills, Procter & Gamble, and Frito-Lay are fighting a savage, relentless war to expand the space given to their product displays and to reduce the space given to competing brands. They use rebates, coupons, free advertising, special displays, and whatever other tactics they can think of to persuade grocers to go along. What have you got to put up against their clout? The same problem of getting shelf space applies to clothes, toys, appliances, books, and most other retail items.

Other distribution channels, whether retail or business-to-business, are also getting congested. Wholesalers, manufacturer's reps, even direct mail: All are overloaded with suppliers and looking for vendors they can cut. New faces with untested products are not particularly welcome.

If you are proposing to introduce a new product (or just a new brand of an existing product), getting a distribution channel is likely to be one of your major problems. A sophisticated investor will want to see that you are aware of this problem, have considered it, and have a rational approach to dealing with it. As Ken Deemer of InterVen Partners says, "New ventures are usually weak on marketing strategy. These days a formula approach isn't good enough. Distribution channels are clogged; you need a unique approach." Because of this, InterVen likes to see ventures develop strategic partnerships with larger firms that already have established distribution channels.

Don't forget export markets—and foreign competitors! We work in an increasingly global economy, and many venture firms are now expecting business plans to have a strategy for early penetration of foreign markets. If you think getting distribution for your products is tough in the United States, wait till you try Japan.

Key Facts About Your Customers

- ☐ What needs did your customers express in your market survey?
- ☐ In what order did they rank those needs?
- ☐ How are customers currently satisfying these needs?
- ☐ What do customers dislike about the currently available products/ services?
- ☐ How do customers locate products of this type? What advertising or publicity media get their attention?
- ☐ Where do customers go to purchase products of this type?
- ☐ If distributors or other middlemen are needed to access the customer, what are their characteristics and requirements?
- ☐ How price-sensitive are customers?
- ☐ What payment method do customers consider normal?

Market Research as a Practical Proposition

As we've seen, there is a great deal of information about your customers that is critical to planning your new venture. Investors will want to know the answers to the kinds of questions we've outlined above. But, beyond that, they will want answers that can be backed up by tangible evidence. Guesswork won't do; theories won't do; opinions (yours or experts') won't do.

You need facts. The only way to get them is to do market research.

Market research starts with background work. To determine the number of potential customers, for instance, you can turn to various published sources. If you're selling square ball bearings to machine-tool manufacturers, for instance, various industry references will tell you the total number of such firms in the country. If you're opening a shop to sell tomatoless pizzas in Orange County, U.S. census figures are available to tell you how many people live within five miles of your proposed location. (Finding out how many of them are allergic to tomatoes may be a bit more difficult.) Markets considered interesting—that is, big markets—are studied by professional market research firms, and these studies are published—usually at very high prices, but they can be worth it. The major conclusions about size and growth rate for each market generally show up in the trade press, and are collected for easy reference by such outfits as Predicasts.

This sort of library work is only the beginning. It won't even start to answer many important questions. To get the information you need, you will have to conduct your own market research.

You can, if you have the funds, hire a professional outfit to do a survey for you. However, even if you are able to take this route, you will need to know how the process works in order to supervise it properly and get your money's worth. So here's a brief overview of the three major steps involved in the market survey process.

1. *Define your market and develop a method to identify and locate prospective customers.* You must then select a *random* sample from this base. This is important: You must select not the best prospects, nor the prospects that are easiest to reach, but a *random sample* of prospects. The size of the sample need not be very large usually.

2. *Conduct the survey.* The best results are obtained by interviewing the subjects in person, but this can be very time-consuming and expensive. Mail surveys are cheaper, but the

response rate is generally low. (It can be improved by putting a small gift or a dollar bill in the survey envelope.) A telephone survey is a good compromise, but you cannot ask many questions over the phone without taxing the subject's patience.

3. *Analyze the results*. A small survey will not give you a high statistical reliability; sales projections are never as accurate as you'd like, even when based on good market research. But the really important objective is to *understand your customers,* and if your survey questions were well designed you should get some very useful information in response to them.

This is only a brief overview of the market research process; for specific instructions, consult some of the references in the Bibliography at the end of this chapter. Whatever you do, do market research. Actually talking to customers is a terrific reality check, and you'll be surprised how impressed investors will be.

Third, the Customer

With the third Key Question we finally come to the subject that most business plans start with: the product. Most entrepreneurs are infatuated with their products. Inventors and engineers especially tend to succumb to an obsessive fixation, in which the customer—whose need is the only justification for the product—is considered almost an irrelevant nuisance.

The most difficult task in putting on an Enterprise Forum session, in fact, is to get the presenter to tell the audience about his *business* instead of spending twenty-four minutes of his twenty-five-minute time allotment talking about how neat his product is, how it works, and why its technology is so ingenious.

The third Key Question asks: What is your product? What does it do? And, above all, *how does it satisfy the customer's need?* If you plan to sell a type of product that's been around for a long time, this question is fairly routine. However, you must explain, then, what is new about your approach. If it's an old, standard product, why should customers buy it from you rather than from their established suppliers? Perhaps because you sell it cheaper, or because your quality is higher, or both. Perhaps you offer a wider selection of models or in some other way appeal to the customer's need for convenience.

> One of the most successful innovations in the junk-food market was not a new type of potato chip but a new way to serve the customer's convenience—Arco's AM/PM Mini-markets, which give motorists the opportunity to top off their tummies along with their tanks.

If your product is new, your homework assignment is to get customer testimonials. *You* may be convinced that your new barbecue widget solves all the customer's frankfurter problems, but your unsupported assertion won't cut the mustard. Even the use of market research data in which prospects ask for specific features is inadequate. The only reliable evidence for product value is the testimony of customers who have actually used the product. Careful selection and monitoring of beta-test sites is therefore critical.

Of course, investors will want to see some evidence that you really will *have* a product, especially if you are starting a high-tech business. Will it actually work? If your great invention is merely a gleam in your eye, or even a set of drawings, investors are likely to be skeptical. You'll get a much better response if you can build a working prototype before you seek funding. Then ask yourself: Can I make it at a reasonable cost? In today's competitive markets, your gadget is unlikely to succeed unless it is designed so that it can be manufactured efficiently. And will it be reliable? If your early models are full of bugs, you may never get a foothold in the market. In many areas of business, particularly if you are addressing a consumer market, you may have to satisfy concerns about product liability. Investors won't see much return on their money if the government bans your product for safety or health reasons.

Key Facts About Your Product/Service

☐ What does your product actually *do?*
☐ What features does it have?

☐ How do these features translate into benefits for the customer?
☐ What makes your product/service distinctively different from competitive offerings?
☐ How much will your product cost?
☐ What stage is product development at?
☐ What steps have you taken to ensure product reliability and quality?

A problem of marketing strategy arises when a business is based on an invention or on proficiency in some area of high technology. As we previously mentioned, the inventor-entrepreneur usually has an instinctive tendency to think in terms of the versatility of the product. "Look at all the different things this could be used for. Think of all the markets we could enter." When experienced investors hear this, they jump up and run for the exit. They know this multimarket approach is disastrous, and want to see just the opposite strategy.

As one venture capitalist, who is himself a trained engineer, put it: "The hard thing is not technology—it's developing a *customer base*. The way you make money is to build a customer base and then sell them new things, *not* to sell the same thing to new markets."

Successful businesses regard their customer base as their most important asset. We see a lot of failed inventors: Generally these people seem to regard their gadgets as their only resources and are obsessed with finding new uses for them. Successful inventors, by contrast, are able to let go of their first contraptions and invent new things. Have confidence in your inventive ability; there's more where that came from.

The Credibility Question

Up to this point, all you have accomplished is to convince the investor that there is an *opportunity* for your venture. You've demonstrated that there is a market, that there are customers who have a need and are willing to pay to have it satisfied, and that you have a product that will satisfy that need. Now, with the fourth Key Question, the focus shifts to *you*.

As founder and leader of the management team of the new venture, you've got to establish your credibility. You've shown that there's an opportunity, but have you got what it takes to exploit it? Just who *are* you, anyway?

In our interviews with venture capitalists, perhaps the single most consistently and strongly expressed criterion they mentioned was *quality of the management team.* They do not want to see any second-string players on the field. And they are concerned not just with the company's officers. Ideally they would like everyone involved—management, lawyers, accountants, previous investors, if any—to be out of the top drawer.

Venture Capitalists on Management

We heard it over and over again.

> "We want leadership. Management should have past accomplishments. We need a CEO with vision, someone able to put together a plan."

> "I want a team with a proven record. And I want them to surround themselves with the best: top lawyers, a Big Eight accounting firm, and strong people in all the infrastructure like the board, technical advisers, and so on."

> "Do they have direct management experience in the same field? And have they come from winners? We want people who have previously been successful at successful companies. We check on their education and stability of employment. *I've never seen a small company with too much management.*"

Several investors commented that it's better to come in with an incomplete team of first-rate people than a complete team with some weak players. As Tom Peterson of El Dorado Ventures puts it, "I'd rather see three good people, and help them hire three more, than get six people, of whom three must be fired."

In fact, many venture capital firms, especially those that do early-stage financings, expect and even welcome the need to help complete the management team. Some will locate the necessary managers themselves; others will hire a search firm.

However, there is a dark side of the Force. Venture capital firms won't hesitate to dump founders who, in their opinion, don't measure up.

When Founders Exit . . .

Several venture capitalists were very frank with us about their way of dealing with managers who can't hack it.

> "More than 50 percent of founding CEOs are replaced. Most are pushed—or at least nudged."

> "Unfortunately, in spite of all our care, we often see an entrepreneur's behavior change after the initial financing. So when we close a deal, we make the founders give us undated resignations."

> "Almost all early-stage CEOs get dropped within a few years."

> "We have had to replace the CEO in over 50 percent of our deals. But in many cases he goes voluntarily."

As you assemble your management team and the other people who are going to work with you in the venture, it would be wise to keep in mind these investor attitudes. Select carefully.

"Competitors? What Competitors? Oh, *Those* Competitors!"

Now comes an even tougher question: What about the competition? It's not enough for you and your team to be good; you've got to be better than the opposition.

The modern economy is intensely turbulent. Technology moves fast; changes are radical; and surprises are common. Brass-knuckle competition is the rule in most industries. It is getting very hard to find a safe, comfortable berth in which you can make a gentlemanly profit without engaging in unseemly conflict. Investors know this; most venture capital firms have lost money in startups that underestimated the competition. So if you want to get financed, you can't afford to be cocky.

At the homework stage, this means knowing your competition. Note that your competition is *anyone who can satisfy the customer need you are aiming at.*

> One company proposed to install picturephones at hotels, airports, and so on. Consumer demand for these picture pay phones was a bit iffy, but the founders felt that there would be strong interest from companies wanting to do teleconferencing without going to the expense of building their own installations.
>
> Viewphone's business plan pretty much dismissed the competition from other phone outfits. But, as one of the panelists pointed out, the real competition for Viewphone was the airlines.

Who are your competitors? How big are they? How strong are they? What are the advantages and disadvantages of their products? What products will they introduce in the future? Remember, you'll be competing against what they bring out at the time you enter the market, not against what they have now.

How is market share divvied up now? You're proposing to take a share of this market yourself. Which of your competitors, do you think, is going to lose share in order to make room for you? Why? Answering these questions can be a sobering process. But by investigating these issues, you develop *credibility* with investors. By doing this homework properly, you show that you are serious, realistic, and objective.

You have further work to do. You must convincingly demonstrate that you can produce the product. If you are planning to sell some new high-tech widget, what stage is product development at? What about future products? Can you present evidence that you know how to do R&D on schedule and on budget? What about scaling up to production? What do you know about modern quality control methods and other production issues?

Once you've gained credibility, you're ready for the final question.

Key Facts About Your Credibility

☐ What are the backgrounds of the members of your team?
☐ What actions have your team members taken to demonstrate their commitment to the venture?
☐ Who are your competitors? Provide full profiles.
☐ What are the current market shares of your larger competitors?
☐ What are the competitive products/services and their advantages and disadvantages?
☐ What innovations are your competitors likely to introduce in the near future?
☐ If your product development is not complete, what stage are you at? Are you currently on schedule and on budget? How long will it be before you are ready for market?
☐ Is your product protected by patents? If not, what is to prevent your competitors from copying it?
☐ What new products do you propose to introduce in the future? What is your development schedule and budget?
☐ What are your manufacturing plans (or service delivery operations plan)?
☐ What is your production/operations budget?
☐ How do you plan to finance capital equipment? By equity, or loans, or leasing?

The Financial Structuring

You perhaps won't be too surprised to hear that financiers are very interested in financial data and projections. In general, they are going to demand three types of financial information.

Historical Financials

Obviously if your venture is a pure startup, it has no history. But if you've already started operations, even if you have few sales and no profits as yet, your company has a history, and a set of financial statements should be assembled.

Sometimes entrepreneurs are reluctant to include historical financials because they don't want investors to see how badly they screwed up while they were learning the ropes—or because they don't want investors to know how desperately the company needs cash *right now*. A surprising number of entrepreneurs don't *have* any decent financial statements. However, there's a single, very good reason to disclose your financial history: No matter how much you'd like to conceal it, you can't get away with it.

Pro Forma Statements

Projections of future financial results make up the heart of your venture's plan. Let's begin by clearing up a common misconception. The purpose of pro forma financial statements is *not* to predict the future performance of your company. Investors don't believe in fortune-tellers and don't expect you to be one. What your pro formas provide is a *model* of the business.

A good set of projections functions as a simulation of your proposed business that will allow the investors—and you—to answer all sorts of important questions. What will your break-even point be? How will your cash flow behave at different growth rates? What will happen if you collect your receivables at sixty days instead of forty-five? If development of your second product slips by six months, will the company go broke?

Investors will compare your projections with the results they've seen in similar companies. Does the model you've set up correspond to the reality of comparable ventures? If not, why not?

Your pro formas give the investor a fast way to check on your homework. All the work we've described so far is necessary to provide the input assumptions for your financial model. If you skip any of it, the deficiency will be obvious in your spreadsheets.

Take, for instance, the top line—sales. If you haven't done market research, your sales projections will be pie in the sky.

INVESTOR: Now, I see here that you're projecting sales of
$100 million in 1992. Where does that figure come
from?

ENTREPRENEUR: Well, *Dataquest* says the market in 1992
will be $5 billion, and we figure we'll have 2 percent of
it.

INVESTOR: I see. Why 2 percent? Why not one percent?
Or 50 percent? Or 6.8 percent?

ENTREPRENEUR: Uh, well, we thought 2 percent was a
reasonable number.

At this point, the venture capitalist is likely to suddenly
remember an important appointment elsewhere. How much
better if you can say: "Well, our market survey indicated an
average sale of $118,000 including peripherals, with a 12 percent
response rate and 5.3 sales calls needed to close. Now, if you'll
refer to page 84, you'll see that in 1992 we're projecting our
sales force at. . . ."

The financial projections in a typical business plan are full
of holes, evasions, and contradictions. One sees record-breaking
sales achieved—without any money being spent on a sales force
or advertising. One sees new products being developed—without any R&D funding. The assumptions on which the numbers
are based turn out to be pure guesswork, imagination, or wishful
thinking.

The key to getting good pro formas is developing good data
for input. If you've actually talked to customers, you'll have
solid information that can be used for projecting sales and selling
costs. If you've investigated production costs thoroughly, you
can get a reasonable estimate of your gross margin. If you have
worked from past experience to get realistic numbers for the
time and money needed for new product development, you'll
have a real R&D budget. Putting everything together becomes
relatively easy, and you end up with projections that can be
defended.

The Deal

Your next step is to figure out what to ask for from investors.
Many entrepreneurs go to investors without knowing how much

money they really need. Often they have only a vague idea that with so many million dollars they could get the business going. Others have done some detailed initial cost calculations and added a reserve, but haven't thought at all about future growth.

Once you have developed a good set of financial projections, based on real information, you can easily determine your real capital needs. Your cash flow projection will tell you how much cash will drain out of the business before you reach a positive cash flow. That, plus a cushion, is the investment you need. With less, your company will go broke—even if it achieves profitability. With more, you are giving up more equity than you need to. From your pro forma financial statements you can see where the money will be going and how it will be used. This will provide the necessary information for the "use of funds" section of your business plan.

Key Facts About Your Financial Plans

- [ ] If your company is already in business, provide historical financials including profit and loss, balance sheet, and cash flow statements.
- [ ] What are your sales projections for the next five years?
- [ ] What are your production costs? And your gross margin?
- [ ] What are your selling costs (including advertising, sales commissions, and so on)?
- [ ] What is budgeted for R&D expense?
- [ ] What are your assumptions on capital equipment financing? And on interest or lease expense?
- [ ] What are your assumptions on depreciation methods?
- [ ] What are you allowing for G&A (general and administrative) expense?
- [ ] What is your tax model?
- [ ] How do your projections compare with the standard financial ratios in your industry? Explain any discrepancies.
- [ ] What does your break-even chart look like?
- [ ] When is your venture projected to turn profitable?
- [ ] When is your venture projected to achieve positive cash flow?
- [ ] What are your financing needs?

Bibliography

Breen, George, and A. B. Blankenship. *Do-It-Yourself Marketing Research,* 3rd ed. New York: McGraw-Hill, 1988.

Merrill, Ronald E., and Sedgwick, Henry D. *The New Venture Handbook.* New York: AMACOM, 1987. This text covers the entire venture development process, with a strong focus on "homework" issues, including a chapter on market research.

Pope, Jeffrey. *Practical Marketing Research.* New York: AMACOM, 1981.

Robert Morris Associates. *Annual Statement Studies.* New York. This standard reference provides average financial ratios for a variety of industries.

Stone, Bob, *Successful Direct Marketing Methods.* Chicago: Crain Books, 1979. This is an excellent guide to direct marketing, covering the entire subject. Among other topics, the book explains test marketing by direct mail.

Viladas, Joseph M. *The Book of Survey Techniques.* Santa Barbara, Calif.: Havemeyer Books, 1982.

2

Writing the Plan

A few macho diehards still think business plans are for wimps. But most of today's entrepreneurs at least pay lip service to the need for a business plan.

Writing a business plan serves as a sort of preflight checklist for your venture. Before you take off, you want to make sure that your vehicle is flight-worthy—and so do your passengers, the investors. Writing a good business plan requires a thorough investigation of all the important issues; that makes it less likely that you'll overlook any critical factors.

Your business plan should accomplish several purposes. To begin with, it serves as your venture's resumé. Like a job hunter's resumé, a well-written business plan can get you an interview, a foot in the door. This is the advertising or promotional function of the plan.

In many cases the business plan must also serve as an educational document. Every industry has unique characteristics, and no investor can know everything about the one you propose to enter (though some may pretend to). You will therefore need to tactfully convey the important facts about the background of your business to the investor. The more innovative your venture, the more important it is that your plan serve this teaching function.

During the financing process, the business plan will also serve as a handy reference guide to information about your venture. An investor commonly works on a dozen or so deals at any given time, and sometimes the details begin to run together in his head. He can keep the facts straight by referring to your well-organized business plan. He must also do extensive investigation for his "due diligence," and your plan is a root document for the information needed.

Before you write the plan—in fact before you even write the outline—you should carefully define what you want your plan to accomplish as a sales document, as an educational document, and as a reference document.

The Business Plan as Advertisement

Your first objective is simply to attract the attention of investors. It's not easy. There's a term you should know: "deal flow." Most investors are drowning in it, particularly venture capitalists. Their desks are piled high with business plans. People who want to talk to them about putting up money to build prototype perpetual motion machines and other neat gadgets are ringing them on the phone incessantly. They must sift through all these proposals to find new opportunities while keeping an eye on the investments they've already made (many of which are floundering).

We asked a variety of venture capitalists and other investors how long they spend on an initial look at a business plan. The typical answer was "about ten minutes." So it's crucial for your plan to quickly and clearly project what your business is and why it is attractive.

Your job is to write a business plan that will cut through the clutter and persuade investors to make time in their busy schedules to talk to you in person. It can't be done with gimmicks. The experienced investor has probably seen plenty of attention-getting tricks: business plans assembled with pop-up cutouts, business plans on videotape, business plans accompanied by singing telegrams. Forget about stunts like this and concentrate on your real sales point. All you need to do is convey a simple message: *This is a good deal.*

There's no hard-and-fast formula you can use, because investors differ as to their definitions of a good deal. The same proposed investment that makes a venture capitalist salivate will make a banker nauseous. Before you start to develop your venture advertising message, you must decide on the type, or types, of financing you will be seeking, and understand the interests and requirements of investors. (We cover this topic in detail in Chapter 4.)

However, there are three key factors that are pretty universal in their appeal to investors, and you should make sure your plan projects all three of them.

1. *"This is your kind of deal."* Investors are specialists and they simply will not even look at deals that are outside their line of business. If you go to a venture capital firm for a loan, or to a bank for an equity investment, you are doing things backwards and you won't get to first base. You want your plan very quickly to specify that you are looking for the type of investment the investor makes; that you are entering an industry with which the investor is familiar; and that the size of the investment is within the means of the investor.

2. *"We are credible people."* In spite of our fervent personal enthusiasm for entrepreneurship, even we must concede that some entrepreneurs are . . . just a tad on the flaky side. Unfortunately, these people tend to be the loudest, most aggressive, and most persistent characters in the business culture. When you are vying for the attention of investors, these are just the people you do not want to look like. It is crucial to project that you and your team are mature, competent, rational, and reliable.

3. *"This venture has a unique advantage."* It's true there are times when a tulip bulb craze sweeps through the investment world, when venture capitalists go temporarily insane and happily pour money into "yet another disk-drive company" or "yet

another gene-splicing company." In normal times, however, you'll probably find it difficult to get investor attention unless you can present some sort of special business advantage. All sorts of things can serve as this unique booster: a patented gadget, a world-renowned expert on your team, a proprietary manufacturing process, anything in fact that gives you a convincing edge over the competition. Keep in mind that a 10 percent improvement is not enough; you need something at least 50 percent better to force your way into the market against established competitors.

If your plan quickly and convincingly presents these three factors in a form carefully tailored to the investor's needs, you've passed the first hurdle.

How Investors Look at Business Plans

When investors look at business plans, how do they operate? What do they look for? What do they want to see? We asked venture capitalists and other investors to tell us how they evaluate business plans. There were some consistent trends, but also some interesting individual differences. Many investors have special criteria they use. Here are some of the comments we got on this topic.

> "I look first at the Executive Summary, then at the resumés of the management team, then at the financials."

> "What's *special* about the business—what's its unique advantage? Then I want to know about the people. After that, the market—its size and growth."

> "I look at the financials first—not in detail, just a quick look at the sales projections. Are they ambitious enough? I want to see them looking for $50 million in sales within a few years; otherwise they're not venture capital material. Then I look at the Executive Summary to see what business they're in, and after that the resumés of the founders."

"What business are they in? More than half the time, I can't tell from the plan. Is it a *business*—or just a product? What are their five-year revenue goals? We want to see a $100 million potential. What are the pedigrees of the founders? In my first pass at the plan, I also want to see a 10 to 20 percent market share projected, an international marketing focus, and proprietary protection for the product."

"What is the business? Who is the management? I want to be able to get this from the Executive Summary. A new business needs an order-of-magnitude improvement in price/performance ratio to succeed; I want to see ventures with an unfair advantage in the market. And give me a team with a proven record; there's no room for error, and we don't want to finance on-the-job training for entrepreneurs."

"What is the business? Then I look at the people. I want to know about the market, especially the source of their competitive advantage. If it's 'we sell it cheaper,' that's not my guy."

A good principle to keep in mind is that investors in a new venture want to see low *market* risk. If your company is a technology startup, or any kind of new product venture, shrewd investors will accept the technology risk. If you can't make the product work, they'll find out quickly and lose relatively little money. But if you can make the product work, but can't sell it, it may take years—and oceans of money—to find out the horrible truth. So as you write your plan, aim your major reassurances at the market risks.

The Business Plan as Educational Aid

You, as an entrepreneur, are probably pretty much engrossed in your new venture. You've thought about it, worked on it, planned and analyzed and brainstormed until it is as familiar as your desk top. It's easy to forget that others—specifically, investors—don't understand it as well as you do. Facts, theories, or concepts that you take for granted may be strange and unfamiliar to them. So your plan needs to serve an educational function.

Your business plan provides the best opportunity for tactfully instructing investors. If they come into the meeting with you with some ridiculous misconceptions, correcting them in person may be awkward. Much better if they get straightened out while reading the plan so nobody witnesses their ignorance. Write into the plan enough background material so that investors will not have to ask stupid questions.

By explaining the background in the plan for your venture you also get a chance to demonstrate your competence. You are able to show that you are familiar with the environment in which you will be competing, that you are not a novice.

Since your plan should not be too long, you will have to limit your educational material to the essentials. In general, they will fall into three categories.

1. *An analysis of the industry you plan to enter.* Briefly explain how the business works. What are the key success factors in this line of business, the classic mistakes to be avoided?
2. *If you are in a technology-based business, some explanatory material in that area.* What are the important issues or objectives in this field of technology? Why is your innovation important? What are the trends and how does your project fit in?
3. *Special issues your venture raises.* Whatever may be unique or unusual or unexpected about your plan requires explanation. If, for instance, everyone else in your industry uses distributors, but you plan to sell by direct mail, don't just assert that this is the best way to do things. Preemptively deal with the questions that will be raised. Go into the background and justify your decision.

Realize that you must take the initiative in educating investors about your business. It is not their responsibility to learn; it is your responsibility to teach.

The Business Plan as Reference Book

There's something about money that makes the people who handle a lot of it very quantitative. Perhaps measuring everything in dollars and cents gets them in the habit of looking for hard, tangible, measurable facts.

All too many business plans are exciting but vague. At first reading, it may make the venture look terrific. But when an investor gets serious, and gives the plan a second look, it seems to lack substance. It turns out to be full of generalities. "The market is growing rapidly." How rapidly? Who says so? "Our device represents a quantum leap in the technology." How much of a leap? What's the figure of merit? "The competition is negligible." Who are your competitors? How big are they? What are their market shares?

A business plan that presents solid facts, not opinions, numbers, not superlatives, evidence, not guesswork will enhance your credibility with investors enormously. You don't have to load down your text with huge piles of data. However, all your key claims should be based on specific facts and backed up by real evidence. If you can't do this, you haven't finished your homework.

A guiding principle here is: *Don't make the investor search for key facts.* The essential information needed to make an investment decision should be in the plan, organized so that it can be readily located. Always make it easy for the investor to find the information he needs to say "yes."

Organizing the Plan

At this stage you can begin organizing your plan. Take a sheet of paper and write down your answers to these preliminary questions:

1. What are the key points I want to get across that will make this venture attractive to the investor? Specifically, let's project that this is the kind of deal this firm does;

that we are credible as a team; and that we have a unique business advantage to exploit.

2. What background must be covered to ensure that the reader fully understands our plans? Industry structure? Maybe technology? Are we doing something out of the ordinary that requires special explanation? Above all, let's clearly explain what the business is.

3. What are the key facts that we must be sure to include? What information will the target investor need in order to make a positive decision?

These are the overarching requirements your plan must meet and against which you will have to check your work.

Your next step is to develop an outline. All sorts of "canned" standard business plan outlines are available. We are about to suggest one ourselves in Exhibit 2-1, but don't use any of them—ours included—as a straitjacket. Businesses differ, and the plans for them must differ accordingly. Always be ready to adapt the structure of your business plan to fit any special aspects of your venture.

That said, we feel that virtually every business plan should answer the Five Key Questions and that it should be organized around the order we have given. By putting the customer first in your plan, you give encouraging evidence that the customer will come first in your business. This is an attitude you'll do well to project to investors at every opportunity.

Exhibit 2-1. Merrill & Nichols's new, improved, industrial-
strength business plan outline.

Executive Summary

(Key Question #1: Who are your customers?)

I.. The Market

(Key Question #2: What do your customers need and want?)

II. Market Strategy

(Key Question #3: What are you selling and why will it satisfy your customers?)

(Continued)

Exhibit 2-1. (Continued)

   III. The Product

       (Key Question #4: Who are you and why can you beat the competition?)

   IV. The Competition

    V. The Team

   VI. The Technology

  VII. Production and Operations

       (Key Question #5: How much money will it take to accomplish your business goals, and how much money will your business make?)

 VIII. Financial Data, Assumptions, and Projections

Even the bare-bones outline shown in Exhibit 2-1 must be adapted to specific conditions.

If, for instance, you are already in business and are looking for second-round or later financing, you should add a section to your plan that will briefly summarize the history of your venture. Section VIII should include a set of historical financial statements preceding the projections.

If your business is not technology-based, Section VI may be unnecessary. However, you may still wish to devote part of the document to your plans for development of new products or services.

The Executive Summary, a very important part of your plan, presents special problems. It should be the last part of the plan you write. It will be the first—and, if not well done, the last—part of your plan the investor reads. For this reason, we've devoted all of the next chapter especially to this subject.

In addition to the main body of your plan, you will probably want to include appendixes that delve into various subjects in more detail. These might include extensive breakdowns of market information or other numbers, more extensive resumés of the founders, lists or tables too long to be placed in the main text, and supporting documents such as magazine articles or scientific papers that help justify your claims. In this way you can keep the plan short and readable while still including necessary supporting material. This brings us to an oft-asked question: How long should a business plan be?

Procrustes, Where Are You Now That We Need You?

Contrary to what you may hear, there is no standard optimum length for a business plan. The appropriate length for your plan depends on several factors.

Generally speaking, the more complex your venture, the longer your business plan will have to be. If you expect your business to be small, simple, and routine, there's no need for a lot of prose to describe it. On the other hand, if you are planning a nationwide rollout with multiple products, a complex distribution strategy, and rapid technological obsolescence built in, you're going to need quite a bit of space to explain how you got yourself into such a mess.

The complexity of the deal may also influence the length of the business plan. A straight equity venture capital deal may require only a short plan. If the same business is financed by corporate partnering, all sorts of intricate complications will arise and the plan will need to lengthen to cover them.

The more innovative your venture, the longer your plan will have to be. When you propose to enter a commonplace business in a conventional way, investors are already familiar with most of what they need to know to evaluate your prospects. If your product employs radically new technology, or your marketing strategy is novel, your plan will have to expand to make room for some educational background material.

Finally, there are fashions in business plans as in most other things. There was a vogue in the 1970s for ponderous tomes; later there was a reaction in many areas in favor of extremely short plans. And of course there are individual variations. One venture capital firm will get a warm and fuzzy feeling from a plan that contains a half-meter-thick stack of spreadsheets; another may pride itself on its fast, snappy investments based on a few sentences scrawled on a napkin. Regional differences play a part too. Areas like Silicon Valley have almost reduced entrepreneurship to a standard routine; abbreviated plans are welcome. In other parts of the country, where the procedures are not so familiar, investors need to be reassured by a plan that dots all its i's and crosses all its t's.

Having thus skillfully evaded the question, we can merely hint that between twenty and thirty pages for the main body of your plan is a reasonable length. In the end, it depends on how well your plan is written. If you've got a good style, your reader will enjoy even a long document and maybe wish for more. A badly written plan can seem endless even if it's actually only a few pages.

How to Present Your Pro Formas

Many entrepreneurs have the somewhat cynical notion that investors consider the main text of the business plan merely as a footnote to the financial projections. Things aren't quite that bad, but certainly your pro formas will get careful scrutiny before an investor starts writing a check. So let's say a few words about your presentation of this important part of your plan.

The meat of your financial projections consists of three statements: the income statement (or P&L); the balance sheet; and the cash flow statement.

The format of the income statement as desired by venture capitalists differs slightly from the standard. They, and many other investors, like to see depreciation broken out as a separate item instead of being buried under expenses or cost of goods sold. This makes it easy for them to verify your cash flow projections.

Putting a balance sheet in your projections is a real nuisance and many entrepreneurs prefer to skip it. However, it's a valuable addition, and essential if you expect to take on much debt.

Most important of all—so much so that some say it should

be the first thing presented—is the cash flow statement. A primitive cash in/cash out summary is often used. If your pro formas are prepared by someone with an accounting background, you'll probably have a "Statement of Sources and Uses of Cash" or "Statement of Sources and Uses of Working Capital." The format isn't terribly important so long as the reader can clearly understand how your business generates and uses cash.

Most financial projections show only pretax income. It's better if you can take taxes into account, especially since they can have a tangible effect on cash flow. But you'll probably need professional help to do so. Tax projections are to be taken with a grain of salt in the out years, what with Congress changing the law every year and the IRS and FASB (Financial Accounting Standards Board) springing little surprises on us almost weekly. But taxes are a part of the business environment. Don't forget trifling details like sales taxes, property taxes, excise taxes, unemployment taxes, and so on.

If your company is already in business, historical financial statements must be presented. The pro forma statements should of course match the format of the historical ones so they can be compared.

The basic three financial statements should be presented at a fairly high level of aggregation, especially if your business is a complex one. The detail should be provided in supplementary statements, such as departmental budgets. (Just because it's more convenient for you to develop the projections in the form of one enormous spreadsheet in the computer doesn't mean that it's convenient for the reader to see it all on one sheet.)

The standard rule is that financial projections should extend five years into the future. The first year or two should be broken down to the monthly level; the remainder can be reported in quarterly increments.

In general, the key point is to make the financial section of your plan as clear, and convenient to use, as the nature of the material presented permits. Be sure to set out your assumptions clearly and provide notes to explain any unusual points.

Here are some additional suggestions. Get your spreadsheets printed sideways so that at least one year will go on a sheet. Don't use foldouts if you can avoid them. Be sure the print is sharp, and don't photoreduce to the point where a magnifying glass will be needed to read the page. Finally, provide clear labels for each row and column; don't make investors puzzle out your spreadsheet abbreviations.

What You Should Project Financially

Now, what sort of fudge should you serve up in your pro formas? What will investors find most delectable?

If you've done your homework, you should have some pretty solid figures on which you can base your projections. However, there will still be plenty of room for you to exercise your judgment. Many of the assumptions you plug into your spreadsheet will be more or less arbitrary. You can generate extremely optimistic numbers, or extremely pessimistic numbers, or something in between.

A study of startup sales forecasts by two Georgetown University professors showed that most projections aren't very accurate. The typical forecast overestimated first-year sales by 28 percent. The ventures studied spent an average of $38,000 on market research, but spending more money didn't seem to help accuracy. Still, it's interesting to note that the most accurate projections were made by entrepreneurs who considered accuracy important—in other words, you can do it if you try.[1]

The Catch-22 of venture capital is that optimistic sales and profit projections will result in rejection of your plan because they are unconvincing, while realistic projections will result in rejection of your plan because your company won't achieve standard venture capital growth goals. So what can you do?

1. "Sales Projections: Facts or Wishful Thinking?" *The Wall Street Journal,* July 7, 1989.

With financial fudge, as with chocolate fudge, the key criterion is *consistency*. Remember that your financial projections are not a fortune-teller's prediction; they are a simulation. It's less important that they look lucrative than that they make sense. Everything has to fit together.

The most obvious deficiency of the typical set of financials shows up in the cash flow. It's positive. The projections show that as soon as the investment money comes in, all the company's problems are over. All the projections have standard "hockey stick" graphs. Sales start to grow like mad. Profit margins are terrific and net profit grows like mad. And cash flow immediately turns positive and it too grows like mad.

Investors are willing to believe in rapid sales growth. They're even willing to believe in rapid profit growth. What they often don't believe is the rapid cash flow growth, because they know that with rare exceptions *fast-growing companies have negative cash flow*. It's mature, stable businesses—"cash cows"—that throw off cash. Growth companies, even when profitable, usually need repeated infusions of new money to finance all that expansion.

So when the venture capitalist sees that in Year Five you're projecting sales of $100 million, profits of $30 million, and a cash flow of $20 million pouring out, his willing suspension of disbelief breaks down. He knows that something must be wrong somewhere.

Projections that show high growth coupled with hugely positive cash flow suggest that the management team has been sloppy with its financial assumptions, that it has omitted to take into account major costs, or, worse, that the founders don't really understand how the business works. They also suggest that management lacks objectivity and may succumb easily to fantasy. Finally, this sort of projection implies that management has not faced up to the need for future financings for the business's growth, something that may present serious problems.

Your pro formas will be most attractive and yet credible if they show very fast sales and profit growth coupled with a cash flow more or less at the borderline. It is likely that your company will have to go out for several additional rounds of financing, and your cash flow projections should reflect that.

Yes, there *are* occasional examples of high-growth companies that throw off cash. If your venture turns out to be one of these exotic creatures, that's great. But in that case, you almost certainly don't need venture capital; you should be looking for other sources of funding.

Business Plan Projections—An Objective View

Digital Equipment Corporation is of course the classic example of the venture capital-backed technology growth company. Appropriately, DEC maintains an active program of support for new-venture OEMs (original equipment manufacturers). Tom Austin, who has run this program for DEC, sees a lot of business plans. Here's his viewpoint on pro formas.

> "The first year projections are optimistic, but if you work like hell you can make it happen. The second year projections are wildly optimistic. For Year Three, the projections are out of touch with reality. For Year Four, they're totally outrageous, usually projecting 50–60% pretax profit.
>
> "Realistic projections would show the price of the product *decreasing* with time due to competition. Projected costs should *increase* with time to reflect inflation as well as increased marketing costs to meet competition. As a result, margins realistically should be projected to decrease; you should expect your margin to be cut in half over the first two years."

Salaries and Other Specifics

One nice thing about starting your own business is that you can set your own salary—or try to. There are no hard-and-fast rules on what company officers can get paid, but as a practical matter investors start to get antsy when salaries approach the six-figure range. CEOs of small companies generally draw somewhere around $100,000 per year, but there's room for variation. One investor told us he expected the CEO to earn between $80,000 and $150,000 per year.

Obviously various factors are taken into account in deciding on a specific figure that's appropriate. If you're stepping into the CEO slot from a big company where you were dragging down a small fortune in salary, you can probably get paid at the high end of the entrepreneurial scale, but it will still mean a pay cut. On the other hand, if you're fresh out of school, better figure on a salary that is less than stratospheric.

Of course bonuses and other incentive payments can be negotiated, but don't expect too much along these lines. The idea is that your big gains should come from appreciation of the company's stock, not from your annual compensation. Investors don't want managers who figure on drawing a nice little check every month; they want people who are looking for the big play. As Ken Deemer of InterVen Partners puts it, "We want to invest in entrepreneurs who want to become rich."

When it comes to perks, investors tend to be a bit on the Calvinistic side. Founders who think executive efficiency calls for a company Porsche and a Learjet don't make a good impression on investors. A sensible attitude toward general business expenditures is also appreciated. Investors like to see you project a reasonable frugality in purchases of office facilities, laboratory equipment, and production machinery. "We like a low-burn-rate plan," says Chuck Cole of Julian Cole & Stein.

But venture capitalists can also be firm about the need to spend money where they think it counts. If you are a technology-based business, you'll be expected to project significant R&D costs—5 to 15 percent of sales or even more, depending on the industry. And you'll definitely be expected to commit significant funding to marketing and sales. Whatever your business, you will be expected to understand your industry and to know not only where you can save money but when *not* to be tightfisted.

One high-tech company was turned down because its founders planned to locate in an area with low land costs to save money. The venture firm felt that it should have chosen a more expensive location, in an area with very attractive

living conditions, so that the startup could attract top scientists to work for it.

Defining the Deal

How much should you say in your plan about the deal? Here is
an area where we found vigorous disagreement among the
investors we interviewed.

> "Put a valuation on the company. And prepare a 'greed
> plan' for share distribution."

> "Don't show a valuation in the plan. Don't try to tell me
> what your company's worth or what my return will be; I'll
> figure that out."

So what should you do? If you can discreetly determine the
attitude of the firm on this issue before you make your approach,
do so. But in general it's probably best to leave the valuation
question out of the plan and have it ready on a separate,
supplementary document; whip it out if the investors ask for it.

Style and Content

When it comes to actually writing your plan, keep in mind a
principle we've mentioned before: *Make it easy for the investor*
to get a positive impression of your venture. A plan that is
turgid, filled with jargon, or badly organized is not just a turnoff;
it's an excuse for the investor to stop reading, put your plan in
the out basket, and take a look at the next plan in the in basket.
Make your plan a pleasure to read, and it is more likely to get
read.

Getting Professional Aid

There are individuals and firms that will write a business plan
for you. Fees vary, but a few thousand dollars is typical. If you

can afford it, you may be tempted. Should you write your business plan yourself, or hire an expert to write one for you?

There's no question that a well-written plan can give you a very substantial leg up with investors, and a poorly written plan can pretty much ruin your chances.

Yet there are strong arguments against using a professional business plan writer. For one thing, many of them don't do a very good job. Writing a business plan is, like many kinds of writing, a specialized task. An author may be a whiz at westerns but unable to create convincing science fiction. In the same way, many excellent writers just don't have the specific skills needed for writing business plans, especially knowledge of the audience.

Furthermore, business plan writing pays very badly, even worse than other types of writing. (And receivables from startup entrepreneurs are about the least collectible one can have.) It's hard to make a living at it unless one skimps on preparation and writes very fast using a standard outline. So if your plan is commercially written, it will tend, at best, to resemble the other products of the firm that created it; it will be attractive and clear, perhaps, but not distinctive.

Finally, investors expect a plan to reflect the personality of the founder. When they spot a commercial plan—and they can spot them quite well—they tend to be turned off, just as employers are by a commercial resumé.

We therefore advocate that you write the plan yourself. That's not to say, however, that you shouldn't get professional help. A qualified consultant can assist you in defining the information you need and in organizing your plan. Outside firms can help by assembling data for you, especially in such areas as market research and competitive analysis. If you can afford it, getting pro formas generated by a first-rate professional accountant will greatly improve the financial section of your plan. You should do the actual writing yourself (or have the best writer on your management team do it). But hiring a professional to *edit* your text will almost always be a good investment.

Your entire management team should get involved in the development of the plan. Everyone should have assignments for gathering information. (For a startup, this is a good way to test the quality of potential co-founders before a commitment is made.) Ask each of them to write a rough draft of the sections pertaining to their responsibilities. Have them help out with the editing and proofreading too.

> In preparation for his presentation, one entrepreneur re-treated to his apartment to rewrite his company's business plan. He stayed completely incommunicado for over a week, emerging just before his presentation with a new plan. None of the company's other managers had any input; this lone technologist insisted on retaining total control of the plan, as he insisted on total control of the business. The plan turned out to be full of contradictions and omissions. The Enterprise Forum panel was not impressed; neither were investors. The company received no further funding and was forced into bankruptcy.

As we shall see, the typical financing takes longer—much longer—than most entrepreneurs expect. In the process, your business plan may have to be revised several times. Once you start getting feedback from investors, you will probably find that your first version, which you thought was perfect, is deficient. New facts will come in; you'll refine your financial projections; new members will join the team, and maybe some old ones will depart. So your business plan is likely to be in a continual state of flux.

What's more, your funding approach may change. You discover that you can't raise as much money as you first antici-pated and decide to ask for less. There go all your financial projections! Back to 1-2-3 for a new set of spreadsheets. Your financing strategy may change and you'll have to adapt the plan to appeal to a different set of investors. Maybe you wrote your plan to appeal to a specific venture firm that likes to see a plan that projects growth by acquisitions. But it turns you down, and you now try another firm that wants to see a green-field startup and pure internal growth. You have to rewrite the plan. Then you decide to get bank financing for some equipment, and you need an entirely new plan designed to be attractive to bankers.

If you expect, and plan for, these repeated revisions, you won't find them so frustrating. You'll want to maintain a good record of the changes you've made and to be prepared to explain to suspicious investors why you made them. Don't forget that you'll have to keep track of the various revisions of your document and of which version was sent to which potential investor.

A real business plan is a living document, constantly growing and evolving. It has to be, to match the growth and evolution of your venture. Be prepared to live with the process.

> While writing this book I've been setting up a major venture capital-backed deal. The business plan went through five major rewrites and countless minor revisions. What's more, bank funding is a significant part of this deal, so I had to write an entirely separate plan to provide the information the bank needed.

Six Keys to a Good Business Plan

What are the requirements for your business plan as a written document? We can summarize them as follows:

The Good Business Plan

- Clear
- Complete
- Concise
- Candid
- Conservative
- Clean

1. *A business plan should be clear.* Eschew obfuscation, as the saying is. Remember that your reader is probably nowhere near as familiar with all the ins and outs as you are.

There is a story that Napoleon kept a very stupid officer on his staff solely to check the clarity of his military orders. He would show every order to the officer in question, then have him explain what it

meant. If the explanation was incorrect, Napoleon would take back
the order and rewrite it.

You can test your business plan in the same way by asking
someone who is ignorant of your industry or technology to read
your rough draft and decide whether it is basically intelligible.

Inventors, computer buffs, and other techies are notoriously prone to write plans that are filled with impenetrable
jargon. If your venture is technology-based, make a special
effort to minimize the use of technical terms in your plan. Where
you do use scientific or engineering terminology, explain it as
you go along and be sure to include a glossary.

Another menace to document clarity is what might be called
"Wall Street Style." People who have spent too much time in
Lower Manhattan develop a tendency to talk like an offering
memorandum: "The Company may also consider using a portion of the net proceeds for the acquisition of businesses or
technologies related to the Company's business. Although the
Company has from time to time engaged in discussions with
respect to possible acquisitions, the Company has no agreement,
understanding, or commitment and is not currently engaged in
negotiations with respect to any such transaction. Pending use
of the proceeds, the Company intends. . . ." Some entrepreneurs try to simulate this sort of prose in their plans because
they think investors expect it, or because they feel it will make
them sound more sophisticated. It's better to speak English. A
business plan is not an offering memorandum (unless you make
it so, which is unwise) and shouldn't sound like one. When you
go public and need an offering memorandum, your investment
bankers will write one for you, never fear.

You should give careful attention to the organization of your
plan. Again, you know the whole story and can start anywhere.
The reader doesn't and must start at the beginning. So be sure
the early chapters of your plan don't assume knowledge that
you won't provide until later in the document.

Don't hesitate to use graphics in moderation to improve the
clarity of your text. A few well-designed graphics or drawings

can be very helpful. You may even want to insert photos if they are essential to get across an important point. Don't, however, waste space with color portraits of your founders or pictures of your many happy employees whistling while they work.

2. *A business plan should be complete.* Your plan should discuss, at least briefly, every critical issue for your venture. Any omission is like a blank time period on a job hunter's resumé; it will raise suspicions that may be difficult to dispel. Indeed, you may never be given the chance to dispel them. You can't cover everything in depth, or your plan will become unwieldly. But be sure everything of importance is at least mentioned.

If you find yourself having trouble keeping the length down, examine how you balance your discussion. Usually there is room for cuts in the description of the product and its features. On the other hand, most plans contain too little information on the founders' past track records. Remember, you're trying to get the investor to hire you as CEO.

3. *A business plan should be concise.* Whatever debate there may be over the proper length for a business plan, one thing is sure: It shouldn't be any longer than it has to be.

The most difficult task for a writer is shortening a manuscript. One thing you can do is eliminate any topic that isn't essential. For instance, your plan does not need to discuss details of the deal; a couple of sentences explaining how much capital you think you need and the form in which you intend to raise it will generally suffice.

Relentlessly blue-pencil any form of hype. Many plans can be lightened up by 10 percent or so just by going through and striking out all the self-complimentary adjectives. Don't tell prospective investors how rich you're going to make them; they can calculate that themselves from your financials. Minimize evaluations in your plan. Don't try to tell readers what they're going to think; tell them the facts.

You'll be surprised how much you can shorten a plan by cleaning up the style. If you're hard up for space, go through the text and mark every sentence that's in the passive voice; switch them to the active voice and you can often pick up half a

page or so. If you need to cut more, go through the plan again
and underline every sentence that uses the verb "to be." Rewrite a third of them, using action verbs; you'll gain some room
and also improve readability.

4. *A business plan should be candid.* Do not omit, hide,
gloss over, or, worst of all, falsify any negative factors about
your venture. No matter how minor, even trivial, the drawback
may be, if you conceal it and get caught you're probably finished
with that investor and any others that he talks to. (There is also
the risk, in some cases, of going to jail.)

It pays to be frank about any problems you fear. Some
business plans even have a separate section titled "The Downside" or "What's Wrong with this Venture." No sophisticated
investor is going to believe that your venture—or any venture—
is risk-free. By taking the initiative in discussing the negatives,
you demonstrate your objectivity and integrity. You also get a
chance to mitigate any damage by immediately bringing up your
plans to deal with the problem.

Trial lawyers long ago learned this strategy. If your witness has
a credibility problem, such as a prior conviction for perjury, bring it
out yourself and defuse it. Don't wait for the opposition to expose
it during cross-examination.

To be specific about a very common problem: Don't deni-
grate the competition. A plan proclaiming that "we have no
competition" has a real credibility problem; there is *always*
competition. Especially amusing are the all-too-common plans
that state that the competition is moribund but then go on to
project a 3 percent market share. If competitors are so weak,
how are they holding 97 percent of the market? Your plan will
be most convincing if you demonstrate that you have carefully
investigated your competitors and that you do not underestimate
them.

5. *A business plan should be conservative.* Once investors

have bought into a company, they don't like surprises. But if surprises must come, they prefer that they be pleasant surprises. So your plan will be regarded more favorably if your projections are conservative.

Many plans display a sort of false conservatism that accomplishes nothing because the original assumptions are all based on fantasy. If translated into plain language, the message of these plans would be, "We could assume $100 billion in sales, but let's be 'conservative' and assume only $10 billion." An assumption is not conservative just because it is smaller than some other unwarranted assumption; it is conservative when it is based on *facts*.

6. *A business plan should be clean.* Your business plan should definitely be presentable. Cosmetic factors are not trivial. But you won't benefit by being too fancy.

Real-world business plans, as we've mentioned, are fluid documents, constantly being revised as new information comes in or flaws are found. So if your plan shows up bound in leather with gilt lettering, the recipient is likely to be a bit skeptical.

> We're not making this up. We've seen several plans permanently bound with very expensive covers. Some five-percenters and public relations outfits run what in effect are vanity presses for business plans. They produce, for hefty fees, very professional-looking books. A hard-bound plan full of four-color photos can impress the hell out of a naive entrepreneur client, but it's not very practical as a money-raising document.

Moreover, investors are always wary of entrepreneurs who appear too fond of spending money. If your business plan looks expensive, they'll start to wonder about your tastes in office furniture and company cars.

Be considerate of the investor's convenience. Investors *work* with business plans. They read them, put them in files so they can find them, make copies for associates to study, and so on. An outsize, unbound, or badly arranged plan can be a real annoyance.

We recommend that you reproduce your plan on a high-

quality copier and use an inexpensive press binder or three-ring
binder. As for the document itself: In these days of desktop
publishing, document escalation is a factor you will have to take
into account. Standards for written presentations, including
business plans, are definitely higher than they were. Like it or
not, you'll be competing with some pretty snazzy-looking plans,
and you should put some effort into making yours look good.

Because your plan is likely to be heavily and repeatedly
revised, use of a word-processing program is practically a must.
Use a high-quality printer for your final draft; if you don't own
one, you can probably borrow one for long enough to print one
document. If you can afford, and know how to use, desktop
publishing software, you should certainly take advantage of it.
Just don't get carried away with multiple fonts and exotic
graphics.

It's generally a good idea to number copies of your business
plan so that you can control their distribution.

Business Plan Blunders

We asked investors to tell us how *not* to write a business plan.
What errors should the entrepreneur avoid?

> "I try to look past the deficiencies of a bad plan to see if
> there might be a good business behind it. But if the plan
> indicates that the entrepreneur is not in contact with reality—
> for instance, if a ridiculous valuation is put on the company—
> that's it."

> "Bad grammar, bad writing, and above all unimpressive
> resumés. When the CEO is a retired military man whose
> qualifications are that he could assemble and disassemble
> weapons in the army . . ."

> "Nepotism. High salaries for the management team. Man-
> agement with no background in the industry. And I don't like
> to see founders who are too old."

> "I'm not positive that there's always a correlation between
> a good plan and a good company. But I have no trouble

immediately rejecting a deal where the entrepreneur clearly didn't bother to put any effort into the plan. Puffed-up resumés are a negative. I remember one plan where the founder told us what a genius he'd been since childhood. But he never finished college and his track record in business was not impressive."

"We don't want to see family or friends in the business. If the plan is too slick, or full of hype, we reject it. We care about cosmetics, and bad English in the plan is a definite negative. *Anything* off-color is a negative. We don't like a deal that's too messy or complex; no five-percenters. We don't want to see projections with high salaries for management—say, over $150,000 for the CEO."

"It's a danger sign if the plan is too slick; write your own. Avoid massive financial projections, especially if they don't have a solid foundation. I'll bow out if there's a broker or a five-percenter involved. I don't want to see any husband/wife teams or family entanglements. We don't fund ventures whose strategy is to capture a small share of a big market; and we don't like companies that are aimed at the *Fortune* 500 market, because big firms are late adopters."

Parting Advice

Before you finalize your business plan and start to peddle it, do three things.

1. Have at least one independent business friend—not one of your team—review the plan and give you a candid evaluation.
2. Have someone edit the plan to make sure your text is clear and your grammar clean. Try a college English professor; they work cheap.
3. Have the plan proofread by as many people as you can persuade to read it. (Merrill's Law: *The average number of typos per page of double-spaced manuscript is the*

reciprocal of the number of different *people who have proofread it.*)

Case Studies

Having a bad business plan is like having bad breath: The people you most want to impress (the investors) will never tell you why they rejected you. Giving entrepreneurs objective, informed, and candid critiques of their business plans is one of the prime functions of the MIT Enterprise Forum and similar organizations. It can be an unsettling experience for an entrepreneur, but the panels, which usually include at least one venture capitalist, provide invaluable advice on the best way to improve a business plan.

In the following four case studies (taken from the CalTech/ MIT Enterprise Forum), the panel comments we summarize are very typical of the criticisms venture capitalists and other investors make of bad plans and will give you a compelling impression of some common mistakes to avoid.

Case 1: High-Tech Swimming Pools

The first company proposed to make energy-efficient swimming pools by exploiting new developments (some of them based on aerospace work) in materials technology and improved designs. They were seeking $2.4 million in venture capital.

The panel immediately zeroed in on the venture's market strategy.

"Your business plan says you're 'targeting' homeowner swimming pools, and 'targeting' hotel chains, and 'targeting' several other market segments. In fact, you're 'targeting' everyone but yak herders in the Gobi desert."

"Your marketing section reminded me of a Yellow Pages ad for an auto repair shop I once saw: 'We Specialize in Everything.' "

"Segment your market. Then pick a segment and go after it."

The panel strongly approved the founder's hands-on approach to the market, but warned that he was overestimating the significance of the "interest" he'd generated with prospective customers.

"Your sales numbers are totally unsupported. The letters from possible customers are a nice addition to the plan, but 'expressions of interest' mean nothing. It costs them nothing to write you a letter, but you'll hear a different story when you ask them to cough up some cash."

"High-end swimming pools are a selective, specialty business. It's highly cyclical. And distribution channels are a problem; there's very high turnover in the business."

The founder's qualifications were impressive.

"You have a marvelous background. You've got terrific credentials as a designer and you're obviously an aggressive salesman."

The operational plan, however, came in for criticism.

"Don't saddle yourself with buildings and capital equipment at this early stage; put your money into design and into selling."

"It's a very clever manufacturing concept. But I think your schedule is highly optimistic. You're planning on putting in a lot of new tooling to manufacture these things—and new tooling is rarely trouble-free."

The founder was using an intermediary to seek capital, and had professional assistance in writing the plan. These were perceived as strong negatives.

"The business plan is a very professional presentation from a visual perspective. But you didn't write it. I'd rather have a plan written by the entrepreneur even if it's not so smooth. And using a finder is not a good way to get financed."

The pro formas were also considered inadequate.

"All you have is a P&L [profit-and-loss statement]. No balance sheet. And, especially, no cash flow. Without a cash flow projection, it's unclear where my investment would be going and whether it's going to last."

In the end, the panel members were not optimistic about this venture, in spite of their respect for the founder's qualifications.

"It looks too much like a solution looking for a problem."

"The plan leaves me feeling that this will be a tough row to hoe."

"I don't think you will find financing for this business. I'd recommend that you seriously consider applying your technology to a more receptive market, such as aerospace, where you already have some experience."

Case 2: Electronic Displays and Signs

The second company had a technology for high-resolution, low-cost electronic displays. It was at the startup stage but already had a few sales.

Again, the panel recommended a tighter market focus.

"Your business plan describes a $2.9 billion market, but apparently that includes everything from disco videos to billboards. What is the segmentation?"

"I couldn't figure out from your plan what you are selling: hardware installation? or advertising?"

"Fasten on one market segment where your product has a clear advantage. Keep in mind that it's hard to persuade people to take down obsolete signs; I'd recommend that you concentrate on new signs."

In fact, marketing overall was considered a major weakness.

"Your're pushing your advantage in cost per pixel. Does the customer care? I'll bet customers are concerned with cost per sign. What are the benefits to the customer?"

"Looking at the business plan, I do not see anything about a patent or any other barrier to entry. You've got strong competition—what's to prevent them from copying your product?"

"I look at your management team in the plan—good people— but what have you got? CEO, chief operations officer, vice-president for manufacturing, director of engineering. I see four overhead heads, and nobody doing sales!"

"It's nice that you're getting 'positive articles in trade publications.' But that does not indicate that anyone is going to buy your product."

The panel found major problems with the financial projections, the result of poor assumptions on the marketing side.

"Your products sell for tens of thousands of dollars. That makes it a capital purchase decision for the customer, which means a long sales cycle. This means you'll need a lot more working capital than you've projected."

"This business is very service/reliability-oriented. You're going to have costs for maintenance, for service, for meeting warranties. That should be reflected in your financials."

"You've grossly underestimated the amount of capital required."

The panel recommended that the company try to team up with a large national advertiser who could provide it with a distribution channel and relieve it of some of its heavy capital costs.

Case 3: A Credit Card Checking Device for Retailers

A third startup venture had developed a point-of-purchase credit card checking device for retailers. Sophisticated encryption technology was used in combination with personal identification numbers (PINs), as in bank automatic teller machines. The company was seeking $3.8 million in venture capital.

The panel aimed its criticism of the business plan primarily at marketing issues.

"In the business plan your market is characterized as 'vast'— $2 billion. You forecast getting a 1 to 2 percent share. Venture capital is not attracted to small players in huge markets."

"The business plan did not identify any competitors. If your product is that unique, why is only a 1 to 2 percent market share forecasted?"

"You're basing your product pricing on what is charged for 'comparable electronic complexity.' What has that got to do with it? What are customers *willing to pay?"*

"You have nothing in your plan about sales and distribution strategy."

"Recent tests of utilization of credit cards show that use of PINs is not *being accepted by the public in retail transactions. That's crucial to your market strategy. I dug up that information in five minutes from readily available public sources. The fact that you didn't discuss it in your plan doesn't say much for the thoroughness of your marketing studies."*

"You have been working on this technology literally for years. Yet you have never talked even to one potential customer, let alone done a real market survey."

The panel was impressed by the qualifications of the founders, but not by their commitment.

"The management team shows great technological and business strength. And they are all comfortably employed in large organizations. Where is the commitment to this venture?"

"You have no prototype; no beta-test sites; no marketing; and no founder funds committed. Why is this supposed to be interesting to venture capital?"

Case 4: An Ultrahigh-Tech Computer System

A fourth company developed ultrahigh-tech hardware/software packages that made it possible for computer systems from different manufacturers to talk to each other. The company sought $6.5 million in venture capital.

The panelists found the business plan heavy going.

"All of the current buzzwords are used freely: 'office automation,' 'LANS,' 'relational data bases,' 'open networks standards,' 'applications software.' The result is pure technobabble."

"Jargon."

"The business plan is disorganized."

Panelists couldn't get a clear grasp of the market from their reading of the business plan.

"There is no market description. I didn't see any market research at all."

"What business are you really in? The computer communications market is much too large. You need to specify the segment you're going to approach."

The CEO was regarded as highly qualified, a top expert in the field, but panelists noted one powerful turnoff for venture capital financing.

"Having family members [the founder's wife] on the management team is a red flag."

The pro formas came in for criticism too.

"The business plan provides lots of financials, but they are confusing and don't provide essential information. For instance, before I put in $6.5 million I'd like to have you tell me what it's going to be used for."

"The financials project growth from zero to $25 million in five years for sales of your new product. There is a 2.5-year

development cycle for product introduction, yet a $10 million profit is forecast for Year Five. This is unrealistic."

These ventures are typical of those rejected by venture capitalists not because the businesses are necessarily bad but because the plans are so deficient that investors cannot effectively evaluate the business. Enterprise Forum panelists conscientiously read the business plans assigned to them, no matter how poorly written they are. Venture capitalists simply won't bother.

Certain themes appear repeatedly in critiques of Enterprise Forum presenters: lack of market focus; failure to back up grandiose sales projections with market research; unintelligible plans; and financial projections that are incomplete and inconsistent. These case studies should give you a more tangible feel for some of the major business plan mistakes to avoid.

Bibliography

The Chicago Manual of Style, 13th ed. Chicago: University of Chicago Press, 1982. You never can tell when the reader of your plan will be one of those obnoxious characters who knows the difference between a comma and a semicolon and who gets upset if you use "presently" when you mean "at present." Checking your work against standard references like the *Chicago Manual* may protect you from appearing uneducated or sloppy.

Delaney, Robert V., Jr., and Robert A. Howell. *How to Prepare an Effective Business Plan*. New York: AMACOM, 1986.

Rich, Stanley R., and David Gumpert. *Business Plans that Win $$$*. New York: Harper & Row, 1985. Advice from seasoned and realistic authors makes this book a valuable guide to development of the business plan. It goes beyond the plan, also, to discuss important aspects of running the business.

Tufte, Edward R. *The Visual Display of Quantitative Information*. Cheshire, Conn.: Graphics Press, 1983. The availability of computer graphics programs has resulted in an incredible proliferation of unintelligible graphics. Tufte explains the difference between good and bad visual displays and shows how to get your information across with clarity and efficiency. Anybody with a need to communicate by means of graphs or charts should own and study this book.

3

You've Got Fifteen Seconds to Sing

After you've put in months of work writing a business plan, it's only natural that you should want to see the thing *read* by investors. Most business plans aren't; they are glanced at and returned. Only a few get real attention. The Executive Summary frequently makes the difference.

By a tradition, the origins of which are lost in the mists of antiquity, every business plan should begin with an Executive Summary. This gives the reader a brief overview of the contents of the plan. As a practical matter, harried venture capitalists use the Executive Summary to decide whether the plan is worth reading. So, in a sense, the Executive Summary is the most important part of the plan. We therefore devote a separate chapter to this subject.

The Goal

The purpose of the Executive Summary is to induce potential investors to read the rest of the plan. So, unless you want to alienate them at the outset, avoid the three don'ts:

1. *Don't be prolix*. The whole point of the Executive Summary is to provide a *short* summary of the plan. If you put in

three or four pages of dense text in an attempt to include all the important information from the plan, the investor won't even read the Executive Summary, let alone the plan. A good rule of thumb is that anything over 500 words is too long. You should shoot for 250.

2. *Don't tease.* There's a temptation to go to the opposite extreme and withhold essential information from the reader. The implied message is, "To find out what you need to know, you'll have to read the whole plan." This is not a good idea. Investors are busy and don't like to play games. They're put off by being teased.

3. *Don't hype.* The Executive Summary should summarize the plan, not evaluate it. Some entrepreneurs feel that the plan has the information and that the function of the Executive Summary is to advertise it, to tell the investor how wonderful the venture is and how rich everybody will become. Again, this is completely counterproductive. The Executive Summary, like the rest of the plan, should be informative, not evaluative. The tone should be enthusiastic but businesslike.

A Simple Rule

Just as with the business plan as a whole, you should be suspicious of canned formulas for writing an Executive Summary. Each venture is unique, and there are times when an innovative approach is required. However, we find it valuable to have some sort of basic rule to use, at least as a starting point. Here's an approach that will usually generate a pretty good Executive Summary.

REFER TO THE FIVE KEY QUESTIONS ON WHICH YOUR BUSINESS PLAN IS BASED. TO EACH QUESTION, WRITE A TWO-SENTENCE ANSWER. THAT'S YOUR EXECUTIVE SUMMARY.

The value of this approach is that it ensures coverage of the essential information about your venture while tightly restricting length.

To Make It Enticing

So far, we've developed a method for making your Executive Summary complete but concise. This is not enough; it should also be an effective means of enticing the investor to read on. Once you have a rough draft of your Executive Summary, you should review it with the investor's concerns in mind. Go over what you've written and ask yourself these three questions:

1. *Does the Executive Summary make it clear that we are proposing the kind of deal that the investor does?* For instance, if the plan is being sent to venture capitalists, the Executive Summary should clearly state that the venture has very ambitious growth goals (for example, $50 million sales within five years) and that an equity investment is desired.

2. *Does the Executive Summary clearly project the qualifications of the management team?* Investors rate the importance of management quality higher than any other factor when they evaluate businesses. So be sure you don't skimp on this section of your summary. This is one area where adding an extra sentence or two may be justified.

3. *Does the Executive Summary explain what the business is about and how this venture's approach is unique?* It is astounding how many Executive Summaries fail to state *what the business is*. The reader is left scratching his head. "Is this outfit going to sell chips, boards, or complete computers? Or maybe software? Or maybe some combination? And what's this about '*Fortune* 1000 customers'? Who is going to use what they're selling, and for what purpose?" (And by the way, watch out for snappy answers like "We sell solutions." That's fine for customers. But though investors may know the economics of the circuit board business or the software business, they have no way to evaluate the prospects of the "solution" business.) You must tell the investor what you're selling and to whom you're selling in specific terms. What's more, you must successfully project the unique advantage you have that will make your venture successful—what you've got that the other guys ain't got. You should be able to explain what your business is about while standing on one foot.

None of this is easy. Writing a good Executive Summary is like putting ten pounds of garter snakes in a five-pound bag. By the time you finish, you'll turn to revising your financial projections as a refreshing vacation.

Some Examples

To show you a little more about writing Executive Summaries, we've persuaded three computer software ventures to let us use theirs as examples. We've critiqued them and developed a makeover for each one.

PAX MODULAR SYSTEMS EXECUTIVE SUMMARY (Original Version)

<u>Introduction</u>

This business plan summarizes all pertinent information related to a funding request to facilitate the expansion of <u>Pax Modular Systems, Inc.</u>

<u>Pax Modular Systems</u> designs, markets, and supports proprietary computer systems "on-line" that enable personal computer owners to gain 24 hour access to electronic marketing materials, customer support data, or to purchase products and services using a major credit card—24 hours a day.

<u>Pax Modular Systems</u> designs these standalone electronic marketing systems for all types of businesses. In addition, the Company has designed and implemented several co-operative on-line marketing networks for those organizations that are two [sic] small to purchase their systems. This concept operates in a similar fashion to organizations that charge up to $7 for the use of their FAX machines. As a result, <u>Pax Modular Systems</u> generates monthly rents ranging from $66-$150 for space on its highly popular co-op electronic marketing systems.

Pax Modular System's existing client base includes:

COMPANY NAME	TYPE OF BUSINESS	APPLICATION
XEROX CORP. Santa Clara, CA	Develops CAE software	Customer Support Marketing/ Sales
C.S.P.I. Boston, MA	Manufactures array process- ing equip.	Customer Support Marketing/ Sales
DEALER-NET Los Angeles, CA	Resells vehicles for use by auto dealers	Networking, Sales Dealer Support
THE RECYCLER Los Angeles, CA	Publishes con- sumer newspa- pers	Accepts user data and Elec- tronic Mail
CIE TERMINALS Costa Mesa, CA	Manufactures data terminal equipment	Customer Support Marketing/ Sales
FUTURENET/ DATA I/O Chatsworth, CA	Develops CAE software	Customer Support Marketing/ Sales
MERCURY COMPUTER Philadelphia, PA	Information brokers to com- merce industry	On-line mail or- der 24 hour da- tabase
HUGHES AIRCRAFT Long Beach, CA	Military Con- tractors for Gov- ernment	Internal data- base and inter- nal mail

For the most part, the Company functions as a value-added dealer of PC hardware and software and develops custom applications and software to maximize the effectiveness of the products. As a result, the Company can be defined primarily as an organization selling proprietary knowledge and systems.

As stated, the Company maintains several co-op advertising networks and rents advertising space enabling all sizes of businesses to benefit from 24 hour exposure without the overhead and maintenance of their own systems.

The Investment

Pax Modular Systems has invested substantial time and money to demonstrate that a large and expanding market exists for its products and services. Based on almost no advertising or a promotional budget, good success has been achieved. The Company is now seeking to obtain the required funds to enter full scale operation, establish profitability, and dominate this new market.

Pax Modular Systems is seeking debt financing of $400,000. Along with a note payable, the Company will offer warrants for Company stock that may be exercised by the investor(s). The Company will negotiate the exact terms of the investment and the projected payback period with qualified parties.

Pax Modular Systems welcomes investor participation in the management of the Company. The extent of this participation will be predetermined and agreed upon in writing, prior to the finalization of the investment.

The Management

Currently, all business operations are handled by Mr. Brian L. Berman, who holds several degrees including an MBA from the University of Redlands and has served in a variety of technical and management positions with established companies throughout Southern California. Mr. Berman is also a recognized author and lecturer and is currently the Chairman of the San Fernando Valley Section of The Institute of Electrical & Electronics Engineers (I.E.E.E.).

As the Company grows, qualified employees will be retained to assume other responsibilities in the organization. Mr. Berman's role will evolve into that of a Chief Operating Officer and responsible for long range planning.

Sales Forecasts

On-line information systems and related applications have established themselves as valuable marketing tools for growth oriented companies. The success of other on-line systems such as the SOURCE and PRODIGY prove that businesses and consumers utilize these data services frequently when properly marketed.

Currently, the industry reports that on-line database facilities are generating over $2.1 billion in annual revenues. As personal computer ownership and modem usage proliferates, on-line systems will experience a proportional level of growth.

Based on past performance, Pax Modular Systems has developed projections of sales and expenses. Though a higher level of growth is anticipated, the Company realizes that these services will take time to generate interest and profitability.

Summarized projected income statement

	Year 1	Year 2	Year 3
SALES	485,000	977,000	1,380,000
COST OF GOODS	125,000	255,000	370,000
GROSS PROFIT	360,000	722,000	1,010,000
OPERATING EXPENSE	384,285	505,600	543,100
EARNINGS (PRE-TAX)	(23,685)	216,400	466,900

Pax Modular Systems considers the viewing of worst case scenarios to be an important management tool. The effect of economic downturns, lower than anticipated sales, higher costs and other variables will be considered as future plans are developed.

Commentary on Pax Modular Systems

The original Executive Summary for Pax is badly bloated. It's easy to shorten because much of the text doesn't really say anything. Take, for instance, the first paragraph, which states essentially, "This is an Executive Summary." All this dead-wood should be cleared out.

Pax, at the time this statement was written, was a one-man show with very low sales. The Executive Summary tries to put a good face on the situation, which is fine, but it tries too hard. The result is a defensive tone. The portentous prose and re-peated invocations of "the company" seem to mimic Wall Street offerings. But for a small deal of this sort, an informal tone is more likely to be effective. This company (as the original sum-mary says) was not venture capital material; it simply didn't have the necessary ultra-ambitious growth objectives. The plan should therefore be written to appeal to the private investor.

For our makeover, we took a different tack in presenting Pax's situation. Describing the company's sales efforts as "test marketing" eliminates the negative of low sales, and allows emphasis of an important positive: Here is an entrepreneur who has thoroughly investigated the market and has hands-on expe-rience with how it works.

Neither the list nor the table should be present in the Executive Summary; their contents should be summarized. The section on investment should also be abbreviated; it is not only too long but much too defensive. Finally, many typos and grammatical errors should be corrected.

PAX MODULAR SYSTEMS EXECUTIVE SUMMARY
(Improved Version)

Many businesses need to offer twenty-four-hour access to customers, employees, or distributors, but cannot afford the expense of three shifts of phone operators.

Pax Modular Systems designs, markets, and supports on-line computer systems that allow personal computer owners to get information or make purchases over tele-phone lines. These turn-key systems can be rented or pur-chased. Pax also organizes cooperative marketing networks for retailers—electronic shopping malls.

Pax has conducted active test marketing of its concept

for over a year. Current clients include the Xerox Corporation, which is using a Pax system to provide customer support; the Recycler, a newspaper that uses a Pax system to accept classified ads; and Hughes Aircraft, for which the application was internal mail. By working with these and other clients Pax has developed detailed information about what it takes to succeed in this market.

Brian L. Berman, Pax's founder, is an MBA with management experience in several small electronics companies.

Pax seeks $400,000 in the form of debt with warrants to finance its market rollout. The company expects to become profitable in its second year of operations and projects sales of $1.38 million and profits of $467,000 in its third year.

CIM REALTIME SOFTWARE EXECUTIVE SUMMARY
(Original Version)

CIM RealTime Software holds exclusive worldwide marketing rights to sell, license, and distribute Trak It (TM) and Trak Fac (TM) factory automation software. CIM RealTime Software seeks an investment of $500,000 to $1 million of seed capital for marketing and advanced product development. CIM RealTime Software has the capability of becoming an industrial leader and a highly successful, money-making company.

These software programs address the production tracking niche of computer integrated manufacturing (CIM), and they provide a key ingredient of the just in time (JIT) manufacturing concept advocated by the industrial leaders of today. As its goal, computer integrated manufacturing (CIM) consolidates the islands of automation in a factory into a complete whole. The Trak It (TM) and Trak Fac (TM) software programs are applicable to about 300,000 factories in the United States, specially in large, multi-plant companies that use batch-processing manufacturing techniques.

Trak It (TM) uses the DOS operating system, and Trak Fac (TM) uses the Unix operating system, providing access to all segments of the market. Moreover, while there is competition out there, there are few competitive software packages that are mature.

Apollo Computer Inc. has recognized Trak Fac's capacity for problem solving in the factory by inviting CIM RealTime Software to participate in its 1989 FactoryView marketing campaign. Currently CIM RealTime Software is one of six Point Solution Suppliers for Apollo's "paperless factory" concept. The FactoryView marketing campaign is a forum to create product awareness in 12 U.S. cities and 2 Canadian cities. It will provide national visibility, immediate product credibility, and direct access to distribution channels. Taking advantage of the Apollo connection gives CIM RealTime Software a unique opportunity to dominate the market before the competition can organize.

There are currently six products that make up the CIM RealTime Software product line. They are:

PC/DOS and MS/DOS

Trak It (TM) I * Production Tracking Manager
Trak It (TM) II * Service Center Manager, and
Trak It (TM) III * Perceived Quality Manager

Unix Operating System

Trak Fac (TM) I * Production Tracking Manager
Trak Fac (TM) II * Service Center Manager, and
Trak Fac (TM) III * Perceived Quality Manager

The I, II and III series of programs are similar—almost identical—except that they run on different operating systems.

These programs are extremely fast, custom data-base software applications with extensive capabilities for data collection, information retrieval and reporting. These programs have been under development for four years, and they have matured on the shop floor in some of the largest electronic manufacturing plants in California, such as Western Digital, Fairchild, and Intel. Currently the software is providing big benefits for a local data equipment communications company.

To our knowledge, no competing software package incorporates the comprehensive capabilities required to track production in a large, high volume manufacturing facility—on a personal computer. Trak It (TM) and Trak Fac (TM) software addresses the 85 percent of all manufacturing plants that are still paper driven. The software can be implemented without changing existing factory procedures and without buying expensive computer hardware. The software is designed for serialized products and the electronic manufacturing community. Manufacturing Resource Planning (MRP II) programs are seen as complementary products, completing the computer integrated manufacturing picture.

Every factory trade journal today repeatedly preaches the crucial need for U.S. manufacturers to decrease labor costs simply to stay even with world competition. Trak It (TM) and Trak Fac (TM) software offer the manufacturer important, money-saving advantages, including the ability to:

—Decrease labor costs
—Reduce inventories
—Improve lead times
—Provide quality control

CIM RealTime Software's marketing plan for 1989 includes:

I. Participation with Apollo Computer Inc. in a strategic marketing alliance to help create the "paperless factory."

II. Penetrating the additional computer hardware markets, such as other Unix compatible systems, the MS/DOS (compatible) market, the OS/2 (IBM) market, and the emerging multi-tasking environments.

III. Penetrating the medical manufacturing market, pharmaceutical industry, and hospital/physician traceability market with two new modules to the Trak It (TM) and Trak Fac (TM) family, Lot Tracking Manager (LTM). On a per capita basis, this market niche has the potential for twice the volume of sales of Phases I and II combined. One factor driving this market is the Food & Drug Administration's good manufacturing practices, which require product traceability for seven years.

CIM RealTime Software is preparing to introduce these factory automation software packages into the business-to-business market for the emerging computerized factory of the future. Our participation in Apollo's FactoryView program must begin immediately. To capitalize on this marketing opportunity, CIM RealTime Software needs immediate start-up funding.

There is a vast, untapped market out there for CIM RealTime Software's new applications programs. You can profit by helping us to tap this market now, to increase the product sophistication for the future. In five years, we plan to harvest the rewards through an initial public offering.

Commentary on CIM RealTime Software

At over a thousand words, CIM's Executive Summary is far too long. The prose is very wordy, continually reiterating the name of the company and of its products; it sounds like a television ad that tries to drive a brand name into the viewer's brain through relentless repetition.

Although a lot of information is presented, the reader has some difficulty understanding just what is being sold, and to whom, and why customers buy the products. The Executive Summary should more forcefully present the nature of the business.

CIM was seeking venture capital, as the closing mention of a projected initial public offering hints. Unfortunately, the summary fails to provide the key information that would entice a venture capitalist. To provide classic venture capital payoffs, this company would have to reach the $50 to $100 million range within five years. That's a pretty big company for the software industry; how are they going to do it? What about the management team? How about proprietary protection of the products? Market size and growth, as well as distribution problems, are glossed over in the Executive Summary. Finally, professional investors would like the entrepreneur to know, and clearly explain, how much money he needs and what he's going to use it for. "An investment of $500,000 to $1 million" is pretty inexact and suggests that the financial planning is a bit fuzzy, to say the least.

The statement that CIM "needs immediate start-up funding" or it will lose the Apollo partnership opportunity projects an invitation to investors to take advantage of the company's urgent need for cash. It's like hanging a "kick me" sign on the founder's back.

This Executive Summary does explain, at least briefly, why customers need the product. The name-dropping is handled well, and the founder projects that he understands the industry and knows what he's talking about. There's another plus: The summary is mostly factual, only occasionally lapsing into evaluative self-praise.

For our makeover we tightened up the presentation and pulled some key information out of the body of the business plan, which had some very solid material in it. We also shifted focus to the market and its needs, and clarified the investment objectives.

CIM REALTIME SOFTWARE EXECUTIVE SUMMARY (Improved Version)

Competitive pressure—domestic and foreign—is pushing U.S. manufacturers toward computer-integrated manufacturing (CIM). Current concerns, including quality control, just-in-time systems, and government requirements for production tracking, make computerization of factory record keeping necessary.

CIM RealTime Software has developed products that automate production tracking by serial number, as well as tracking service and repair work. These programs, Trak It and Trak Fac, run on PC or workstation platforms under either MS-DOS or Unix. They are inexpensive, fast, and highly flexible, unlike competing products that run on minicomputers or mainframes. CIM is thus in a position to dominate the major segment of the market—the 314,000 manufacturing plants with less than 100 employees.

CIM's founders are Mike Powell, who previously operated a company selling bar code and other data collection equipment to factories; and Dr. X, who has worked as a programmer at a major software firm.

The Trak It and Trak Fac software has been successfully tested at customers like Intel and Fairchild. Apollo Computer has agreed to enter a marketing partnership with CIM and make the company one of its Point Solution Suppliers for its "paperless factory" concept. CIM seeks $1 million in venture capital to finance market rollout and development of follow-on products.

ABC SYSTEMS, INC. EXECUTIVE SUMMARY
(Original Version)

Healthcare providers including hospitals, physicians, and health maintenance organizations face the challenge to improve the quality of patient care and the economic necessity to simultaneously increase productivity. Action is required to meet the aspirations of the public for better medical care while responding to the urgent demands of federal and private insurers to trim costs. Computerization of patient care data management is the best strategy to accomplish these objectives. ABC Systems, Incorporated offers a series of proprietary software systems which specifically address automation of clinical data management.

Computerization of patient care, as differentiated from administrative functions, represents an exceptional business opportunity in the healthcare computer industry. The

U.S. market for computer application in patient care has increased from $147 million sales in 1979 to $725 million in 1986. Sales are projected to grow to $1.625 billion in 1990 and to over $2.5 billion in 1993. Clinical data management software accounts for 20 to 30 percent of the total, leading to an estimate of a $500 to $750 million market for 1993. ABC Systems expects to capture at least 5 percent of this market to reach annual sales of $24 million by 1993.

ABC Systems' proprietary programs, developed and proven in fifteen European hospital installations, comprise two basic systems, "Softdoc" and "Softhosp," which provide electronic patient charting, clinical data management for medical specialties, complete clinical image management, and research and statistics capability for the electronically-stored data base. These systems will materially improve the operations effectiveness of the health provider leading to enhanced quality of care and reduced operating costs.

Presentations by ABC Systems have been made to physicians, administrators, nurses, and consultants resulting in the imminent prospect for two entry installations in Southern California hospitals, one of which is part of a large California-based chain. Since incorporation in early 1987, ABC Systems has organized its Tomorrowland, California office, conducted an intensive market evaluation program, developed five product applications for the U.S. market, hired a sales manager, and demonstrated its products to several potential customers. A number of key organizational and marketing problems have been thrashed out and resolved.

The business plan presented herein is the result of this fourteen-month effort. Management now wishes to raise $850,000 from private investors to take advantage of the opportunities defined in the plan. These funds will be used for the two entry installations, to add additional market, service, and development personnel, to purchase additional demonstration hardware, and to provide required working capital.

Commentary on ABC Systems, Inc.

There are a number of good points in this company's Executive Summary. The length is reasonable. There is not much hype. The summary starts out by talking about the need in the market and places heavy emphasis on market size and customer contacts. All in all, this is an above-average specimen.

Still, there are several significant deficiencies.

In the whole discussion of the market, ABC's summary fails to explain clearly *who the customer is.* Exactly who buys the product? Why? What does the product do for buyers? Other crucial marketing questions are not addressed, notably, what the company's competitive advantage is.

By adopting the "5 percent of a humongous market" approach, the company shoots itself in the foot right at the start of its plan.

The Executive Summary has nothing—not a word—on the qualifications of the company's management team. The only hint given in this area has somewhat negative connotations: "A number of key organizational . . . problems have been thrashed out and resolved." Accurately or not, this suggests that the founders have been in conflict, a possibility not alluring to investors.

The founders clearly state how much investment they want, the type of investor, and how they plan to use the funds. However, it would be helpful to mention the type of investment proposed. Incidentally, $850,000 is near the high end of the range for private investor deals.

ABC Systems, finally, doesn't project quite the right image to investors. They claim as accomplishments that they've set up an office and hired a sales manager; yet they still haven't even got beta sites, let alone paying customers. They would have done much better to make some sales, *then* rent an office. They need to put a better face on their position. To impress investors, you should brag about the sales you've made, not about the money you've spent.

For our makeover, we clarified the customer focus of the

business and showcased the value of the company's products to the market. The market share projection was made attractive by redefining the market to a smaller segment. We also put in a description of the management team; the founders were strong people and there was no reason to hide their light under a bushel. The nature of the deal and the prospects for profit were made a little more explicit. Finally, we tried to put the company's history and achievements in a better light.

ABC SYSTEMS, INC. EXECUTIVE SUMMARY
(Improved Version)

The health-care industry is under intense pressure from government and health insurers to cut costs and improve productivity.

ABC Systems has developed microcomputer software to store and retrieve clinical data for hospital patients. These programs can handle all patient care data, including temperature and other vital signs, doctor and nurse observations, and even graphical data such as X rays.

Computerization of patient care data offers major benefits to hospitals, including improved efficiency, reduced labor costs, and prevention of lost or misplaced records. It also improves hospital revenues by providing efficient documentation to support reimbursement claims under the Diagnostic Related Groupings (DRG) and other regulations.

Twenty-six percent of nonfederal hospitals have at least partially automated their patient care records. The market for patient care software is estimated at about $300 million and strong growth is expected. The current trend is toward replacement of mainframe and minicomputer systems with microcomputers. ABC Systems expects to dominate this segment of the market because its products provide comprehensive data handling and connectivity to other hospital data systems. The company is currently arranging for entry installations at two California hospitals. Co-marketing agreements are being discussed with hardware and systems vendors.

The management team of ABC Systems includes Dr. Nemo (CEO), who previously founded, and built to $40 million sales, an engineering contracting company; Dr. Erewhon (COO), who has fourteen years experience as general manager of computer services companies, including clinical information management; and Mr. Anon (director of sales and marketing), who previously sold information systems to hospitals. Outside directors and technical advisers include prominent industry figures who can assist in market penetration.

ABC Systems seeks $850,000 in funding from private investors in the form of convertible preferred stock. These funds will be used to finance the entry installations, support market rollout, and provide working capital.

4

Your Financing Options

Raising money is not an end in itself. You are raising money for a purpose: to start or grow your business. So before you approach investors, there are certain important questions you will need to settle.

1. *What will you use the money for?* It's been said that people spend money for three reasons: because they have to spend it; because they want to spend it; or simply because they have it to spend. Entrepreneurs, we've learned, raise money for all three of these reasons, but, considering what outside capital costs you, only the first is really valid. You should have a very clear, specific idea of why you need money and what you are going to do with it; that's the purpose of having a business plan.

Sometimes a stock market frenzy occurs and money is poured into certain industries—for example, biotechnology in the early 1980s—with a complete disregard for the merits of the companies receiving it. If you are fortunate enough to encounter such an opportunity, go for it while you can; you can figure out what to do with the funds later, while investors are sleeping it off.

Uses of Funds

☐ Working capital—money to finance expansion of inventory and accounts receivable in a growing firm
☐ Capital equipment—manufacturing equipment, office equipment, perhaps land and buildings
☐ Acquisition—money to buy firms so as to expand the business
☐ Marketing expenditures—funds to expand sales by rolling out new products or entering new markets
☐ R&D funding—investment in the development of new products, production processes, technological improvements
☐ Seed money—funds to investigate new business possibilities

It is important to classify your capital needs because *how* you raise money depends on what you intend to use it for. Many entrepreneurs naively rely on equity for all their financing needs. This is not a good way to finance your company. Take, for instance, a high-tech manufacturing company that is growing rapidly. It has a need for additional working capital to handle the accounts receivable and inventory that go with increased sales. If it goes out for venture capital to cover this need, it may get it. But as growth continues, the amount of working capital needed expands relentlessly. Soon additional financing is needed. Each time the company goes out for equity money, the founders get diluted. What's needed is a financing route that can grow automatically with the size of working capital needed. Debt financing, such as a line of credit, is one possibility.

A simple way of looking at financing needs is the balance-sheet principle (see the balance sheet shown in Table 4-1). Match up the assets you need with the proper type of funding (liability) for that asset.

2. *How much money are you going to raise?* If you took the trouble to develop good financial projections, you should

Table 4-1. The fund-raising balance sheet.

Assets	Funding/Liability
Cash	
Accounts Receivable	Customer financing, receivables loans, factoring
Inventory	Vendor financing, short-term loans
Equipment	Long-term loans, leasing
Acquisitions	Cash flow- or asset-based loans
Marketing expansion	Strategic partnerships, equity
R&D	Strategic partnerships, equity
Seed money	Equity

have a good estimate of the amount of money you actually need. In fact, you should also know what it will be used for and when you'll need it. (Many venture capital investments, for instance, are "staged"; the money is disbursed in lumps as your company meets certain milestones.) Now you must decide if that's the right amount of money to raise.

You may wish to try to raise more. Having an extra cushion in the bank can make you feel much more comfortable. More important, financial projections are not infallible, and they have a nasty habit of turning out to be in error in just the wrong direction. A reserve for contingencies can be a lifesaver for your company.

It's especially important to keep the need for a reserve in mind when your financing is going well. When investors are very cooperative and eager to fund you, it's tempting to minimize the financing to retain equity. You think, "If we need more money in the future, we can come back to these nice chaps for it—they're so eager for stock." Surprise! If your company gets into trouble, even mild trouble, those nice, openhanded chaps will turn into tightfisted misers. At that point every three thousand ducats will cost you another pound of flesh. Get your reserve while you can.

You should think about getting extra funding while the getting is good for another reason: Your company has (you hope) a future. It's not enough to satisfy the immediate need for cash; you must plan ahead for future needs. As your company grows, you'll need additional capital to finance its expansion. Raising a little extra cushion now can strengthen your bargaining position next time you raise money. Of course, it will cost you. This leads us to another crucial question for your financing plans.

3. *What are your objectives in terms of equity, safety, and control?* Money isn't free. You will have to pay a price, probably a stiff price, for the funding you need. What are you prepared to give up?

Generally speaking it is rarely possible to finance an entrepreneurial venture without selling some part of the equity. New companies are high-risk investments and few investors are willing to accept the risk without a corresponding opportunity for exceptional gains, which can only be achieved by an explicit or implicit equity participation in the venture. The more equity you sell, the smaller your proportion of the eventual reward when the company succeeds. To the extent that your motivation is purely financial, you will have to decide to what extent the higher growth you can achieve with additional financing will compensate for the reduction in your portion of the pie.

There's a standard saying that "it's better to have 10 percent of a billion-dollar business than 100 percent of a million-dollar business." This is true as far as it goes, but things aren't always that simple. Although it's not widely appreciated, from a strictly financial point of view the amount of investment that will maximize the growth of the business is higher than the amount of investment that will maximize the founder's return.

Of course your motivation as an entrepreneur is probably not purely financial. You may value the growth of your company as a good thing in itself, even if higher growth will diminish rather than increase your personal financial rewards. Some notable entrepreneurs have made that choice.

You may also be concerned about safety. As we've seen, by surrendering some additional equity, you can obtain a cash cushion that may save the company in a crisis. But safety considerations also affect your decisions on nonequity financings. You can reduce your need to give up equity by financing growth with debt. But the higher the company's debt load, the higher your risk. Once again this is a matter of the entrepreneur's personal preference. Many are surprisingly—sometimes excessively—conservative, preferring to carry little or no debt.

The structure of your financing ultimately is likely to be determined by your evaluation of the questions of *leverage* and *control*.

Leverage vs. Control: The Case for the Plaintiff

Classically, "leverage" has referred to the use of "other people's money" in the form of debt. The power of leverage can readily be seen from a simple example using the accounting equation:

$$Assets = Debt + Equity$$

If the company is 50 percent leveraged and assets are $1 million, we have:

$$\$1 \text{ million (assets)} = \$0.5 \text{ million (debt)} + \$0.5 \text{ million (equity)}$$

If the company becomes successful and, say, doubles in size, the new equation is:

$$\$2 \text{ million (assets)} = \$0.5 \text{ million (debt)} + \$1.5 \text{ million (equity)}$$

So the equity in the company triples in value, though growth was only doubling. Of course, leverage works both ways; if the company loses money and assets are halved, the equity will be not halved but totally wiped out.

Still, leveraging the company with debt brings a double benefit. Not only does it multiply the effectiveness of the equity as long as the company is successful; it also reduces the need to surrender equity to investors. Every dollar of debt is a dollar worth of equity that needn't be sold.

The term "leverage" may also be used more loosely to discuss the use of equity investments. At least in principle, the more capital your company has, the faster it can grow. Thus you may be able to set up a small shop out of your own pocket, which over the decades could become a tidy little business, without any outside investment. However, the same business, with a couple of million in venture capital, might become a dominant force in the industry and a member of the *Fortune* 500. In the latter case, you as the founder might end up with only a sliver of equity, and yet be much wealthier than you would be in the first case. Is this not leverage?

Leverage vs. Control: The Case for the Defendant

Yet few entrepreneurs are in business purely for the money. Most of them are concerned, more than anything else, with *control*. In fact, the closest thing to a universal trait of entrepreneurs is the need for independence, to make their own decisions instead of being subject to outside authority. To the extent that you leverage your company, you will be surrendering some degree of control.

To the naive entrepreneur, possession of 51 percent of the company's stock constitutes control. In actual practice, things are not so simple.

Venture capitalists and other professional equity investors are adept at fashioning deals that will give them effective control of their investments. Often, of course, the valuation of the venture will be such that the investors will end up with the majority of common stock. But even if the founders are left with a majority, the investors are likely to keep a few tricks up their sleeve. There is, for instance, "vesting": The founders' stock, in most venture capital deals, is "released" only over a period of years. Or the rules for election of the board of directors may be written so that investors are guaranteed a majority regardless of the stock ownership situation. Or the investment may be in the form of "heads we win, tails you lose" convertible bonds that can be used to smash the company if management proves recalcitrant.

Venture Capitalists on Control

Our venture capital sources were up-front about the question of "control."

> "Venture capitalists insist on control of the company."

> "Venture capitalists believe in the 'Golden Rule': he who has the gold, rules. Entrepreneurs had better understand that the investors control the company."

> "We have no interest in running companies. We don't think we're very good at it. But we have control and we replace the CEO when necessary."

As a practical matter, their bark may be just a bit worse than their bite. Though it's difficult to do a seed or very early-stage financing without giving up control, your position is much stronger in later-stage financings. If you can bootstrap your company to a viable size before going out for equity, you may well be able to keep control. Even at an early stage, if your venture is an exceptionally hot one, with several venture firms bidding for it, you may be able to dictate some terms, including effective control. In any case, even when they have formal control, venture capitalists show a clear reluctance to coerce founders; it's unpleasant at best, and even though they get their way the incident can poison relations with the management team. They may insist on having control, but they exercise it only as a last resort.

You might turn for relief to debt financing, but even here control issues arise. Loans generally come with "restrictive covenants." They can impose all sorts of requirements—that the company maintain certain cash levels, for instance. There's generally a lot of fine print and it's easy to slip into "technical default," at which point the loan becomes due and payable. Then you do as you're told or go under. To make sure you remain pliable, your friendly banker will generally decline to make a true long-term loan; instead you'll be required to "clean up" your line of credit once a year. Of course that's just a formality—unless you get out of line, in which case the requirement can easily turn you into an obedient appendage of the bank.

And yet, control in the end is more subtle still. Just as you cannot guarantee control by retaining 51 percent of the company, so investors cannot guarantee control by legal maneuvers. In the final analysis, "control" of a company is a fluid, intangible force. True authority derives from knowing what to do and having the guts to do it. As long as you have the self-confidence to run your company, and the ability to produce good results— or at least results no worse than you've predicted—you are likely to maintain effective control.

Neither venture capitalists nor bankers want to run companies. The typical venture capitalist is frantically busy just serving on boards and looking out for new investments. If a management team fails and he has to step in as CEO, he has a problem. To begin with, he's blotted his copybook: The management team, which *he* endorsed, he now says is so bad it has to be replaced. Taking over involves a very unpleasant confrontation. Running a company is a terrible drain on his time. He's tied up with work he doesn't much like. And—horrible thought—what if *he,* the brilliant venture capitalist, fails to turn the company around? What a loss of face!

In the same way, your loan officer definitely does not want to slip your company into the Workout Department's in basket; it's an admission that he goofed. What's more, it may expose the bank to the possibility of a lawsuit. There is a recent trend toward holding banks responsible for client companies' problems to the extent that the bank interferes in the management of its client.

You should be concerned with control, and careful to keep the issue in mind as you structure and negotiate your financing. But don't be too paranoid on the subject.

How Investors Behave—And Why

Before we start enumerating the many financing options available to you, let's take a moment to consider the basic roots of investor behavior. There are essentially four classes of people you may encounter as you search for funding. Members of different groups may exhibit different behavior.

1. *People with money.* These are individuals, or corporations, or even government agencies, who are investing their own money. Because money tends to be secretive and protected, investors of this class are the hardest to find, to contact, and to talk to. However, because they are dealing with their own money, they can make quick decisions. They are also often more flexible and willing to consider innovative ventures or financing terms because they are less restricted by rules imposed from outside.

2. *People who control a fund of other people's money.* Venture capital firms almost always fall into this category, and so do banks and even some nonprofessional investors. These investors are generally more accessible than they're reputed to be. Their institutional nature makes them relatively resistant to innovation, however. They have procedures, which were set up intentionally to restrict their freedom of action in handling the money they manage, and these procedures must be respected.

3. *People who raise money ad hoc for each deal.* Here we have, for instance, Wall Street investment banking firms that assemble the financings for takeovers and leveraged buyouts. However, the same sort of technique is also sometimes used for venture financings. Because each deal is custom-crafted—not only in which money sources are approached but also in the

structure of the transaction—these groups can be very flexible. On the other hand, the customized deal process is a great deal slower than a standardized deal, and of course it takes time to raise the money, so the financing tends to take longer.

4. *Finders*. These people neither have nor raise money; they merely try to locate investors for the venture. Because they put little or nothing at risk themselves, they are very easy to find and not at all difficult to commit.

Obvious though it may be, many entrepreneurs never take into account the behavioral differences of various investor types. But, as we shall see, adapting your approach to the investor's specific needs is a key factor in successful financing.

Your Venture's Life Cycle

As you consider your financing options, you should take into account more than your current financial needs. Think about the future also.

The life cycle of a successful growth company proceeds through a series of stages, and for each stage certain kinds of financing are available. The diagram shown in Figure 4-1, adapted from one used by Tom Turney of NewCap Partners, illustrates financing stages and how they correlate with the growth of your company.

Of course real-life companies don't always follow a smooth track; they boom and bust, go through sudden sales surges and suffer major crises. Also, real-life investors are not absolutely consistent; often they break their own rules for one reason or another. But this diagram can give you a rough overview of how funding options change as your company matures.

An Investor Bestiary

Entrepreneurs are very ingenious people and over the centuries they have come up with some unusual and innovative ways to

Figure 4-1. Financing stages.

COMPANY LIFE CYCLE

| Seed | Startup | Low Volume | High Volume | Expansion |

EQUITY SOURCES

Family and Friends

Private Investors

Venture Capital

Mezzanine Capital

Public Markets

DEBT SOURCES

Finance/Leasing Companies

Commercial Banks

Private Debt

Public Debt

raise money. We can't possibly cover all the possibilities for
financing your venture. But we can urge you: *Don't limit your
options arbitrarily.* Many entrepreneurs start the money hunt
with blinders on; we see them walk past piles of money, unheed-
ing, muttering to themselves, "Venture capital, venture capital,
gotta find venture capital." Venture capital is terrific, but it isn't
available, or even appropriate, for most companies. The vast
majority of new companies are financed in other ways.

Here are some of the major sources of funding available to
you—and this is not by any means an exhaustive list.

Investment Sources

- ☐ Founder pockets
- ☐ Family and friends
- ☐ Customers
- ☐ Vendors
- ☐ Joint ventures
- ☐ Corporate partners
- ☐ Bank loans

- ☐ Nonbank lending
- ☐ Leasing
- ☐ Government sources
- ☐ Private placements
- ☐ Venture capital
- ☐ Public offering

To bring some order to this zoo, we may somewhat arbitrarily classify capital sources into four families.

1. There is what we might call *bootstrap financing*. You can dig into your own pockets, put the bite on your family and friends, or get your customers to help out.
2. You can resort to *cooperative financing*. There are people out there—perhaps more than you suspect—who have a stake in your success. Your vendors are prime examples; they want you to survive and grow so that you can buy more from them. You may be surprised at how much they'll do to help you if you ask them nicely.
3. There are various forms of formal *debt financing*. Not only banks but all sorts of other organizations lend money. There are expedients such as leasing that don't look like loans, though they really are.
4. If you want to be a traditionalist, you can seek *equity financing*. Venture capital is the most prominent source, but it's not the only source.

In this book, we concentrate on the most complex and difficult financing avenues, such as venture capital, because we feel that's where you will need the most help. We'll therefore give short shrift to some of the other types of financing, but we do want to mention them because they are so often ignored. And you should keep this fact in mind: Even if your primary financing comes from venture capital, by utilizing other financing techniques you can reduce the amount of money you'll need to raise and, often, the amount of equity you'll have to give up.

Bootstrap Financing

The most immediate of all financing sources is your own wallet. It's also, of course, the least desirable. Why should you risk your own money on some harebrained scheme if you can find someone else foolish enough to put up the funds? Generally speaking, you should try to minimize your personal investment in your venture. Since your salary from the startup may be unreliable, even nonexistent at first, your savings will be needed to support yourself, and your family if you have one, until the company has a stable cash flow. (Of course money you invest may be drawn out as salary, but then you have to pay taxes on it.)

Even so, *Inc.* magazine in June 1989 reported that the founders of *Inc.* 500 companies—high-growth champions—got the bulk of their startup capital out of their own pockets. Stodgy old banks supplied funds for many others. Venture capitalists weren't even in the running. The initial investments were surprisingly small, less than $10,000 for a third of the companies, less than $50,000 for another third.

But don't rely too heavily on such statistics. The *Inc.* 500 companies are *very* atypical.

If you go to your friendly banker for a loan for your new business, you'll almost certainly be turned down. Bankers lend on credit records, and a new firm has no credit record. But *you* have a credit record, so you can use your personal borrowing power to raise funds for your venture. In our modern economy, most middle-class people, particularly professionals, have credit pressed on them by eager lenders. You can often raise a substantial sum with a second mortgage on your house. You can accept one of those offers you get in the mail every couple of days for a personal loan with no collateral and no questions asked. And don't forget your credit cards; some successful startups have simply been charged to VISA.

Another route is that used by immigrants. Many immigrants, who often don't have credit, use credit clubs like the Korean *kye* to finance their businesses. Each member of the group puts a moderate sum in the pool each month; the entire pool is then given to each participant in turn. Sometimes more complicated forms, which may involve interest rate auctions of loan, are used. If you happen to know a lot of other entrepreneurially inclined people, you might want to consider setting up some such arrangement.

Of course, drawing down your meager savings or loading yourself up with debt and putting the money into a high-risk venture is not exactly prudent. But in the very early stages of a venture—the seed-money phase, when you don't even know whether there's a market or whether your invention can be built—the risk is so high that most other forms of financing will be closed to you. Even if you can raise money elsewhere, the investors may insist that you have your own funds at risk.

You may be able to tap your family and friends for small-scale financing. You should exercise great care in doing so, however. Failing, going through personal bankruptcy, and having to start over in life, is not a very pleasant experience. But it beats failing and having your maiden aunt, or your retired father, or your old college chum go through personal bankruptcy. Don't let those who love you risk more than they can afford.

For informal financings you want a structure that provides some level of safety for the investor, a risk bonus, and a shot at really big returns if the venture is successful. You would also like to avoid giving up equity (not only because it's bad in itself to do so but because having amateurs as stockholders can poison the deal if you later seek professional capital).

One way of doing this is for the investor to give you a loan at a higher-than-market interest rate. In addition, there is paid, during the life of the loan (not forever!), a percentage of sales. This way, if the company takes off, the investor will get a tidy little bonus.

These small-scale financings are limited only by the resources of the people you know and your own imagination. But
watch out for a common pitfall, the profit percentage. Avoid any
structure that calls for paying out a percentage of the profits.
Such provisions will usually poison your chances of future
professional financing. They can also lead to arguments and
disruptive fights with your backers. The problem is that "profit"
is not an objective number; it's an accounting construct.

> Movie actors and directors learned this the hard way. Major
> stars used to sign contracts in which they were promised a
> percentage of the profits from the film. Lo and behold, the
> studio accountants found that even blockbuster successes
> somehow lost money. Now all but the most naive film stars
> insist on a percentage of the *gross*.

Bootstrap financing deals should be kept as simple as possible. Tie any payments to clearly defined, objective numbers
that everyone can agree on, such as sales.

The Ideal Financing Source

If using your own funds is the worst type of financing, the best
is to get customers to fund you. How? Any which way you can
think of.

Suppose your venture needs working capital—money to
finance accounts receivable and inventory. Try asking customers
to pay cash on the barrelhead. Presto! No accounts receivable.
But you're not being aggressive enough. Ask them to pay in
advance. Presto! No inventory carrying costs.

Impossible, you say? Nonsense! You never know until you
try. So screw your courage to the sticking place and see what
you can get. Advance payments are ideal, but a long-term
contract (or even just a purchase order) can give you a substantial boost. Sometimes your customers will help to finance a key
piece of production equipment so that you can supply them
more quickly. Or they'll pay all or part of the cost of your R&D.
Or they'll have their people run tests for you, free. Ask!

Who would think that a major pharmaceutical house would violate its standard purchasing procedures to place a large order with a small shaky supplier it had never used before— and pay half in advance with months to wait for delivery? But it did; the company needed a rare chemical for an important research program and the only other supplier was even less attractive.

The really good thing about customer financing is that you can't even try for it without talking to your customers, which is no bad thing for an entrepreneur to do. Wheedling advance payments or other goodies out of your customers will automatically make you aware of, and attentive to, their needs. After all, your justification for being in business is satisfaction of customer needs.

This is such a good point that it's worth emphasizing. A lot of the startup entrepreneurs we encounter are practically obsessed with making a good impression on venture capitalists. If they spent half as much time worrying about what their customers wanted as they do worrying about what investors want, many of them wouldn't even *need* venture capital.

What if you try for customer financing along these lines and can't get it? Well, if your customers aren't willing to give you a hand, *that tells you something*. It tells you that you had better very seriously consider going back to the drawing board.

To the extent that you can get customers to finance your business, you reduce the need to resort to repugnant expedients like selling equity to venture capitalists. But even if you can't cover all your financing needs in this way, it will give you a marvelous boost in approaching other money sources. Whether bankers or venture capitalists, investors are tremendously impressed by ventures that arouse enthusiasm among their customers.

Many entrepreneurs fail to exploit customer financing because they fear to reveal any financial weakness to their customers. Customers certainly do worry that a small vendor might fail and leave them holding the bag, especially if they've paid in advance! But even if you put up a bold front, it's hard to bluff any but the most naive buyer. Chances are that they have a

D&B report—a Dun & Bradstreet credit check—on you, and a
pretty good idea of your financial situation. If they *don't* have
hard information, they'll generally assume the worst. So what
do you gain by pretending to be as solid as the Bank of England?
You'll probably find that your customers respond better to a
frank explanation of your situation.

Cooperative Financing

It's worth taking a moment to understand the basic concept of
cooperative financing. Normally when we think of raising money
for a venture, we visualize investors who are in it for the money.
For most professional investment sources, this is essentially
true. A banker may focus on the book value of your company,
the net worth as shown on the balance sheet. A venture capitalist
is more likely to be concerned with market value, with how
much your company could be sold for in the stock market. In
either case, these are purely financial criteria of value. Their
valuation of your company depends more or less solely on its
financial prospects, and their decision is made (at least in theory)
solely on the basis of the money they expect to make.

But "value" is subjective; it has different meanings to
different people. We know that a house, an automobile, a
painting, or a stamp may have an appeal to a specific person—a
special aesthetic appeal, for instance, or a sentimental value, or
a collector's value—which allows it to command an unusually
high price. In the same way, some people or organizations may
value your company more highly than purely financial considerations would "justify" because it offers some unique benefit to
them. To the extent that you can get financing from these
"cooperative" sources, you can get better terms than from
investors who are solely concerned with financial return. In
other words, these are sources that will pay a *premium* over the
market price in order to invest in your company. This is the
basic advantage of cooperative financing. There are a number of
ways you can apply this approach. We'll tell you about a couple,
but we encourage you to use your creativity in thinking of
others.

Vendor Financing

The foremost candidates for cooperative financing are your vendors. Smart companies are always on the lookout for opportunities to develop new, growing, and loyal customers. More often than you might think, they will make special concessions for startups. Easy installment terms or delayed payments are common. Sometimes, when a bank won't give you a loan to buy a big piece of equipment, the vendor will take the paper itself. (The collateral is more familiar, and more secure, to vendors than to the bank; they know where to sell it if they have to take it back, because they're in the business.) The vendor may provide you with valuable services, such as engineering support to get your manufacturing process working. Or he may help you with marketing by steering you to prospective customers or putting out joint advertising.

Most entrepreneurs are much too timid about exploiting their vendors. They believe that a new venture must deal with vendors on less favorable terms than established companies because it's small and weak and has no track record. It ain't necessarily so. Again, you never know until you try. Some large companies, such as computer manufacturer Digital Equipment Corporation, have installed special, systematic programs to develop startup customers. Smaller vendors can also be very receptive, especially if they're hungry. Ask!

Keep in mind that you have vendors for more than raw materials and equipment. Promising startups can often obtain basic business services at steep discounts. For instance, most of the Big Eight accounting firms are now making a special effort to attract new businesses. They can offer not only standard accounting services such as financial statements and audits but consulting in various areas. They can help you with management recruiting, computerization, marketing, even writing your business plan. If your venture looks promising, you can get the equivalent of thousands of dollars in seed money this way—and give up no equity for it, *and* get a boost in credibility from your relationship with a big-name firm.

Strategic Partners

There are other opportunities for cooperative financing. As the American economy becomes ever more complex, new types of business arrangements are developed and play increasing roles.

"Strategic partner" arrangements are drawing increasing interest as a means of financing. The idea is that your small company can team up with a much larger firm that needs something you've got. In turn, you get access to big-company resources—not just money, but marketing clout, manufacturing capabilities, and so on.

> A classic example of a successful strategic partner arrangement is provided by the case of Conner Peripherals, a maker of disc drives for personal computers. Though the founder, Finis Conner, had sterling credentials as a co-founder of two successful companies in the industry, he could not raise venture capital on satisfactory terms. So Conner entered into a partnership with Compaq Computer. Conner got $12 million in funding on much better terms than the venture capitalists had offered. Compaq got a reliable supplier of a key component for its computers—and a very profitable investment.

If your venture has a technology focus, you may be able to get important assistance from other organizations interested in the same technology. Research costs money, a lot of money, especially when it's done within a bureaucratic organization. What's more, the most useful applied research is commonly generated by independent, practical-minded, and obstinate scientists and engineers—a personality type that large corporations find hard to attract, keep, or put up with. Odd as it may seem, a small company can sometimes develop technology faster than a huge organization with unlimited resources.

Big companies are often willing to negotiate some sort of agreement that will give them a "window" into your technology. For instance, Japanese firms have recently begun making venture capital investments in Silicon Valley companies at inflated prices, aiming not so much at capital gains from the investment as at getting their hands on advanced technology.

A larger company may find other motives for possible cooperation with your venture. For instance, you and your "corporate partner" may find mutual interests in manufacturing. Here you are with your new semiconductor design, wondering where you're going to find $100 million or so to build a fabrication line. And there's Megalithic Silicon Devices with a major product clobbered by the Japanese and a whole factory standing idle eating up cash every month. "Uh . . . can we talk?" A lot of big firms have excess capacity, and they really don't *like* layoffs even though it sometimes seems that way. Look around. Manufacturing leverage of this sort can *substantially* reduce your capital needs *and* the amount of equity you have to sell to raise it.

> One presenter, who wanted to become a "micro-brewer" of a local, specialty beer, avoided the cost of building a brewery by arranging for his brew to be brewed at the plant of one of the major beer companies.

Most valuable of all for a small firm is setting up joint marketing arrangements of one sort or another. You'll recall that the biggest hurdle for a new product is getting distribution. An arrangement in which you develop and manufacture a new widget, and your huge corporate partner uses its financial clout and army of salesmen to push it into the market, can offer both of you substantial benefits.

> CIM RealTime Software, a startup presenter, developed valuable software for computer-integrated manufacturing. Software, of course, must run on hardware—the "platform." CIM chose Apollo workstations as a platform. Even though CIM was a startup, it attracted significant help from Apollo in the form of a joint marketing agreement. The arrangement offered Apollo a product to help it sell computers to factories; in turn, Apollo's reputation and marketing clout offered CIM an enormous free boost.

Remember that the decisive risk factor for a new company is *market risk*. The toughest job you face is getting sales. Marketing and sales, because of their heavy overhead requirements, are often far more costly to initiate than R&D and manufacturing. The most likely source of failure for your venture is lack of sales. So an opportunity to have a large company take part of the load can play a crucial role in your success.

There are, of course, dangers in such arrangements. Your partner's sales force probably will not have as much enthusiasm for selling your product as for selling its own. Consider taking special measures to motivate these people. Relying on your partner for distribution and sales can insulate you from your market. Don't abdicate your responsibility for marketing; be sure your people are active participants and get plenty of customer contact. And maintain an outside, independent sales effort, even if only a small one, to keep your hand in.

Setting Up a Corporate Partnership

It's difficult to lay down strict rules about this sort of deal because so many types of arrangement are possible. For example:

- *R&D partnering arrangement.* You do the research; they pay for all or part of it. Maybe they also help by giving you access to expensive instruments in their labs. When the product is ready, they market it and pay you a royalty.
- *Co-marketing.* Your product complements theirs. Maybe it's software that runs on their hardware, or vice versa. So they do the marketing for you. They get improved sales because your product enhances the demand for theirs, and you get your product sold without major marketing expenditures.
- *Direct investment.* If there's a good fit in technology or market, the partner may want to put some money into your firm, buying a minority position in the equity or possibly even giving you a loan.

You might worry, of course, that your corporate partner could end up being overly influential, using its much larger size and clout to dominate your venture. In this case, you could consider a joint venture, a new entity owned jointly by you and your partner. They put up the money, you put up the technology or whatever you have to contribute. In this way you have a better chance to maintain your independence and freedom of action.

But sharing a bed with an elephant has its hazards, whether you're in a four-poster or a water bed. Structure the deal as you will, the tie to a large partner will limit your freedom of action at best; at worst, you may get crushed. Be sure to take some basic precautions.

Corporate Partnering Precautions

☐ Check out your partners in advance. Have they done this sort of deal before? How did they behave? Are their previous partners happy?

☐ Secure your contact arrangements. What *person* in the corporate partner will you be dealing with? What are the odds that this person will still be there, and still be your contact, five years from now? If he or she departs, who will be the replacement?

☐ Agree on *specific* goals with the partner. Get everything in writing. Get a lawyer, one experienced in these deals, to vet the contract.

☐ Put in place an explicit grievance procedure in advance.

☐ Make a list of all proprietary technical or marketing information you are putting into the deal. Write in explicit protection for your rights.

☐ If the partner will own stock in a joint venture, and especially if it will own stock in your company, restrict its right to transfer stock to third parties.

☐ Write up and sign a prenuptial divorce agreement and property settlement to minimize the chance of an expensive court fight if, or when, the partnership breaks up.

A corporate partnership, like any partnership, is most likely to be successful if the two parties are (as scientists like to say) "orthogonal." You should seek a situation where you and your partner have different interests and different goals. This is the best way to ensure that you will complement each other rather than compete with each other.

What About Foreign Partners?

Most entrepreneurial companies don't set up agreements with foreign companies until they're pretty well established. Once you have developed a good market position in the United States and are thinking about expanding overseas, you look into getting local partners in various countries to help out. But that's changing; today, many venture capitalists like to see ambitious companies planning for growth into foreign markets almost from the start.

Conversely, foreign firms generally haven't shown a lot of interest in getting into deals with startups. However, that too may be changing. The United States, as the world's premier entrepreneurial economy, is getting quite a reputation, and businessmen in other countries are starting to think that it might be a good idea to get a piece of the action.

Many high-tech companies, particularly in the biotechnology area, are attracted to working with overseas partners because of regulatory considerations at home. The United States is one of the slowest countries in the world to approve new drugs and medical devices, for instance. By working overseas, a company can get into the market years earlier. In this way it not only gets sales much sooner but gains experience that can be applied when it finally is allowed to market in the United States.

The variation among foreign countries and their companies is enormous. However, there are a few common traits you can expect to encounter.

Generally, it is easier to get cooperation for deals that involve importing goods into the United States than for deals based on exports, especially to developing countries. Setting up production in the host country is also looked on with approval.

Many foreign companies are particularly interested in getting their hands on American technology, and their governments often actively encourage them. For instance, India quietly arranges joint ventures between U.S. and Indian firms, which will use American technology to produce goods for Indian markets. Then the Indian government imposes import restrictions so that the new company will have a monopoly. These transactions can be quite lucrative if your ethical standards will permit you to engage in them.

Obviously setting up an overseas partnership will be greatly facilitated if you or one of your co-founders (or at least an employee) can speak the language of the country in question. In this multiethnic country, the ready availability of people who hail from practically any country on the planet creates a real advantage for foreign deal making.

Working with a foreign partner does have its complications, however. Cybergraphics, a maker of computerized newspaper publishing systems, illustrated the problems that you may face. Cybergraphics had strong financial, technological, and manufacturing ties to Australian interests. The company's CEO gave us an earful.

Cultural differences made communication with the Australians troublesome on occasion. Just the difference in time zones was a significant nuisance. The distances involved made business interactions expensive and caused problems in coordinating production. The foreign connection also interfered with getting additional financing for Cybergraphics. Though American venture firms like to see companies with foreign customers, they are much less receptive to working with foreign investors.

The Complexity Factor

During the 1980s there was quite a vogue for corporate partnering. It can provide decisive advantages to a young venture, and there's only one real drawback—but that one is a dilly. Corporate partnering is just about the most complex form of business arrangement ever devised by the mind of man. The two companies must coordinate all sorts of policies, from quality-control standards to advertising themes. A corporate partnership is extraordinarily management-intensive. You and your co-founders will have to spend a significant fraction of your time— generally between 120 percent and 150 percent—on developing and maintaining the relationship with your corporate partner. It can be worth it, but be sure you're prepared to pay this price.

Spin-Offs and Variants

You may already have a good candidate for a corporate partner: your current employer. If the idea for your venture was generated by your job, your employer may get its finger in the pie whether you like it or not. If you need to use its technology, equipment, or customer lists, you might want to consider cutting your employer in.

There are some real advantages to selecting your employer (or possibly a former employer) as a corporate partner. One of the biggest drawbacks to corporate partnering is the difficulty of finding out, and understanding, what's going on in the big organization. What do they really want? What are their long-range plans? Who really wields the power, and how will internal politics affect the way they deal with you? If you are an insider, you will understand your corporate partner much better than someone who sets up the deal from outside. What's more, your contacts within the organization, and their familiarity with you, will make it much easier to initiate and settle on the deal.

Of course, there is the little matter of timing. If you take up the possibility of starting a company with the support of the firm that employs you too soon, you may suddenly find yourself out on the street. If, however, you are cautious and delay your approach until your plans are more advanced, they may yet turn you down and you'll have to go back to the drawing board. There's no perfect solution; you must use your knowledge of the situation to decide how much risk to take.

Debt Financing

Not so long ago, if you wanted to borrow money you automatically thought of a bank. Today, you have a wide variety of options.

As we mentioned before, the key to effective use of debt financing is tailoring the type of debt, and the source, to the purpose for which you wish to use the money. Look at the asset side of your balance sheet: Where will the money be invested?

If you're using it to purchase fixed assets such as manufacturing equipment, you should obviously look to long-term debt for financing. If the money's going into current assets such as inventory, a short-term loan is indicated. If you plan to put the money into a nonbalance sheet account such as R&D or marketing, debt financing generally isn't appropriate; these are activities that should be financed out of your equity base.

In general, lenders are both conservative and hard-nosed. Their top priority is getting back the principal. Your first task in qualifying for a loan is to convince the lender that you can and will pay it back. Don't overestimate the significance of collateral. The lender does not want to get stuck with the collateral except as a last resort. Your credit record—a demonstrated track record of paying back loans—is a much more important decision factor than is your collateral.

Lenders are next concerned with interest, obviously. They make their money by borrowing money at relatively low interest rates and lending it at relatively high interest rates. What entrepreneurs sometimes fail to appreciate is that when they borrow money they are doing the same thing—or at least, they'd better be! If you can't invest the money you borrow to get a *higher* rate of return, don't borrow it.

And be sure you know how much interest you're paying. Banks commonly require a "compensating balance"; that is, part of the money you borrow must remain in your account and cannot be spent. So your real interest rate should be based on the principal you actually have control over. This can add several percentage points to your effective interest rate.

Lenders also have another route to profit: *fees*. The terminology varies: "points," "origination fees," "service charges," or whatever. You can be sure of one thing: The lender gets some of your money up front. It's important to realize that fees are now a significant and increasing portion of lender profits. They used to make almost all their profits off the "spread"; now fees have become very important. This focus on the immediate and highly tangible cash flow brought in by fees has biased the thinking of many bankers and other lenders, making them amenable to doing loans that might not make sense if the interest

rate spread were the only consideration. You should take this
into account, and make use of it when you have the opportunity.

Banks

The most substantial lending source is still, of course, the bank.
Banks tend to be asset-based lenders; they still like bricks and
mortar. That's the reality, but in dealing with bankers keep in
mind also the fantasy. Bankers like to think of themselves as,
what they once were, character-based lenders. They retain a
nostalgic affection for the idea of a long-term banking relationship, with the bank knowing its customers and assisting them
with wise counsel as well as money.

Unfortunately, very few banks fit this model any longer
because of their personnel policies. To be a character-based
lender, a bank must have career loan officers who can develop
stable relationships with customers. Today, the average loan
officer at a big money-center bank has a half-life measured in
months. Then it's off to another department or another branch
or maybe another bank. Unless you are very lucky, your loan
officer will be replaced by someone else before you really have
a chance to become acquainted. Plan for this. Says one banker
we interviewed:

> "Loan officers generally are trained in larger banks, which
> have high personnel turnover. Then they often move to smaller
> banks, sometimes taking their customers with them. Since loan
> officers have incentive compensation, they are motivated to
> develop long-term relationships with firms that perform well."

The banking industry used to be pretty homogeneous. Today, bankers are, more and more, specializing. If you want a
loan, you'll be wiser to investigate the possibilities and find a
bank that's concentrating on borrowers of your type than to
walk into one that happens to have a branch in your neighborhood. Some banks seek only large customers; some want to
serve family firms; others are looking for growth companies.

"The large banks are secured lenders; they make asset-based loans requiring strong collateral. They prefer customers who are at least in the 'middle range'—with between $20 and $200 million in sales.

"Smaller banks are more likely to be relationship lenders; they're more inclined to get involved with management and try to advise the company and assist its growth. Sometimes they do cash flow-based lending. Their typical customer is a company in the $2 to $20 million range with a single, dominant entrepreneurial founder."

Furthermore, banks are becoming specialists in specific industries—if not by intention, by default. If you are, let's say, an electronics company, and the *only* electronics company among your bank's customers, your banker is not going to understand your business. Better switch to a bank that has lots of electronics firms as customers.

In general, banks are not enthusiastic about loaning money to startups. The rule of thumb is that you'll have to go in with three years of financial statements. It definitely helps if your company is profitable. Also, banks want to see some tangible capital like production equipment—not just for collateral, but for assurance that you're for real and won't evaporate. A company with no physical assets can look fly-by-night to a banker.

Your best bet for finding a receptive banker is *not* to choose a bank from the Yellow Pages. Bankers, like other types of investors, rely heavily on referrals. Lawyers and accountants, as always, are good referral sources. You should also seek introductions via your customers and suppliers, who have considerable credibility in recommending you. Says the same banker:

"Banks *have* to loan out their deposits to make money. A typical small bank will seek to do about 20 percent of its loan volume from new customers, the rest from existing customers."

Not surprisingly, the best way to appeal to a banker is to look solid.

"Smaller banks, which are most receptive to small or young businesses, tend to specialize. They mainly look for an

entrepreneur who wants to keep control, who has boot-
strapped or self-financed his early growth. They like companies
that are manufacturing- and product-oriented. High-tech and
high-growth businesses are not as attractive to a banker as a
company with reliable, quality earnings and a moderate growth
rate. Banks want to see a founder who's in for the long haul,
with no hint of a 'take the money and run' attitude.''

At first, the savings and loan association had its own turf—
housing loans—and didn't invade the domain of the commercial
bank. The distinction between these two types of financial
institutions gradually eroded and many S&Ls began to make
commercial loans. As this is written, the industry is in crisis.
Congress has legislated a "solution," but nobody knows what
policies will be when the dust has settled. S&Ls are worth a
look; they can be hungry for business, and you shouldn't neglect
the possibility.

Other types of lending outfits exist to serve specialized
needs. Many growing companies, for instance, have cash flow
problems because of their ever-increasing receivables. Too many
of them make the mistake of going out for venture capital or
other equity financing. This merely defers the problem; as
growth continues, the new cash gets tied up in receivables and a
further resort to investors becomes necessary. A fast-growing
company should instead look into direct receivables financing.
If you borrow money against your receivables, your credit line
can automatically expand as your business grows, thus relieving
you of the necessity to give up equity or spend all your time
looking for more cash.

Unfortunately, new ventures generally find it hard to do
receivables financing. We talked to Craig Isom, a partner at
Arthur Andersen, about the options available.

"Getting receivables financing is an uphill climb for young
companies. If you can get it at all, it's very costly—at least two
points over prime. And only your 'qualified' receivables will be
financed. That means no foreign receivables, and nothing over
sixty days.

"For those loans, the rule at most banks is that your
company should have been profitable for at least three years.

The size of the proposed loan must be large enough to make it worthwhile for the bank. Smaller banks will sometimes lower these standards, but you must be in the black, and they'll demand collateral and personal guarantees in addition to the receivables."

Alternatively, you can sell your receivables. (One oft-neglected way for a retail company to sell receivables is to sign up with the major credit card companies.) Of course, receivable-based lending is expensive—effective interest rates of 20 to 40 percent are not uncommon—but this is often a secondary concern for a fast-growing firm. Again, calculate your return on the money; if your margins are high enough, it will often pay you to borrow even at usurious rates to maintain your growth.

It is also possible, in certain cases, to borrow money against your inventory, the other moiety of working capital. The key factor is the liquidity of the inventory; if you sell highly specialized goods with limited markets, you probably won't be able to borrow against inventory, except, just possibly, from your suppliers.

Recently, the practice of cash flow-based lending has developed. The idea here is that the important factor from the lender's point of view is the free cash flow of the business, out of which debt must be serviced. If the free cash flow is sufficient, to hell with where it comes from; the loan is OK. This form of lending is commonly used for LBOs (leveraged buyouts) and other acquisitions.

Bank Loan Collateral Traps

Here are a few things to watch out for when negotiating a bank loan.

Obviously you should resist giving collateral if you can. Probably you can't. But try to restrict it to a corporate commitment and avoid giving a personal guarantee. Above all, dig in your heels if the bank wants your spouse to co-sign; it can save your house, and maybe your marriage.

Check out the wording of a guarantee very carefully. Look out for a clause stating that the guarantee applies to "past, present, and future loans.'' This means that even if you pay off the loan, they have your guarantee for any future loan to the company, without having to ask you for it or even mention it to you. If you leave the company, and several years later it goes into default on a loan, you could get a nasty surprise.

Keep in mind that once you've guaranteed or collateralized a loan, it is very difficult to free up your assets. Even if the company prospers and the alleged justification for the security dissipates, you'll never get your bank to release the collateral. So bargain as hard as you can when you negotiate the loan.

Nondebt Debt

Before you buy a major piece of equipment, or even a minor piece of equipment, ask yourself whether you really *need* to own it. In fact, do you really *want* to own it? Whether production machinery or office equipment, many items in these days of fast-moving technology, computers especially, become obsolete very quickly. You can be stuck with something that's out of date and has to be replaced before you have even paid off the loan. Why not consider leasing instead?

Leasing equipment will cost you more than buying. And leases are often hard to arrange for nonstandard items of equipment. But a lease gives you more flexibility, can reduce your worries about maintenance, and generally doesn't show up on your balance sheet.

There are companies that specialize in buying equipment and leasing it out. Your vendor can probably refer you to one. Many vendors do leasing themselves. Some of the big venture capital organizations, such as Hambrecht & Quist, have set up leasing affiliates. Your accountant is another good source of leads to leasing firms.

There are two types of leases for equipment: operating and capital. The operating lease is a ''real'' lease, in which the lessor retains title to the equipment. A capital lease or ''lease-purchase'' is essentially equivalent to buying the equipment on loan, and must show up as a liability on the balance sheet. The only advantage is that there is no down payment.

Doing a big leasing deal can be difficult for a young company. You need a credit rating, which means that you need a history. Still, you can lease a lot of small office stuff like copying machines and personal computers, and it often makes sense to do so, particularly for items that become obsolete rapidly.

If your company is backed by venture capital, leasing outfits are sometimes willing to deal with you even though you have no credit history. In this "venture leasing" mode, you'll probably have to give warrants or some other equity kicker to the lessor.

> A leasing deal can also be done with private investors. In one company, a major piece of laboratory equipment was purchased by the father of one of the founders and leased to the company. The investor got higher payments than he would have from a certificate of deposit, and was able to offset the income with depreciation for tax purposes. The timing worked out nicely to fit the change in his tax situation as he retired. The company got an essential item of equipment without expending any of its precious equity.

Incidentally, what we said about owning equipment applies even more strongly to real estate. When you buy land and buildings, you are entering the real estate business. Is that your business? Do you expect to be competitive in real estate speculation against the professionals? Do you really need to tie up all that capital? If you're thinking about buying your premises, think again.

"I'm From the Government and I'm Here to Fund You"

All sorts of money is available from government sources—federal, state, local, and even foreign. It's impossible to list all the varieties here, and in any case such a list would be obsolete before we could get this book into print. However, here are some options you may wish to look into.

The traditional Small Business Administration loan is nowadays very difficult to get; the federal budget is tight, the SBA's funding is very limited, and competition for the remaining funds is fierce. The situation isn't helped by the fact that the SBA's direct loan program has a default rate, by one estimate, of 30 percent. (Commercial banks, by contrast, have a default rate of about 2 percent.) Still, the SBA made about 30,000 loans in 1988. In addition to loaning money directly, the SBA can guarantee bank loans. You can get a good reading on the current situation simply by calling the SBA office in your city.

Though the SBA is not the limitless money fountain its supporters would like it to be, state and local governments are taking up a lot of the slack. Impressed by the ability of new and small companies to create jobs, they are setting up everything from "business incubators" to venture capital funds.

Loan money may be available from various government sources to accomplish certain social or economic goals. For instance, if you are locating in a depressed area or slum, government money may be forthcoming. Many state governments now have seed-money venture capital funds. They are also setting up business incubators and providing other services for new firms. Some states give research grants to high-tech startups.

You may also be able to get assistance if you plan to export (from the U.S. Government) or import (from the foreign government). Some cities, including Los Angeles, have loan funds to assist small companies in financing foreign trade.

Some foreign governments have what are called "offset" programs. They will accept exports from the United States, but only if they receive guarantees that companies in their country will get some business too. Thus, when a major aerospace corporation sells jets to another country, it may be required to buy some of the parts from firms in the purchasing country; these are "direct offsets." It may also have to arrange to import other goods, sometimes completely unrelated, into the United States. If you're in a position to be helpful in this process, the aerospace company or the foreign government may subsidize you.

"Set-asides" remain popular with governments. These require agencies to place a certain percentage of their purchases or grants with small businesses or with companies owned by minorities or women. Attractive though such business may seem, you risk becoming a helpless appendage of the government. In principle, firms that receive "8a" or similar set-aside business are expected eventually to grow to the point where they can be weaned from their government privileges and become independent. In practice, as the recipients themselves loudly assert, such companies generally cannot survive if their special status is discontinued.

Probably the most effective set-asides are SBIR (Small Business Innovative Research) grants. All U.S. government agencies having R&D funds are required to set aside money for grants to small technology-based firms. The grant application process is simplified and there are few strings attached. You give up no equity and you can retain patent rights to the technology you develop.

To participate, you must apply for a Phase I grant, which is intended to fund a six-month feasibility study. Currently, Phase I grants under this program are limited to $50,000, but this can make a tidy contribution to a startup's R&D effort. Unfortunately, it's difficult to use this for seed money because the "principal investigator" must be employed full-time by the company in order to get the grant, and because of some awkward timing rules. However, once you're in the startup phase, that $50,000 can contribute nicely to your product development budget. What's more, an SBIR grant can assist you materially in raising venture capital. Many investors regard it as a vote of confidence in your company's technology.

Successful Phase I grantees can apply for Phase II grants of up to $500,000. However, to qualify for Phase II you must attach a letter of intent from an investor to fund your venture after completion of the Phase II work.

Competition for these grants is fairly stiff; you face odds of about one in ten for a Phase I proposal and of about one in three for Phase II. Though there are provisions for protecting confidential information, leaks via the anonymous reviewers of proposals may occur. And we're told that payments from the government can be very slow, though you will always get your money in the end.

If you want to pursue SBIR money, write to all the agencies; you'll be surprised at how broad the interests are and at how

unusual some of the topics are. A university tie-in can be
extremely helpful; university researchers know grantsmanship,
and the association will give your proposal greater weight with
government reviewers.

Though government funding agencies are notorious for the
paperwork they demand, in many cases the red tape is no worse
than what will be imposed by, say, a commercial bank. But
getting funded by the government can require a very different
procedure from getting funded by private entities. You may have
to shift your focus from economic to political considerations.
No matter how much the funding agency may talk about investment and risk and return—some of their personnel can do very
convincing imitations of venture capitalists—never forget that
they are political creatures and political priorities dominate their
concerns.

If you want money from a government agency, you must
address that agency's goals. Don't talk growth and profits; talk
jobs, or exports, or relief of poverty—whatever the mission of
the agency is. The race and gender of members of your management team will probably be more important than their experience or talent. Your connections with important political figures
may count for more than the excellence of your technology. You
must recognize this and work with it.

Equity Financing

When all else has failed, when every expedient has been tried,
when you've raised every cent you can by other means, and it's
still not enough, then you have to sell some equity.

In our discussion of the funding process, we concentrate
primarily on equity financings, especially venture capital. One
justification for this is that equity investors have some unique
characteristics. For one thing, unlike most other types of investors, they have a direct and irreversible interest in the success
of your business. They're in the same boat with you, and they
share your intense concern that the boat not sink. Of course,
they may at some point decide to throw you over the side, but
that's another matter.

A related point is that equity investors tend to be more permanent participants in your venture. You are much more likely to switch banks, say, than you are to switch stockholders. Your relationship with a lender is an affair; your relationship with a stockholder is a marriage. Even if it does turn out to be impermanent, the commitment is at a much higher level.

We've already discussed the type of equity investment where the investors have an ulterior motive for investing above and beyond financial ambitions. This applies to co-founders, political agencies, corporate partners, and so on. Let's now consider the classic, standard equity investor.

To appeal to the equity investor, you must of course promise an attractive risk/reward ratio. The size and nature of the risk and reward must be tailored to the investor type. Some equity investors are looking for long shots; others make it a point to bet the favorite to place.

The equity investor, more than any other type, must *understand* your business in order to invest. This simple principle is probably the most neglected rule in entrepreneurial financing efforts. Whether you're approaching venture capitalists or private "angels," focus your effort on investors who have some familiarity with your industry, your technology, and your markets.

Above all, equity financing is dependent on *building a relationship* with the investor. As we pointed out above, the equity investment creates a strong and long-term commitment between investor and entrepreneur. There is an exception— we'll get to it later—but generally you will need to focus heavily on relationship building if you wish to do a successful equity financing.

The Invisible Empire

Let's start by considering the least formal equity market: private placements. There is an inconspicuous, amorphous, and surprisingly large market that buys stock in small companies. The private placement market is very ill-defined; experts can't even agree on what to call it, let alone how large it is. Some estimates, however, place the amount of money involved in such deals at around $150 billion. Much of the private placement pool consists of wealthy individuals who like to speculate in early-stage investments, but many other players participate, including even pension funds. Entrepreneurs locate private placement investors mostly by personal contact and word of mouth. However, some financial firms specialize in assembling such deals.

> My first venture was financed by what you might call a "low-end" private placement. Our initial target was an acquaintance of my partner, a pocket tycoon who'd made his pile in real estate. As it turned out, he never invested. But while I was talking one day to some scientist friends about a different subject, they asked me what I was working on. I told them; they found it interesting and soon volunteered to put in some money themselves. What's more, they introduced me to some people they knew who frequently made venture investments, who also liked what we were doing and later became investors. Our first round raised $80,000 this way. Among the investors were two scientists, a consulting engineer, a free-lance computer programmer, and a college professor.
>
> Working on a more recent project, my partner and I were looking for about $6 to 8 million in a mixture of debt and equity. Here we encountered a much more professional and sophisticated version of the private placement. One outfit we talked to was a New York firm that was ready— for a stiff fee, of course—to assemble the whole deal. Using its massive contact network, it would locate private placement investors—pension funds, insurance companies, and so on—to put up about a third of the sum in equity, and lenders to take paper on the rest.

Private placement investors exhibit varying degrees of sophistication. Some are long-shot players who like "story" companies—ventures based on simple, attractive concepts— that have some "sizzle" to them. Others want to play it very safe and stick to backing businesses they themselves understand.

Most private investors seem to do comparatively little investigation of the entrepreneurs or companies they invest in, but instead rely heavily on recommendations from friends, business associates, or financial advisers. Most of them—more than you might think—are very reluctant to interfere in the operations of the business and, as long as they receive regular reports, probably will not pester management unduly. However, the private investor has his own money at stake and can get pretty upset if the company gets into trouble.

A special case is presented by the private investor who's also looking to participate in management. You may occasionally encounter an investor who wants to put in money *and* become vice-president for this-and-that. Obviously your reaction to this offer will depend on your evaluation of the prospective investor's management qualifications, as well as on such minor factors as whether you already have a VP for this-and-that. You're in effect taking on another founder, and you'll need to take into account how this will affect relations among the original team members. In particular, if the new investor is putting in a lot more money than the other members, he may feel entitled to have more of a say in management decisions, an attitude that can lead to discord.

Selling stock to private investors is *not* an unregulated activity. Generally speaking, the government aims to protect "widows and orphans"—unsophisticated people, particularly those with relatively low incomes. The rich can fend for themselves; nobody cares if they get clobbered. However, the regulations aren't always easy to understand.

Securities and Blue Sky Laws

We asked Lieb Orlanski, a partner in the Beverly Hills law firm of Freshman, Marantz, Orlanski, Cooper & Klein, to give us a briefing on what "blue sky laws" really mean and how to stay out of trouble. The first rule, as you might anticipate, is "see your lawyer!" However, here are some hints.

When you finance your firm, you may come under federal laws, such as Regulation D, as well as various state codes, which are known as blue sky laws. The intent is the same—to protect investors, especially unsophisticated investors—but the exact rules differ.

Restrictions apply to any sale of a "security," which includes not only stock but promissory notes and so on. Professionals, such as venture capitalists and investment bankers, are presumed to know what they're doing. Usually you don't have to worry about them because they fall under appropriate excmptions. Similarly, transactions with co-founders should present no problem. However, if you sell stock to, or borrow money from, your employees, you must follow the rules; they are considered unsophisticated investors. The typical private investor "angel" is also considered an amateur and restrictions probably apply.

What restrictions? That's where it gets difficult, because not only does the federal government regulate securities but each state has its own set of blue sky laws. So you'll have to check up on the regulations in your state. Typically these may require you to provide prospective investors with certain information, limit your solicitations, and restrict transactions that might harm minority stock-holders.

Something more may be involved. If your company is in one state and the investor is in another, the transaction must comply with the blue sky laws of *both* states. That's not all. If you have out-of-state investors, it is considered an interstate transaction and you must comply with the federal law, Regulation D.

OK, so what's Regulation D? Actually, it's not too bad unless you want to raise over $500,000.

The basic idea is that the federal government would like you to "register" your securities before selling them. This is a tedious and very expensive process. Fortunately, you can sell securities without registering them if you meet certain conditions for "exemption." If you are selling less than $500,000 worth of securities, and have no more than thirty-five investors, sale of unregistered securities is fairly straightforward so long as you follow the requirements of Regulation D. Among other things, you may not advertise for investors, and you must file a form (the Regulation D notice) with the SEC. You may also have to provide the investors with a private offering memorandum, the contents of which are mandated by the SEC. Keep in mind that investors may be limited in how they can transfer or resell their stock. The exact requirements depend on the exemption you are using.

Again, get a good attorney and be sure all the requirements are properly met. In general, the government won't prosecute you if you inadvertently fail to meet some technical requirement. However, if you fail to meet the requirements of the applicable federal and state laws, you may open yourself to a recession action, that is, a suit by a disgruntled investor who wants her money back. So you should make every effort to meet all requirements when doing a private placement because you may later want to go for venture capital or other professional money. If so, state and federal regulators will insist on a clean record, and the deal may be slowed or even derailed if you've omitted a legal iota somewhere.

Stalking the Wild Investor

How can you locate private placement investors? At the high end—the professional outfits—your best bet is to make a pilgrimage to New York or one of the other big money centers. Most investment banking firms do private placements. A large, corporate-oriented law or accounting firm can often refer you to an appropriate private placement outfit.

Keep in mind that the big private placement outfits, like other investors, tend to specialize. Many of them are subsidiaries of, or affiliated with, major industrial corporations. If your startup is working on aerospace equipment, you're more likely to get respectful attention from, say, Grumman Ventures than from some random pension fund.

As for the private individual investor, that's a much more difficult proposition. But there are two rules that can help. First, individual investors, probably more than any other type, rely on "lead investors" in decision making. Most of these people have someone they rely on to identify opportunities and check them out. This person will assemble the deal, bringing in friends who have participated with him in the past. It is this lead investor who is the key and whom you must identify. You find such people through networking; stockbrokers are often good sources. So are professional, licensed, personal money managers. Probably the best sources are accountants.

The other rule is to cast your net where there are people who know your business. If you're doing technology, go talk to a lot of people who are familiar with that kind of technology. Try executives from firms in the same industry, academic scientists in the field, and so on. Talk to people who are in the market—salesmen, distributors, customers, suppliers. You should be talking to all these people anyway as part of your market research. Guess what? Quite a few of them have money, or know someone who has money. If you thoroughly investigate your industry and your market, you are very likely to stumble across that key, lead investor.

Keep in mind that private investors have a strong preference for doing investments locally. Apparently they like to keep an eye on things. So look first in your hometown, not on the other side of the country.

Profiling the Private Investor

Who are these private small-business investors anyway? A survey by the Small Business Administration came up with this somewhat surprising profile.

Private investors are overwhelmingly white males, usually with entrepreneurial experience themselves. (Contrary to the conventional wisdom, doctors and lawyers are only a small segment of this group.) They seldom have family ties to the business founders in whom they invest. They back all sorts of ventures, with a slight preference for manufacturing companies, and they favor early-stage companies.

The investors surveyed had an average income of $90,000 per year and a net worth of $750,000. They were mostly *not* retirees; the mean age was 47. On average, they had $131,000 invested in 3.5 companies.

Perhaps most interesting of all, these people claimed that they accepted three out of ten of the investment opportunities they encountered. Either they are much more reckless than venture capitalists (who commonly fund less than one percent of the plans they see) or they are getting far higher quality in their deal flow. Perhaps it's the latter, for 72 percent of these investors say that results have met or exceeded their expectations.

Doing the Private Investor Deal

The private investor is a crucial source of seed money and startup funds. Unlike professional investment outfits, which concentrate heavily on later-stage fundings, private investors do the majority of their deals at the seed or startup phase.

Private investors seldom seek control of the venture. However, they are generally actively involved as advisers, board members, or consultants; often they become employees.

The typical deal with a private investor runs on the order of $100,000. However, many much smaller investments are made, and some are much larger. (The SBA survey found that 7 percent of the deals involved an equity investment of over $750,000.) Most such deals, especially the larger ones, involve several investors.

If you want to do a deal with a private investor, plan on a very simple structure. Normally the deal will involve a straightforward purchase of common stock, plus a loan.

1244 Stock: Protection on the Downside

If you do a placement of stock under $1 million, you should look into issuing it as "1244 stock." Section 1244 of the Internal Revenue Code is one of the few tax breaks for investors to survive the 1986 tax reform. It provides your investors (and you and your co-founders) with a way of salving your wounds if the company goes bust.

Normally a capital loss can be deducted only against a capital gain; if your losses exceed your capital gains, you're simply out of luck. But if stock issued under Section 1244 is

sold at a loss; it can be deducted against *ordinary* income
such as salary. This can greatly alleviate the pain for investors (and founders!) in a failed company.

Section 1244 applies only to "small business stock,"
and certain technical restrictions, not particularly onerous,
do apply. Check with your accountants.

What are private investors looking for? There's a lot a
variation in this diverse group, but on average they are seeking
a return on investment in the 20 to 25 percent range. These
people normally expect to hold their stock for up to ten years.
It's interesting to note that the standard exit strategy is selling
the stock back to the corporation, its founders, or other insiders.

How do you appeal to private investors? It turns out that
they are surprisingly similar to venture capitalists in the way
they evaluate prospects. They want to see a business plan, and
they focus heavily on market viability and founder qualifications, just as venture capitalists do. There is one key difference:
With the private investor, keep the deal simple, explain your
offering up front, and above all avoid any vagueness about how
the investment will work.

One final thing you should keep in mind when doing private
investor deals: They don't mix well with many other types of
financing. For instance, these people strongly dislike involve-
ment with government funding agencies, so better not plan to
pursue both types of investment. Also, venture capitalists tend
to be prejudiced against "amateur" investors, so getting early-
stage funding from private investors can damage your chances
for funding at later stages.

A Hybrid Creature

Turning from the amateurs to the professionals, let's consider
Small Business Investment Companies (SBICs). These are
among the less conspicuous creatures in the investment jungle,
so they're often overlooked.

An SBIC is a federally chartered firm that is eligible to
borrow money with government guarantees. In return, the SBIC

must finance "small businesses" (according to the U.S. government definition, which is very liberal) with equity or long-term debt (five years or more) investments. There is a subspecies called the MESBIC (Minority Enterprise SBIC), which does just what its name implies.

The SBIC segment is surprisingly inconspicuous considering its size and importance. The program has existed for thirty years and financed thousands of companies. It's particularly useful in doing early-stage fundings that venture capitalists are reluctant to back. Since SBICs are a major training ground for venture capital personnel, a seed funding from an SBIC can be a good bridge to later financings.

The 400 or so SBICs may be broken down into three groups. First, there are subsidiaries of bank holding companies. At this time, SBICs are the only way banks can make equity investments. Second, some SBICs are affiliated with venture capital funds. Third, there are pure "spread lenders," who make money by borrowing cheap (due to the government guarantees) and lending it out at higher interest rates.

Approaching and dealing with SBICs is very similar to the way you would handle venture capitalists or any other professional investor. Though their investment objectives are not so ambitious as those of venture capital firms, SBICs have to be wooed in the same way. However, SBICs tend to have a stronger regional focus than venture capitalists, so work the local firms first.

Venture Capital

And now, the moment you've all been waiting for . . . we take up the subject of venture capital.

Strictly speaking, venture capital refers to firms that take equity positions in small and/or young companies; provide some degree of management assistance or oversight to help them grow extremely rapidly; and cash out their successful investments (if any) after a three-to-ten-year period by taking the company public or selling it to a larger company. Before you seek venture

capital, you must decide whether this is what you want done
with your company.

The Venture Capitalist as Whale

You can understand venture capitalists better if you think
of them as being like some species of whale: filter feeders.
The deal flow through a typical venture capital firm is
enormous; the business plans flow in, and most of them flow
right out again. The firm's filter picks up the edible morsels.

Venture capitalists are like whales in other ways. They
commonly travel in herds, following the fashion in investments. And, like whales, they have a language, but it's very
hard to interpret.

The standard venture capital rule is, "Bet the jockey, not
the horse." The quality of your management team is the dominant factor in the venture capitalist's evaluation of your venture.
In fact, it's not unreasonable to define the venture capitalist as
someone who *invests in entrepreneurs.* They are the equity
equivalent of the old-fashioned "character-based lender."

To continue the gambling metaphor, venture capitalists are
not necessarily long-shot bettors. Some are very conservative,
bet-the-favorite-to-place types. Even the seed money funds take
carefully calculated risks and always have an eye out for a sure
thing.

Venture Capitalists and Risk

We've previously described some of the findings from our
own informal and quite unscientific interviews with venture
capitalists. You might be interested to see the results obtained by a thorough scientific survey and statistical analysis. The following data come from a study conducted by Ian
C. MacMillan, Robin Siegel, and P. N. Subba Narasimha.[1]

The survey tested various criteria for venture capital
investment decisions, and asked the subjects to rate them
in importance on a scale from 1 to 4, with 4 ranking highest.
The venture capitalists rated the qualities of the entrepre-

1. "Criteria Used by Venture Capitalists to Evaluate New Venture Proposals,"
Journal of Business Venturing, No. 1 (1985): 119–128.

neur as most important. Specifically, they wanted founders "capable of sustained intense effort" (3.60), "thoroughly familiar with the market" (3.58), and of "demonstrated leadership ability" (3.41). Aside from management qualities, the most significant factors were potential for high returns (3.42), fast market growth (3.34), and a proprietary position in the product (3.11).

Using a technique called "cluster analysis," the authors of this study were able to divide venture capitalists into three groups. First, there are the "purposeful risk managers." These firms try to minimize their perceived risks across the board, accepting only ventures that fit their pre-determined criteria. Very different was the second group, the "determined eclectics," who try to avoid any hard rules and pride themselves on being ready to consider almost any deal. This doesn't mean, however, that they are any easier to persuade. Third, there are the "parachutists," whose primary concern is the liquidity of the deal. Their strategy is to select deals where they can cut their losses if necessary, by bailing out of the company if things start to go sour.

It would seem that venture firms can take very different attitudes, and it would be very helpful in approaching them if you knew which group a particular firm belonged to. Unfortunately, they don't put up signs saying "We are determined eclectics." However, it's not too hard to get a feel for this from people who know the firm.

Few entrepreneurs appreciate the size and diversity of the modern venture capital industry. Old stereotypes from the 1960s still abound. The industry has grown immense. As this is written, there are about 800 recognized venture capital firms in the United States, with around $30 billion under management. Nearly $4 billion of that gets invested every year. The geographical distribution is very lopsided: In 1987, 39 percent was invested in California; the runner-up was Massachusetts, with only 11 percent.

Is High Tech Really Dead?

Many magazine articles in recent years have bemoaned or acclaimed the shift of venture capital from high-tech ventures to no-tech companies. Your attitude toward this trend will no doubt depend on what kind of company *you* are trying to start. But just what is really happening?

According to *Venture Economics Yearbook* (as reported in *Inc.,* January 1989), a shift does seem to be occurring. There has been a significant drop in investment in technology ventures, especially computer hardware and software and other electronics companies. The strongest growth area is consumer-related companies. Medical and health-care companies are also getting more money.

Everybody's in on the act now in venture capital. The classic independent venture capital partnership still plays an important role. But pension funds, insurance companies, and other immense investment pools have diversified into venture capital by setting up their own funds. Major industrial companies have also developed venture capital subsidiaries, which generally specialize in technologies of interest to the parent company. The idea is that these firms can invest more intelligently than the independents because they can draw on the parent's specialized technical and business expertise. Also, they give the parent firm a means of keeping an eye on new developments, and perhaps of buying into them. The parent, in fact, may provide a convenient exit route for some of the venture fund's investments by acquiring them.

"Daddy, Where Does Venture Capital Come From?"

Venture capital is not simply a natural resource, like trees or iron ore. It has to be created. Entrepreneurs seldom appreciate that venture capitalists, too, have to raise money. In a typical example, five partners worked full-time for fourteen months to raise the money for their first fund.

Where does the money come from? We talked to Tony Hoberman, head of venture capital investing at Alliance Capital Management, to find out.

"Venture capital ultimately comes from pension funds, insurance companies, and similar investors. University and foundation endowments often invest part of their money in venture capital; so do some major corporations. A very small proportion comes from individuals.

"Alliance Capital serves clients—including the pension funds of several *Fortune* 100 companies—by managing their venture capital investments. Typcially an institutional investor will decide to put a certain small percentage of its assets into venture capital. Then we will select the firms in which the investment will be made; negotiate the agreements; supervise the investments; and manage the ultimate distribution from the partnerships. We monitor the venture firms pretty closely; normally we'll be on the phone to each venture capital firm at least once a month.

"It's getting harder for venture capitalists to raise money. Some of the bigger firms seem to be able to put together new funds even when they don't have particularly good past performance, but it's very tough for new partnerships with no track record.

"When we evaluate a venture firm, we try to look behind the numbers. If they did well with their last fund, was it due to just one fluke success, or did they show consistent performance? Do the partners have real expertise in the industries in which they invest? Were they lead investors?

"We insist on a clear understanding of what the investment focus of the venture capital fund will be, what industries and kinds of companies the fund will invest in. This has to be recorded from the start in the partnership agreement. The agreement will also usually limit how much money can go into public companies, and limit or prohibit debt leverage. There may be restrictions on overseas investments. Also, we look into general partners and how much time they will commit to the fund.

"Venture capitalists normally get 20 percent of a fund's profits. But more important these days are management fees. Annual management fees are 2.5 percent; that doesn't sound like much until you realize it's on *committed* capital rather than *invested* capital. It takes years for a fund to be drawn down and fully invested. So for the first few years, the fees are a very heavy drain on the client's return on investment. As a result, venture capitalists are under growing pressure to reduce their fees."

Though most venture funds specialize in particular technologies of industries, some are large enough to cover very wide areas. Keep in mind that an increasing number of funds are now focused on nontechnology businesses.

Venture funds also differ in size. The smallest ones run to a few million dollars; below that size, the fund is too small to carry its overhead, such as paying the people who run it. The largest firms have more than a billion dollars under management, although this will invariably be split into a number of smaller funds.

There are also regional styles in venture capital. Most of the larger funds, and some rather small ones, claim a nationwide presence. In practice, this usually means that they have two or three offices, perhaps one in New York and another in California. The majority of firms are definitely local in outlook. They inevitably tend to take on some characteristics of the local style of entrepreneurship, which leads to geographical differences.

Support Your Local Venture Capitalist

We've heard some strange things about regional differences in venture capital. One venture capitalist told us, "There are no *real* venture capital firms outside New York City." Most people in the business, even in the Big Apple, hold opinions rather less extreme. But geography does make a difference. Here are some comments from the experts.

"Entrepreneurs are more sophisticated in Silicon Valley and Route 128, and so are the venture capitalists. The deal flow is much higher quality there than in other parts of the country. New York and Boston firms seem to be more conservative. Here in southern California, venture capitalists are more competitive, less collegial, than in Silicon Valley."

"I suspect that Western firms are less conservative. New York and Boston venture capitalists tend to come from the financial industry rather than an operating background, which may explain it."

"Silicon Valley is a tightly integrated community. They all know each other. One third of the deals there are by 'dragooning,' where venture capitalists draw known talent from existing high-tech companies and set them up in business. This is rare in other parts of the country."

"Venture capitalists in Silicon Valley and Route 128 are more oriented toward early-stage investments. They also rely more on the 'old-boy network.' "

"Southern California venture capital is not cohesive—unlike Silicon Valley and Route 128, which are. New York firms are different in that they are more willing to invest outside their own geographical area—all over the country. Silicon Valley funds seem to use more young associates. Another difference there is that vesting periods for founder stock are shorter because turnover is so high."

A venture capital fund has a life cycle. When the money is first raised, the fund is fresh and new, and optimistic. During the first few years, the investments are made. By the time the fund is three or four years old, the partners will be spending most of their time monitoring their companies, some of which will be doing well, others poorly. In the late stage of the fund's life cycle—when it's over seven, say—the investments will be maturing or dying. The partners will be thinking about cashing out by taking the winners public, letting the losers die, and unloading the ones in between any way they can.

The Walking Dead

From a venture capitalist's point of view, the worst thing your company can do is to succeed—modestly. Most of their investments fall into this group; they don't become the next Apple or Compaq, but neither do they flame out. These are the "walking dead." They present a problem to the venture capital firm because it's hard to exit from such investments. The investors need to get liquid.

What do venture capitalists do with these investments? It

depends. Some companies are doing OK on sales and profits but have a negative cash flow and poor growth possibilities. The venture capitalists will, in these cases, generally just turn off the money valve of their life-support machines and let them die. Ventures that have achieved a positive cash flow present a different problem. Sometimes they are merged with other companies in the hope that the combination will result in enough growth to get to an initial public offering (IPO). Sometimes they are simply sold.

It's worth thinking about this. If you get venture capital funding, statistically the most likely outcome is that your company will become one of the "walking dead." You should keep this possibility in mind as you negotiate your deal. Before you sign your agreement, look at the fine print on the subjects of mergers and sale of the company. Chances are that those clauses will become operative, so understand what the terms are.

Be Selective

Here is a key message: Venture capital firms *are not interchangeable*. There is a tendency among entrepreneurs, and among many of their advisers who ought to know better, to attack the venture capital industry more or less at random. They ask, "Whom can I somehow persuade to read our plan?" instead of "Which would be the best firm for us to approach?" We recommend that you look over the many venture capital prospects carefully, identify those most likely to invest in your technological and geographical area, and figure out how to approach them, rather than merely follow the line of least resistance.

Trends in Venture Capital

Most of the venture capitalists we interviewed have been in the business for quite a while. We asked them to tell us how venture capital has changed and is changing and what the future might bring.

"Venture capitalists are definitely more professional than they used to be. People have been through up and down cycles. The infrastructure that supports deals is more developed. Entrepreneurs are more sophisticated; we're seeing second- and third-generation entrepreneurs now."

"Firms are more specialized now. They're also more cautious, slower to invest. The 'old-boy network' has weakened; venture capitalists operate more independently than they used to. We're also more concentrated on geography; in the old days there were parts of the country that were short of venture capital, and we used to go there to find deals that offered neglected value. Entrepreneurs are definitely more sophisticated, but that hasn't resulted in better deals. Still, I don't agree with the claim that venture capital returns are dropping and must go lower in the future. They've been consistently at 25 percent."

"Entrepreneurs these days have read the books and know the right things to say. The venture capital industry has grown. That means there are more inexperienced partners. There's increased competition for deals, less 'old-boy' and more 'cutthroat.' Deals get made faster to avoid losing the deal. That can cause problems. I remember one disaster where everybody assumed somebody else had done the due diligence. But the competition is making it an 'efficient market.' The trend is to more institutionalized, systematic venture capital investments; it will become less of an art."

"I see a market trend toward institutionalization, with slower decision making. Firms are becoming somewhat more risk-averse, and they have more of a financial (as opposed to operating) orientation."

"There's a lot of talk about consolidation in the venture capital industry; it may even be happening. It certainly is becoming more competitive, and I see venture capital firms now aggressively marketing themselves."

"The industry is much more competitive; venture capital has grown faster than deal flow has. You see price-cutting on top-quality deals. An increasing problem is the technology; it's

getting more advanced all the time, so it's more difficult to
understand it, to get up to speed so you can evaluate it for a
deal."

The Public Market

The basic idea of venture capital is to spot winning ventures
early, develop them, and then sell them, usually by going public,
and reap a humongous profit. Some entrepreneurs choose to
bypass the venture capitalist and go directly to the public offering. It can work, but it can also be very tricky.

Going public can, in principle, give you access to very large
pools of capital. With almost any other sort of financing, you
must locate, interest, and sell the investor. But once your
company is "public," other people take over the market-making
function for you—investment bankers, brokers, specialists, and
so on. So you don't need to concern yourself so much with
building a relationship with investors (this is the exception we
mentioned earlier); your investors are rather anonymous.

That's the good news. The bad news is that when you go
public, you completely lose control over who invests in your
company. Anyone can buy your stock, including naive odd
lotters who haven't got the slightest idea what you're trying to
accomplish with the company, speculators looking for a quick
buck even if it cripples the company's future, and takeover
artists who see a chance to pick up some money by throwing
out management—that is, you—and breaking the firm into
pieces. And anybody can sell your stock, including "shorts"
who spread defamatory rumors about your company to drive
down the price so they can make a killing.

A public company is also subject to heavy regulation. The
IPO (initial public offering) process is slow, frustrating, and
frighteningly expensive. Once you even start going public, the
SEC will control what you can say and what you can't say about
your company's progress and prospects. Stock transactions by
you and the other members of your team will now be "insider
trading" and subject to very tight restrictions. You will have to
expose your company's financial performance and other critical

data to the public—including your competitors. And once you've gone public, it isn't easy (though it is possible) to change your mind and become a private company again.

The market for IPOs is highly variable. There are times when the stock market will buy anything, including companies with no sales, no product, and no management. At other times, the stock market will not touch any IPO, no matter how solid the company or how firm its prospects. There are some regional exchanges—Vancouver and Denver, for instance—where IPO activity is fairly continuous. However, a lot of pretty flaky deals go public in these arenas, and some of their reputation may rub off on you if you go this route.

Going Public: Advice From an Expert

Lieb Orlanski's desk is covered with souvenir "tombstones"—copies of the offering announcements for the many companies that he and his firm have taken public. We asked him to give us his thoughts on the IPO process.

> "Going public will—usually—give you a better valuation for your company. Generally in an IPO you can sell stock for about twice what you would get from a venture capital firm. But there's a downside. Once you're public, everyone sees your numbers—including your competitors. You are under short-run earnings pressure. And being public will generate overhead of about $100,000 per year.
>
> "There are two schools of thought on going public. One says do it if the market will take you. The other says do it only after you've developed a consistent track record.
>
> "My feeling is that the big mistake is doing an IPO that's too small. Considering the costs and the hassles and the risks, you shouldn't go public with an offering that will bring in less than $4 million net.
>
> "That's why it's usually not wise to do an IPO on the Vancouver or Denver markets. The biggest offerings done there are around a million dollars or so. Also, too many penny stocks are questionable, so if you go this route you may be

stigmatized as a company. Blind pools are even more disreputable, and most of them are very small anyway.

"What about public shells? A public shell with no cash in it doesn't have much to offer. Merge with it, and you get the costs and problems of being public, but no money to compensate. It's like kissing your sister. A public shell with significant cash in it is different, but those are very rare."

Consider the Source

We can't possibly cover in detail all the possible sources for venture funding. What we hope we have accomplished is to give you a feel for the basic types of money available and for how the various sources differ in their objectives and criteria. It's up to you to decide which sources you want to approach and how you want to balance your funding among them.

Let us emphasize again that you can greatly improve your company's odds of success, and at the same time retain more equity for yourself, if you look to nonstandard funding sources first. Don't just assume that you "must" get venture capital or "must" get a bank loan. Strive to be flexible, aggressive, and innovative in raising money.

You have probably discovered that the funding process is much more complicated than you thought. But, in compensation, chances are that you have more options for financing your venture than you previously realized.

Bibliography

Bruno, Albert V., and Tyzoon T. Tyebjee. "The Destinies of Rejected Venture Capital Deals," *Sloan Management Review,* No. 27 (Winter 1986), p. 43.

Burrill, G. Steven, and Craig T. Norback. *The Arthur Young Guide to Raising Venture Capital.* Blue Ridge Summit, Penn.: Liberty House, 1988.

Contino, Richard M., *Handbook of Equipment Leasing.* New York: AMACOM, 1989.

Gaston, Robert J. *Finding Private Venture Capital for Your Firm: A Complete Guide*. New York: Wiley, 1989. Based on an SBA survey of private investors, this book is packed with statistics. The author classifies the various sorts of "angels" and describes how and where they invest.

Gaston, Robert J., and S. E. Bell. *The Informal Supply of Capital*. Final report on contract SBA-2024-AER-87, SBA Office of Economic Research, 1987. If you want to go to the source, this is the study on which the preceding book was based.

Livingston, Abby. "State Capital," *Venture* (May 1989), p. 57. This article discusses various state government programs for aiding small and new businesses and provides a table surveying them.

Mangelsdorf, Martha E. *"Inc.*'s Guide to 'Smart' Government Money," *Inc.* (August 1989), p. 51.

Morris, Jane K., and Susan Isenstein (eds.). *Pratt's Guide to Venture Capital Sources*. 13th ed. Phoenix, Ariz.: Oryx Press, 1989. Annual. This is the classic reference book on venture capital. It leads off with a number of valuable essays on the venture capital funding process, then follows up with a complete directory of funds, with names, addresses, the size of the fund, its preferred areas for investment, and other useful data. Indispensable if you're seeking venture capital.

Rao, Dileep. *Handbook of Business Finance and Capital Sources*. New York: AMACOM, 1985. This reference work follows much the same approach as *Pratt's*; however, it tackles all sorts of financing sources instead of just venture capital. The directory coverage is therefore much broader, but also shallower.

Wat, Leslie. *Strategies for Going Public: An Entrepreneur's Guidebook*. New York: Deloitte Haskins & Sells, 1983.

The States and Small Business Programs and Activities. Washington, DC: Small Business Administration. Government Printing Office, 1986. 166–650. This government document provides a complete listing of state-level programs for small and entrepreneurial businesses. All types of programs are included, from loans and grants to business incubators.

5

Running the Gantlet: An Overview of the Financing Process

Some deals simply fall into place without the slightest difficulty. Everything comes together smoothly and rapidly, the parties shake hands, the check is signed, and the financing process is over practically before it started. Unfortunately, such cases are rare.

The more typical deal climaxes a tortuous marathon run through the financing gantlet. You suffer through leads that never amount to anything, investors who never call back, negotiations that fall through at the last minute. You spend sleepless nights revising projections, and fall asleep during the days as you plough through the endless pages of fine print generated by the lawyers. And you do all this while worrying every day about scrounging up enough cash to keep going until the deal finally closes.

The venture financing process is complicated, and getting more so every year. You're likely to find it a grueling effort. But you can avoid many hassles, and improve your odds of getting the money, if you understand how the modern financing process works. This chapter provides an overview that can steer you past some of the worst hazards.

When Should You Start?

This is a question with a very simple answer: quite a while before you will desperately need the money. There's an old joke that a banker is a guy who lends you his umbrella when the sun is shining and takes it back when it rains. The truth is that *all* investors (with the sole exception of pawnbrokers) exhibit precisely this attitude.

The Fundamental Theorem of Fund-Raising

THERE IS NOTHING YOU CAN DO TO REDUCE YOUR CHANCES OF GETTING FUNDED MORE THAN TO NEED THE MONEY.

You must take into account that typical financing deals take a long time to consummate. Venture capitalists, for instance, say that the average time between first approach and closing the deal is about two and a half months. Objective observers say that the reality is more like four or five months. And if the deal is unusally complicated—or, especially, if it involves a large amount of money—six months to a year is a more realistic estimate.

Don't Hold Your Breath

In interviewing venture capitalists, we asked them to estimate how long it normally took from the first contact with a new venture to closing the deal. We got answers mostly in the two- to three-month range.

Then, as a check, we asked specifically how long it took to do the most recent deal that they'd invested in. The answers to this question ranged from five to eight months.

Investors sincerely believe that they move quickly on funding decisions. But it appears that, like most of us, they don't really have an accurate idea of how long it takes to accomplish their tasks. As you plan your funding process, you'd be wise to assume that it will take two to three times as long as expected.

Craig Isom of Arthur Andersen describes the ordeal—not atypical—of one of his clients:

> "This was a classical high-tech garage startup. He attracted interest from a good venture capital firm and, overall, things went pretty smoothly. But it took over a year to close the deal. He survived, barely, by consulting and eating his nest egg."

Your plans therefore should allow for the time needed. Be sure that you are prepared to wait for the money; if your venture—or your family—is starving, your negotiating position will be very weak.

Beware the "bridge loan." Some investors will offer to lend you enough money to keep going while all those tedious details are taken care of before the main deal can close. Guess what happens to you if you are not sufficiently . . . flexible in your negotiating stance?

"Sure," we hear you sneer. "Nice work if you can get it." If you're like most entrepreneurs, you're in a hurry, and usually with good reason. You see a market window; if you don't roll out quickly, competitors will come in and you'll be shut out. You have a chance to buy a company, or a plant, or a patent, and you can't hold the option indefinitely. After all, that "do it now" mentality is one of the basic traits of the entrepreneur, and it's a major factor in making your venture a success.

Ultimately you will have to balance your need to save time with your desire to negotiate the best possible deal. Ideally, you would do all your homework, assemble a complete team, and develop a finished plan before starting the financing process. That way you'd have the strongest position with investors; the more work you do before the deal is cut, the bigger your slice of the pie will be. That's the whole idea of "sweat equity." But getting all your ducks in a row is a time-consuming process.

The alternative is to bring the investors in at an early stage. That way you can run the financing process in parallel with the planning process. You'll save months. Another advantage is that the investors can help out with your work—giving you advice about the industry, optimizing your financial planning, and helping you to complete your team. Of course, you may have mixed feelings about this "assistance." Some of your decision-making power will seem to shift to the investors, and you may not be totally happy about the way in which they wield it. And, since they have done a lot of the work of getting your startup going, the investors will feel entitled to take more of the equity in compensation.

Your decision on timing may not be completely up to you, however. For some kinds of financings, external factors may compel you to move at certain times. If, for instance, you plan to make a public stock offering, you may have to time your entry for one of the periodic "windows" in the stock market when IPOs are viable. If you are borrowing money, fluctuations in interest rates will affect your plans.

> If you are fortunate enough to be starting up at a time when your industry is a fad among investors, don't miss your chance. I remember being invited out to lunch by a Wall Street acquaintance in 1981. He asked me if I was interested in starting a biotechnology company. I told him I was a chemist, not a biologist, and barely knew what a petri dish was. "Damn," he said. "I've got five million dollars that has to be invested in biotechnology by the end of the month."

Whatever your choice, you'll be wise to develop a realistic estimate of the time needed to complete your financing—and to accept it, repugnant though it may be. You may spend months approaching nonreceptive investors before you find the one who will finance you, so the overall financing process will probably take much longer than you'd like.

Developing the Leads

Once you've determined what kind of financing you want to do
and have decided you're ready to start, you must search out
prospects for the deal. How can you find them? How can you
approach them?

There are directories of venture capital firms and other
financial institutions (see the Bibliography for this chapter). You
can compile an initial list of prospects from these sources. Keep
in mind that the financial industry is fluid and new firms are
constantly being formed. Don't neglect them; a brand-new fund
with freshly raised money burning a hole in its pocket and an
urgent need to get some of it invested might be very receptive to
your pitch. Conversely, of course, you should avoid funds that
are fully invested. The small-business magazine *Inc.* regularly
reports on developments in venture capital and publishes annual
directories. *Venture Capital Journal,* which is aimed more at the
investment community, provides excellent coverage of the industry. *Pratt's Guide to Venture Capital Sources* is also a very
useful reference.

Generally speaking—there are exceptions—you should concentrate on local investors. Most firms prefer to have their
investments nearby so that they can keep an eye on them. From
your point of view, flying all over the country to search for
capital is time-consuming, tiring, and expensive. Keep in mind
too that the problems of geographical distance don't end when
the investment is made. You may think it would be nice to have
your financiers in Australia so that they'll be out of your hair.
Well, one Enterprise Forum presenter, Cybergraphic Systems,
which had just that situation, found it not so favorable. Absentee
landlords aren't familiar with the situation on the ground and
often make decisions motivated by their local conditions without
understanding how they will affect their far-flung outposts—
namely, you.

What about those exceptions? Well, you might not think it
from what most writers on financing say, but not all entrepreneurs live in or near the big money centers. If you're setting up
business out in the tuliebrush somewhere, local investment

bankers may not be thick on the ground. In that case, better plan on traveling to the Big Apple or some other den of iniquity to find capital.

Keep in mind that investors, particularly venture capitalists, are not always passive in this process. Because investing has become more competitive, particularly in high-tech areas, many firms now go out and actively look for good prospects. They try to find inventors or other founders early, while the venture is still in the formative stages. Some firms even take the initiative completely; seeing a market opportunity, they will go out and recruit a team of entrepreneurs from scratch to form a company. Once you understand how investors think, you may be able to arrange things so that they chase you until you catch them.

The Notorious Network

Not all investors can be located from print sources. The "angels" who provide private placement money, for instance, almost never show up on any lists. To stalk the elusive investor successfully, you should tie into the complex network of financial professionals.

"Networking" has become a buzzword and millions of hopeful businesspeople are cruising around madly handing out business cards. It doesn't work that way, of course. Networking is not an exchange of phone numbers; it is an exchange of *favors*.

> Ever watch a really superb networker in action? I have. He's a great listener. He fixes his whole attention on his subject with an intensity that's almost frightening. And you can see him continuously taking mental notes. What does the subject *need?* Can he introduce him to a prospective customer? A supplier? The engineer he so desperately needs to hire? His whole focus is on one simple question: What can I do to help this guy? By working at this every day, he's developed a network of hundreds of people who owe him a favor.

If you already have a good position in your local business network, now's the time to tap it. If you don't—well, you might be surprised at how quickly you can get into the network. People will, so to speak, give you credit. The key thing is to demonstrate that you understand what networking is, that your attitude is one of looking for favors *you* can do. Once you begin to project this outlook, you'll soon find that perfect strangers will start calling you up to say, "So-and-so told me you're looking for venture capital. I hear Buzzard & Condor is looking for startups to invest in."

Among your best sources for investor contacts are other investors. If you've got a bank loan already, your loan officer can introduce you to all sorts of other people in the financial industry. (Be careful about asking him to introduce you to other bankers, however.)

Don't forget your fellow entrepreneurs. They are very useful people to talk to and can give you a lot of good advice, quite aside from their potential for contacts with investors. Ken Deemer, of InterVen Partners, advises: "Look for mentors, people who have built successful companies, and cultivate them."

Probably the very best sources are attorneys at law firms that specialize in business work. Seek out those who deal regularly with startups; they work with investors every day and have terrific contact networks.

Venture Network Nodes

In the major entrepreneurial growth areas, certain law firms totally dominate the market for successful high-tech startups. If you can connect with one of their partners, you'll have a tremendous leg up in getting venture capital. Here are some of the leaders in various areas:

Silicon Valley:	Brobeck, Phleger, & Harrison
	Cooley Godward
	Wilson Sonsini
	Ware, Fletcher, & Friedenrich
Route 128:	Testa, Hurwitz, & Thibeault
Los Angeles:	Freshman, Marantz, Orlanski, Cooper & Klein
	Irvin, Cohen, & Jessup
	Riordan & McKenzie

New York: Shereff, Friedman, Hoffman, &
                        Goodman
                     O'Sullivan, Graev, & Karabel

Washington, D.C.: McVey & Sherman

Accounting firms are also excellent routes into the financing network. If you plan to seek major funding, then, as you plan your startup, resist the temptation to get free numbers from your sister-in-law, who happens to be a CPA. Instead, go to a Big Eight firm. They're highly competitive and hungry for new clients, and they'll often give you a break on fees (which, even so, will be backbreaking). The Big Eight have national and even international presence and they work routinely with all sorts of investors, from venture capital outfits to small private investors. Their contacts are superb. And using a Big Eight firm for your accounting will lend your venture instant credibility.

See if your actual or prospective customers can give you some leads. Vendors can be very fruitful sources of introductions, particularly to bankers and other debt-financing sources.

What About Five-Percenters?

"Five-percenter" is the not terribly complimentary term for people who offer to find capital for you in return for a cut of the proceeds. They generally prefer to call themselves "finders"— or sometimes something more impressive-sounding. Keep in mind that anyone who can afford to have business cards printed up can call himself or herself an "investment banker."

How can you tell what they really are? Simple: Do they have any money themselves? And if not, are they engaged by, *and paid by,* the investor? Or are they to be paid by you, either with a fee or a percentage of the investment? If the latter, you're dealing with a finder. Should you use one?

The standard "finder's fee" deal looks attractive. The finder offers to put you in touch with investors and help you to sell your deal to them. If—and only if—the deal goes through, you agree to pay 5 percent (sometimes more) of the proceeds to the finder. If it doesn't go through, or if you locate the money on your own, you owe nothing. So what do you risk?

Well, you risk the whole deal. Having the finder in the circuit makes the investment much less attractive to investors. The investor wants to make a profit on his investment. If he's going to take a 5 percent hit immediately after the deal is made, that will have to be made up out of the company's profits before he even gets back to break-even. Who needs it? He's got lots of other deals he can do.

And, we regret to say, the presence of a finder will generally not enhance your credibility. There are some pretty flaky specimens doing this sort of thing. To be fair, the vast majority are not dishonest; they're naive. They see the prospect of getting a quick and easy $50,000 for "finding" a million-dollar investment and persuade an equally naive entrepreneur to sign up with them. Often they don't even realize that their participation will poison the deal; or, if they do, they go on anyway. They have little to lose, and—never can tell—they might win. It's like buying a lottery ticket.

This is not to say that you should never accept any help in seeking capital or conducting negotiations. There is an increasing trend for consultants to get involved in financing efforts. Some large firms, such as the Boston Consulting Group, have entered this business. (Others, including McKinsey & Co., cite potential conflict-of-interest problems and are staying away from it.) Many small firms and individuals are doing similar work. Often a skilled consultant can provide invaluable assistance.

But if you decide to employ a consultant to assist your financing, it's probably best to dip into your meager funds and pay the fees yourself. If you really can't afford the service, sign an agreement to retain the consultant for future services on very lucrative terms but contingent on successful funding of your company. Try to avoid agreeing to an explicit percentage of the financing. And check out the consultant carefully before you sign anything.

Networking Organizations

A wide variety of organizations provide networking opportunities for entrepreneurs.

The MIT Enterprise Forum has chapters in most major cities. Entrepreneurs and would-be entrepreneurs from both high-tech and low-tech companies attend. So do accountants, lawyers, and consultants specializing in new-venture work, as well as a sprinkling of investors. (See Appendix I for more details.)

> Presenters at the Enterprise Forum should not expect venture capitalists to jump up and start waving their checkbooks. However, more than one company has made useful investor contacts at the Forum. A good example is Triplex Corporation. At its November 1985 presentation, a representative of Union Ventures was in the audience. The result was a $5 million venture capital funding, with Union taking the lead role.

Most cities have one or more organizations devoted to seminars or presentations for entrepreneurs. The quality of their offerings varies widely, but the best offer some good contacts. In entrepreneurial hotbeds you'll find literally dozens of such groups. In northern California, for instance, there are the Silicon Valley Entrepreneurs Club, Berkeley Young Entrepreneurs, the Sacramento Valley Venture Capital Forum, and many others.

Many universities offer programs aimed at entrepreneurs, and the attendees can be fertile ground for networking. College alumni organizations or clubs, especially those associated with business schools, often have networking groups in major cities.

There are also associations set up specifically to assist inventors in developing and marketing their inventions.

Some large technology companies have set up organizations to assist small ventures that might become customers or suppliers. A leading example is Digital Equipment's Technology Executive Roundtable.

Professional organizations can be excellent networking sources. The American Electronics Association is permeated with entrepreneurs; even the staid American Chemical Society has a Small Chemical Business section.

Look into industry associations. Where there's a lot of venture activity, specialized networking groups spring up, such as the Software Entrepreneurs' Forum. There's even a group called Space Entrepreneurs.

City, county, and state governments these days often have offices assigned to promote entrepreneurship. If you have a specific need, they may be able to provide you with key names to contact. Of course the local SBA office is also a resource.

We've mentioned the Big Eight accounting firms. Note that several of them run their own networking organizations. For example, Deloitte Haskins & Sells offers an ''Executive High Technology Breakfast Series.''

There are also groups aimed at networking for specific segments of the entrepreneurial culture, including women, ethnic groups, and racial minorities. If you and your spouse are doing a startup together, you might want to contact the National Association of Entrepreneurial Couples.

Check out the organizations in your area. Pick one or two that look promising and start attending regularly. Don't try to join them all. It's more effective to become well known and well trusted in one group than to be a semistranger in half a dozen.

The Initial Contact

There are several ways of making the initial contact with an investor. Throwing your business plan over the transom is just about the least effective of them.

The very best way to get consideration for your business plan is to become a personal acquaintance of the investor in advance. When you are still in the homework stage, identify prospective investors who specialize in your industry. Then start looking for ways to get to know them. For instance, investors will often attend conferences to keep up with the technology in their area. It won't hurt if you or your techies get up and give a paper when your target is in the audience. When you're doing your marketing studies, you have an excellent excuse to call a few venture capitalists and ask them, as experts in the industry, some carefully chosen, intelligent questions.

Even if they're too busy to talk to you, you'll leave the impression of someone serious, competent, and thorough.

A quite satisfactory entry results from a strong recommendation by someone the investor trusts. An accountant or attorney who regularly works with the investor calls and says, "I've run across a deal I think will interest you. It's called Retroactive Circuits Inc. and they have a really neat idea for going back to vacuum tubes. The team is first-rate. Shall I have them send you their business plan?"

There's another, more subtle way of using an intermediary. Drawing on your Executive Summary, write a two- or three-page letter describing your company to the lawyer or accountant or consultant who knows the investor. In this letter, you ask for advice on some point or other. The intermediary then sends a copy of the letter to the investor, with a cover note saying something like, "These fellows asked me to advise them on their patent application. I thought you might find their project interesting." This technique allows you to dangle your venture in front of the investor without applying any pressure or demanding any commitment.

It isn't always easy to get someone who is known to the investor to actually endorse you. Such people value their financial contacts and are reluctant to tie themselves too closely to a deal that might turn out to be a lemon and discredit them. If your contact is reluctant to recommend you or take an active role, you can at least call the investor and say, "Prudence Pusillanimous tells me your firm is looking for startups that are focused on obsolete technology. Can I send you the Retroactive Circuits business plan?"

Any introduction to the prospect by someone known to him is better than none. But sometimes you just can't get the contact you need, and you have to hit him cold. In that case, your best bet is to try to reach the investor by phone; tell him briefly ("briefly," meaning in not more than a minute or two) what your venture is about and offer to send the plan. This will increase the odds that he'll at least glance at the plan. If he won't accept your phone call, you can send the plan anyway, but it's a forlorn hope.

Making Contact: Investor Comments

We asked a number of venture capitalists to tell us where their deal flow comes from and how the source affects their attitude.

"About 50 percent of the plans I see come in through referrals. But an increasing number result from my request to see something. There's a trend to active search for attractive deals."

"Our first fund did eleven deals, and every one of them came in through a referral—mostly from a couple of law firms we know and rely on. During this period we rejected 1800 plans that came in cold."

"Naturally we like prequalified plans. In fact, I can't recall ever investing in a nonreferred deal. But I will take a phone call from anybody; even that introduction is better than just sending the plan."

"I don't think there's that much prejudice in favor of plans that are referred. It's that the good plans tend to come from referrals."

"The firm I used to be with has done over a hundred deals, none of which came in cold. The firm I'm with now relies heavily on accountants—especially the Big Eight, of course—and lawyers. We make it a point to throw them business from our investments to encourage them to bring future deals to us. We also get referrals from a network of successful entrepreneurs that we've established. We don't much use brokers or finders; there are honest ones, but they're rare. Yes, we still look at unreferred plans, if only to keep an eye on what's going on, but they definitely get a lower priority."

"Most of our deals come from referrals or from our own initiative. There are six or eight law firms in Los Angeles that dominate the network of venture capital referrals. Venture capitalists *do* go to "beauty shows," but we'd like to see better

ones, with high-quality companies. We don't do deals from
finders."

The key point to keep in mind is the need to *initiate a
relationship* with the investor. This must be done with some
care. Some people advocate building a relationship in advance
of broaching the subject of the deal. This is excellent advice, but
only if you have some *independent* basis for the relationship. If
you and the investor know each other because you're both
involved with the Girl Scouts, great. But if you are buttering her
up just to make her feel good about you so that you can hit her
with your business plan—or even if you merely appear to be
doing so—it will probably backfire. Most investors have all sorts
of people fawning over them; money attracts insincerity as
garbage attracts flies. So investors quickly get cynical about
friendly approaches; those who don't, quickly go broke.

Secrecy Agreements

All of us who deal with entrepreneurs, particularly those who
are still in the startup phase, encounter requests to sign secrecy
agreements. Mostly this seems to reflect a certain naïveté. Once
the agreement is signed and the invention or business plan is
unveiled, it generally turns out to be unremarkable. Almost
never is there anything there that really needs to be kept secret.

Not to put too fine a point on it, our advice in most cases is
to forget about secrecy agreements. First, *an idea by itself has
almost no value.* Ideas are cheap; they simply aren't worth
stealing. Second, the people who are most obsessed with secrecy agreements tend to be inventors with perpetual motion
machines and similar devices, so *insisting on a secrecy agreement damages your credibility.* Third, a secrecy agreement, like
any legal document, is only as strong as your lawyers and the
bankroll you have to pay them with. So *a secrecy agreement
doesn't give you much protection anyway.*

Note also that most investors pride themselves on their
professionalism and integrity. It is very unlikely that your proprietary information is going to leak from a venture capital firm

or similar outfit. So they may feel a bit insulted when you whip
out your little document.

That said, there are some precautions you *should* take.
Mark your business plan "confidential," and clearly indicate
any other proprietary material you hand out. Do be careful in
dealing with private, amateur investors, who are not always so
conscientious as professionals like venture capitalists. And even
with venture capital firms, do check that they haven't already
invested in a competitor before sending your business plan!
Detailed information should be handled with discretion; unlike
ideas, solid data that took a lot of work to assemble *are* valuable.
Information about your customers is precious and should be
carefully protected, particularly if the customers consider it
confidential. Finally, and most important, premature revelation
of technological information, with or without a secrecy agreement, can wreck your chance of getting a patent. See your
patent attorney before you open your mouth.

Is There Safety in Numbers?

How many investors should you approach? Well, the obvious
answer is: as many as it takes to raise the money. But there are
some serious questions to consider in selecting investors to
approach. The main consideration to keep in mind is that financiers are clubby; they have a very efficient grapevine.

If you do a simultaneous submission of your plan to several
dozen venture capital firms, you may blow the deal. Everyone
in the area will know about your promiscuous ways. The top
firms will not feel an intense desire to compete with a lot of
other funds for the chance to invest. Instead, you'll attract flakes
and even chiselers—the people who are looking for a one-night
stand, not the ones who want to build a lasting relationship.

But. If you peddle your deal to one firm at a time, you must
take into account that the odds are fairly low that any single firm
will say yes, even for a very good deal. There's a better-than-
even chance that your first prospect will turn you down. Again,
the news will spread like wildfire. From then on, every venture

capitalist you approach will probably be aware that you have already been rejected. It can't help but prejudice your case.

Shall we despair? What's the moral? We are inclined to go with the conventional wisdom: Simultaneous submission to a small number—less than six or so—of *very carefully chosen* prospects gives you your best odds. If your initial approach fails, it may be advisable to withdraw your deal from the market for a few weeks or months, revise your plan heavily, and start afresh.

Still, experienced people advise us that it's better to keep the pot a-boiling, so to speak. Start with half a dozen firms or so, but every time you get turned down, approach a new outfit to replace the one that dropped out.

Living in Suspense

Once you've made the initial contact and got the plan into the investor's hands, all you can do is wait—while, of course, working on other prospects. Generally speaking, the investor shouldn't take more than a few weeks to get back to you. After that time, follow up by phone. They hate saying "no" and if they don't like your plan they'll generally just stay silent and hope you'll go away. If your phone calls aren't returned, that's "no."

What you're waiting for is that initial expression of interest—the request to come in and talk to the investor. Then you face the next step.

Financier Qualification

Most big companies have a function called "vendor qualification." It consists of checking out prospective suppliers: Can they handle the company's requirements? Do they have a good reputation? Are they the kind of people the company wants to deal with? In a similar manner, when you look for funds you should start with a preliminary "financier qualification." The naive entrepreneur may not see the need for this. Any warm body with a big bag of money will do, right? But approaching the wrong investors will, at best, result in a waste of your precious time; at worst, you can get badly burned.

The first item you should consider is the size of the investor in relation to the investment. Investors come in all sizes. There is your Aunt Tillie, who might put in the $100 she saved from her Social Security checks, and there are venture capital firms with half a billion dollars under investment, and everything in between. No intelligent investor will put more than a small fraction of her assets into a single transaction, of course. A fund with $100 million might put as much as $5 million into a single deal. So you must first ask whether your prospect has the money to do your financing. With a professional firm this is simply a matter of looking it up in the appropriate directory. With your Aunt Tillie and other private investors, you should take *active* steps to be sure they can afford to lose their stake. Otherwise, you might face some unpleasant reactions if your venture, contrary to all reasonable expectation, should run into difficulties.

You must also be sure that the investor does the *type* of financing you have in mind (see Figure 5-1). Some venture capital firms, for instance, do only second-round financings and won't touch startups. (But check with the firm before drawing conclusions; what one calls a "startup" another might call "second-round" and a third "seed-stage"; there's no standardized terminology.)

A crucial though generally underestimated requirement is *familiarity with your industry*. Most professional investors are specialists and won't touch a deal in an area with which they are unfamiliar. Unfortunately, they sometimes don't know their limits. No matter what kind of investor you're approaching, do not bother if he doesn't understand your business. If you're setting up a biotechnology company, don't waste time on a venture capitalist who specializes in electronics. If you're expanding your machine-tool manufacturing shop, don't use a bank whose customers are primarily retail service businesses. If you're seeking seed money for an aerospace invention, don't approach a private investor who made his pile in real estate.

You see, investors make decisions on the basis of experience. The successful investor has learned from past deals certain

Figure 5-1. Venture capital fundings broken down by stage.

Stage	Percentage of investment
Seed/startup	13%
Other early stage	15%
Second stage	31%
Later stage	25%
LBOs, acquisitions, etc.	18%

Source: *Venture Capital Yearbook* (as reported in *Inc.*, March 1989), p. 118.

rules of thumb to rely on in evaluating a deal. But that wisdom is based on doing deals in his specialized area. When you try to get money from someone who doesn't know your field, you waste endless hours explaining to him why the rules of thumb he normally relies on don't apply in your business. Even if you succeed in convincing him, there is still the emotional factor. In the end he simply won't feel comfortable, and won't invest.

In dealing with professional investors, keep in mind that you should perform financier qualification both for the firm and for the individual. Your contact, the person you'll be working with in negotiating the investment, should be subject to personal qualification. Does he understand your industry and your business? Does he even have the authority to give you the money? (This is particularly a problem when getting a bank loan; a bank senior executive vice-president has just about enough authority to go to the bathroom without asking permission.) Do you trust this person and feel comfortable dealing with him? You're not just doing a deal, you're building a relationship, and it's a relationship with a person, not a company. If all goes well, you'll be dealing with this chap on a regular basis for years, maybe decades. Better be sure you like him.

Don't rely solely on your own impressions. By the time you get down to serious talks with an investor, you should have some independent sources give you references. Talk to the

CEOs of some other companies he's invested in. Are they happy
with the results? Do they feel they were dealt with fairly? Are
they being harassed or overmonitored? You might turn up some
surprising comments.

Financier Qualification Checklist

☐ Does the firm have the resources to do this deal?
☐ Does the firm normally do financings of this size?
☐ Does the firm normally do financings of this type?
☐ Does the firm have experience in your industry?
☐ Does the firm have an office reasonably near your company?
☐ Does your contact have the authority to negotiate the deal?
☐ Does your contact understand your industry, your technology, and
   your business?
☐ Do you have complete confidence in the integrity of your contact?
☐ Does the firm have a consistently good reputation with intermedi-
   aries such as attorneys and accountants?
☐ Have you checked with other entrepreneurs who have dealt with
   the firm?

Structuring the Deal

In Chapter 4 we discussed the various types of financial sources
you can approach and their characteristics. Sometime early in
the financing process you will have to decide what kind of
financing you will seek and how you would like to structure the
deal.

Of course, it won't be completely up to you. You may find,
as you talk to investors—or as they refuse to talk to you!—that
your deal, as you conceived it, simply is not doable. In that case
you'll have to go back to the drawing board. Even if the basic
deal structure is acceptable, it may have to be modified in the
course of negotiations.

You can of course do a financing that combines various
types of investments. For instance, you might sell stock to get
working capital, arrange a leasing deal to obtain some production equipment, and get a vendor to finance your initial needs

for raw materials. A shrewdly designed multiple-source financing can satisfy your capital needs far more efficiently than a blind reliance on massive equity investments.

On the other hand, it is wise not to make your financing any more complicated than necessary. The more complicated the deal, the more people have to sign on. It can be very difficult assembling all the needed approvals, and as a result complex deals are harder to finance and take much longer than simple deals. Keep in mind also that alternative modes of financing may be most useful if kept in reserve for future rounds.

> A cautionary example is provided by Cipherlink Corporation, a company that developed software to transfer data between different types of computers. When it came to the Enterprise Forum it was seeking additional capital. However, Cipherlink had already exploited several sources of financing. As a result, the company had a very complex financial structure. It had issued common stock, three classes of preferred stock, and warrants, and had also set up an R&D limited partnership. As panelist Craig Isom (a partner at Arthur Andersen) pointed out, Cipherlink had simply used up most of the traditional venture funding sources. The R&D partnership in particular inhibited future equity investments, and the panel suggested that Cipherlink's best remaining option was customer financing.

If you use multiple financing avenues, try to make each financing a separate, independent deal. This is much simpler and more effective than trying to bring together several different players, each with different objectives, and keeping them warm while the due diligence is ground out.

The Road Show

Once you've tickled the fancy of a financier, you have to make a more or less formal presentation of your venture. Developing and delivering a presentation is, as we techies say, a nontrivial task, so the next chapter is devoted to a detailed exposition of this subject. For now, however, we'd like to point out that you are not likely to be handed a check after doing a single presentation. You will probably have to peddle your wares to many people before the financing is completed. You may, believe it or not, get a bit bored with the repetition.

Since you are the seller and the investor is the buyer, you are naturally going to have to suit the time, place, and manner of the presentation to his convenience. If your venture is still embryonic, you should expect to show up at the investor's office. If you already have an operating business, or at least have set up a facility, the investor may come to see you.

As for the time—you wouldn't believe how much venture capitalists travel. It seems they are always just about to take the plane somewhere, or else just off it. Keep in mind that they have their own imperatives. It isn't their money they are investing; it comes from pension funds and insurance companies and other investors. The venture capitalist has to keep his investors happy, just as you have to keep him happy, and that sometimes means canceling an appointment with you so that he can be at their beck and call.

This can cause problems for you if you are doing a startup financing. Trying to get a startup going is much like finding a new job. You don't want to leave the security of your current employment until you have something solid lined up. On the other hand, it can become quite difficult keeping your secret while you are running around talking to investors. Some venture capitalists are quite considerate of would-be entrepreneurs who are in this situation, and willingly meet you outside business hours. Others insist that you show up on short notice to make your presentation at their office, and if you've run out of sick days that's your problem.

Some investors more or less insist that you burn your bridges. As one puts it, "We want to see real commitment to the new venture. If the founder is still hanging on to a job, that's a negative."

You can try to check out this factor in your financier qualification; but in any case, it's wise to plan ahead. Save up your sick days and your vacation to reserve as much time as you can in advance.

You should, at the initial presentation, get a basic go/no-go decision from the investor; that is, he should either want to continue or not, and there's no reason why he can't make that decision by the end of the meeting.

But investors don't like to simply say "no." Who does? What's more, the investor who says "no" knows that the response is likely to be "why?" That's a question he definitely does not want to answer. The investor may have good reason to conceal his motives for rejection. For instance, he may have seen a competitor's plan that has technology superior to yours.

Most of the time, though, the answer is, "I simply don't have confidence in *you*. You strike me as incompetent [or naive, or inexperienced, or dishonest]." Blurting out a truth of this sort can lead to unpleasantness. On the other hand, evading the issue by bringing up some specific deficiency in the plan simply leads to an endless process of reapplication. The entrepreneur goes home and fixes up the marketing section or whatever was cited as the problem, and then expects to be handed a check. Now the investor is once again faced with the need to find an excuse for rejection. Rather than get into this kind of mess, many investors prefer to distract, evade, and then simply hide behind their secretaries.

Seven Standard Investor Euphemisms for "No"

1. "I like your plan, but I can't do anything without the agreement of my partner. Let me talk it over with him."
2. "It's very interesting. Let me think it over."
3. "I know a guy who's a real expert in your industry. Let me discuss it with him and get his opinion."
4. "It looks good to me, but I'll have to send it to the New Projects Committee for their approval."
5. "Your idea is terrific, but right now we're fully invested. Maybe sometime in the future."
6. "This isn't quite in our line, but I'm sure Hyena & Jackal would jump at it. Why don't you give them a call?"
7. "We definitely would like to invest in this venture, but we prefer not to take the lead position. As soon as you have your lead investor lined up, give us a call."

Discount everything nice that the investor says about you, your team, and your plan. It doesn't necessarily mean a thing. There are, however, some fairly reliable indicators of true interest in moving ahead.

Seven Signs of Real Investor Interest

1. Desire to move quickly—like tomorrow
2. Tangible action taken to move ahead
3. Request not to approach other, competing investors
4. Expressed willingness to be the lead investor
5. Request to correct *specific* deficiency in the team or the plan
6. Spending money to help you assemble data
7. Taking out checkbook and asking, "How much do you want?"

Once the investor has taken the initial decision to move ahead, you proceed into the "due diligence" phase of the financing.

Getting Due Process During Due Diligence

The grass, they say, is always greener on the other side of the fence. The entrepreneur is inclined to feel that to be an investor is to be on top of the world. To comfortably position one's posterior on a mountainous bag of money and sit in judgment on new ventures—thumbs up, this one shall live; thumbs down, this one shall die—what could be closer to paradise?

The professional investor, however, doesn't see things quite that way. He is painfully aware that *it's not his money* he's playing with. He is very definitely responsible to the people who put up the capital for his investments. What's more, in many cases the federal government is looking over his shoulder. He has what is known in the trade as "fiduciary responsibility." If he makes an investment that turns sour, that bag of money can become a hot seat; uneasy sits the posterior that isn't properly covered. In the financial industry, posterior coverage is called "due diligence."

Not even the United States government is silly enough to mandate that every investment shall make money. It does in certain cases require, however, that the professional investor, who uses other people's money, exercise "due diligence" to properly investigate each investment. Even where there is no legal requirement, investors are expected—by the people who supply the money—to meet the standards of "due diligence."

As soon as the investor has decided, following your initial presentation, that he wants to move ahead, he will initiate the due diligence process. It is crucially important for you, the entrepreneur, to understand the requirements of due diligence. You want to accomplish two things: First, you want to make it easy for the investor to complete his due diligence. If you don't, it will take him longer, and your financing will be delayed. He may even become fed up and drop your venture. If, on the other hand, you show an understanding of his constraints and work to make his task easier, it will help to build your relationship with him. Second, you want to get actively involved in the due diligence process so that you can assist it to produce a positive answer on your venture.

What are the requirements of due diligence? First and foremost, the investor must investigate you (and the other members of the team) to make sure that there are no skeletons in your venture's closet. If you turn out to be a notorious bunko artist and your CFO has served time for embezzlement, an investor who failed to dig up these little embarrassments would have failed to be sufficiently diligent.

In checking out your team, the investor must also be concerned with your competence. For this reason, it is important to provide the investor with complete and candid resumés. Make the best of your experience, but don't push too hard. If you get caught fudging, it could make it impossible for the investor to do the deal. Also, line up some strong business and personal references. Big names help. The investor wants to be able to say, if things go wrong, "This guy was endorsed in the strongest terms by Lee Iacocca, Carl Icahn, and Andrew Grove. How was I to know he was going to turn out to be incompetent?

Good financial projections are an important contributor to the due diligence process. When the second-guessing starts after a bad investment, the investor doesn't want to hear: "You're a Harvard MBA; how is it you didn't foresee that selling the product at a negative gross margin would lead to significant cash flow problems?" You can improve your chances of financing by making sure the pro forma statements are complete; if they aren't, the investor will have to finish them up himself. And as you put together your financial projections, keep in mind that they should not only be accurate and reasonable, they should be *defensible*. Again, prestigious names help, whether relevant or not. Having a Big Eight accounting firm help you with the projections will cost money, but being able to cite their name will definitely have a positive effect from the point of view of due diligence.

If you're doing a later-round financing, you should make sure you've dealt with any "poison pills" that may have been set up by previous financings. These can include flaky investors in your early rounds, preemptive rights or antidilution clauses, or awkward financial structures like limited partnerships. See if you can tidy up any messes before you talk to the professionals.

Due diligence also means never having to say you're sorry about marketing, production, and technology issues. For instance, the investor may need to investigate whether you really did have that patent application in on time and what the prospects are that the patent actually will issue. Investors may also ask you to prove that your company has never polluted the environment and that you're complying with all relevant government regulations. Sometimes they come up with due dillies that you never imagined.

If you are setting up a technology venture, *be sure you have solid legal control of your technology* before you start the financing process. Techies notoriously neglect to consider intellectual property questions. The result is that deals are stalled when the investors discover that the entrepreneur's former employer, or a university, or the government, or someone else actually owns the technology.

If you've done your homework properly, providing all the information required by the investor for due diligence will be easy. If your plan is well written, he can extract the information he needs without difficulty. What entrepreneurs often neglect is that, *for due diligence purposes, the appearance is more important than the reality.*

This means: Be sure to complete the various legal and other formalities for your startup, no matter how trivial or unnecessary they may seem. Be sure you avoid anything that even smells of impropriety. And drag in every prestigious connection you can reasonably manage, without excessive regard for relevance.

Try to become not an opponent but a partner with the investor in the due diligence process. By taking this attitude, you take a big step in building your relationship.

Putting 'Em Through the Wringer

We found a surprising degree of variation among venture capitalists in the ways they investigate the companies and founders they are considering.

> "We investigate entrepreneurs *very* thoroughly. We'll typically talk to about twenty people—not just his references but many others—for each person under consideration. And we have professional investigators check them out too. We find that about 25 percent, even of our prescreened candidates, have lies on their resumés."

> "We usually don't check the details of resumés, but we do call their references. We spend a lot of time talking to the

members of the management team, and we think we can evaluate them pretty well from that.''

"We do routine checks, including credit references. But what's really important is the founder's character; integrity is crucial, and we have to evaluate that by gut feel. We look at things like how he dresses, his family.''

"We check the resumés of the founders, and we're very thorough on talking to references.''

"We call a few references. But an awful lot of deals are done on a hunch. Frankly, most deals you get into you later regret. Usually it's not for reasons of moral turpitude. The FBI isn't going to help you find out that someone has no market sense.''

Passing a Consultant Without Getting Clobbered

As you run the financing gantlet, the deadliest club that will be swung at you is the one wielded by the consultant. Often, especially in venture capital financings, the investor will go out to a consultant for an opinion on some aspect of your venture's viability. The consultant may be asked to evaluate your technology, your market, your product, or possibly your manufacturing plans. When sought, a consultant opinion is almost always wanted by the investor as a reassuring document for the due diligence process. The problem is that consultants generally are not positive in their evaluations of new ventures.

One consultant, who is frequently retained by venture capitalists, says—off the record:

"I never give a positive recommendation on a company. If I did, and it later failed, my reputation would suffer. On the other hand, if I say it's a loser, the venture capitalist won't invest, so he'll never know if I was wrong.''

If your venture idea is innovative, whether in its technology, its marketing approach, or whatever, your chances of passing the consultant without being pulverized drop to near zero. The type of consultant typically looked for by investors is a person with an established reputation and a big-name-laden resumé. In practice, this commonly translates into a retired senior executive from a large corporation, a person who is not likely to be receptive to radical new ideas from young, entrepreneurial whippersnappers.

How can you get by the consultant without being flattened? There are four things you can and should try.

1. *If you possibly can, keep consultants out of the deal in the first place.* Here is another very good reason for selecting investors who are familiar with your industry, your market, and your technology. They probably won't need to hire a consultant. On the other hand, an investor who is out of his depth in your industry will feel he has to hire a consultant who does understand it, to cover him in his due diligence. If your lead investor doesn't have the right background himself, you should—at an early stage, before he has a chance to bring up the consultant idea—take the initiative by trying to bring in a secondary *investor* who does have the necessary expertise.

2. *Make heavy use of big-name endorsements in your plan.* If you set up a Scientific Board of Advisers for your company with three Nobel laureates sitting on it, the venture capitalist probably will not feel the need to have some random nerd of a consultant perform a feasibility study on your invention.

3. *If you can't avoid the intrusion of a consultant, pack the deck.* Look around for experts in the field who are most likely to be positive about your venture and submit their names (with addresses and telephone numbers—always make things as easy as possible) to the investor, before he has a chance to hire some idiot of his own selection. Make a particular point of selecting experts who have as much prestige as is compatible with intelligence.

4. *If all else fails, employ preemptive overkill.* Don't let the investor send your preliminary, speculative outline to the consultant. He'll murder it. Instead, insist on providing a massive tome that goes into the entire subject in relentless detail. Start

with forty or fifty pages of historical background. Go on to
describe your ideas, backing up every statement that is even
remotely controversial with citations from big-name authorities.
Load it down with every bit of data you've managed to produce,
assembled onto page after page of graphs and tables. Anticipate
every possible objection and blow each away with preplanned
fire. Thoroughly document everything. The idea is to leave the
consultant no opportunity to find a flaw in your work, however
trivial. Ideally, the document should leave him totally intimi-
dated, sure that if he raises any objection it will only be immediately refuted in a way calculated to humiliate him. Naturally
this isn't easy, so it's best to use one of the other three strategies
if you possibly can.

The Follow-Up Meetings

As the due diligence is ground out, you will probably be involved
in a series of meetings with your lead investors. These encoun-
ters serve a number of purposes.

The investor will require an amazing amount of information
about your venture. Every week, if not every day, you'll be
bombarded with new questions to which you'll have to find the
answers—unless, as we may hope, you already know them. This
is another of those times when having done your homework
really pays off, because a question you can answer immediately
won't delay the deal—and give the investor time, and an excuse,
to cool off.

These meetings may also involve introductions. Your lead
investor may want you to meet the other partners in his firm, for
instance. If the other members of your team were not all present
at the initial presentation, you may be asked to bring them in so
they can be inspected. Your lead investor may also want to bring
other firms in to share the deal, in which case the newcomers
must also meet you and your colleagues.

Above all, these meetings contribute to building the relationship between entrepreneur and investor. The investor is
putting his anatomy on the line to back you. He will feel much
more comfortable backing someone he knows than he would

backing a stranger. Your resumé isn't enough. By spending time with you he gets a better fix on those intangible parts of your character that can make the difference between success and failure for your venture—and his investment.

The Multi-Investor Deal

No investor—and this includes venture capitalists—*likes* to make a high-risk investment, such as backing a new venture inevitably is. Some investors do. But they are very concerned with minimizing that risk. One way they do so is to split the deal. If a venture needs, say, $2 million, a large enough firm may put up the whole amount. Or, more likely, two or three or four smaller firms will get together and split the deal among them.

There is an etiquette about such joint investments that you should be aware of. The essential principle is that the lead investor is the key to everything. Deals of this type don't just assemble themselves like a virus particle. They are carefully crafted by the lead investor. You may have in mind a firm or two that you'd like to see included. Fine. Suggest them to your lead investor—but very diffidently. He may not be on good terms with the people you want. Etiquette also requires that the lead investor make the first call to invite another firm into the deal, not the other way around.

If you suspect that your company will have to be financed as a multi-investor project, your strategy must take this into account. You must concentrate on locating and selling a suitable lead investor, because, as we've just said, the lead investor is the key to the deal. But not every firm can or will take the lead. Small venture capital funds generally either do independent deals or take a "follower" position in multifirm deals. Before you even approach a firm, find out if it has experience in acting as the lead in joint deals. If it doesn't, it probably won't be suitable for your purposes.

Who Are the Leaders?

As we've seen, it isn't sufficient to find a venture capitalist; you have to find one who's a leader. What are the odds? We asked some experts.

"About 50 percent of venture capital firms say they take lead positions in deals. The real number is about 10 percent."

"Except for seed funding, you can't expect a venture capital firm to be a lead investor unless it has at least $100 million under management."

"There are few leaders, lots of followers."

Completing the Courtship

The time comes at last—we hope—when you get down to the final challenge: negotiating the deal. Of course, negotiation at some level is likely to be taking place throughout your early discussions with investors. There is no sharp dividing line at which preliminary discussions end and negotiation begins. However, at the early stages investors generally won't be pressing for concessions. They will want to get a rough feel for what you want—how much money you seek—so they can be sure that the deal is appropriate for their firms. They also may ask about your equity objectives, mainly to see if you have a realistic idea of the value of your venture. The heavy questions will be left for later.

We devote Chapter 7 entirely to the negotiating process, so we'll say no more here. However, we'd like to emphasize again that the entire courtship ritual, from first approach all the way through the hot-breathing climax of the negotiations, must be focused on *building a relationship* between investor and entrepreneur.

The Financing Process

- ☐ Business plan finished
- ☐ Financing plan decided
- ☐ Realistic financing schedule prepared and plans made for economic survival during that period
- ☐ Rights to technology secured
- ☐ Preliminary list of financier prospects prepared

☐ Network lines to prospects developed
☐ Introductions to prospects obtained
☐ Plan submitted to prospects
☐ Financier qualification performed
☐ Presentations scheduled
☐ Presentations prepared
☐ Presentations conducted
☐ Due diligence initiated
☐ Investors selected
☐ Negotiations initiated
☐ Deal signed

Striking a Balance

The road to venture capital is long and arduous. It can be tougher than you ever dreamed of to get funding. We know of many ventures where, after months or even years of work, the founders simply got tired of traipsing around talking to investors and getting turned down, and finally just hung it up. Other entrepreneurs find they have a real talent for raising money.

> One of the best we've seen is George Koopman, CEO of American Rocket. Over the years this venture has repeatedly survived apparently fatal blows on its way into space. Again and again it's run out of money and had to slow or suspend development work on the firm's hybrid rocket design—and every time George has gone out and somehow raised enough funds to get it going again. As I said when I moderated one of his presentations, "George is like something out of a monster movie. You see him buried at a crossroads with a stake through his heart and you think 'that's that.' Then the ground starts to bulge . . . clods of earth fly away . . . and George pops up and he's after you again." This kind of talent—and determination—is a real asset to a struggling company.

There is a danger in becoming too involved in the financing process. We've seen entrepreneurs get too enamored of deal making. Meeting with venture capitalists can be exciting; sitting in a luxurious conference room, feeling like a "Master of the Universe," you may begin to find the grimy details of running your company less interesting. The company still needs to be run. The CEO of a growing company must have the maturity to strike a balance between operational work and financing.

Bibliography

Dible, Donald M. (ed.). *Winning the Money Game*. Santa Clara, Calif.: Entrepreneur Press, 1975. This collection of essays on the startup process includes much useful advice on financing, though some of the specific details are now out of date.

Lesko, Matthew. *Lesko's New Tech Sourcebook*. New York: Harper & Row, 1986. Lesko provides a valuable reference work of contacts, complete with addresses and phone numbers, for experts in all sorts of technology, as well as of organizations devoted to entrepreneurship, venture incubators, market research outfits, and so on.

6

Show Time: Making Your Presentation

When you're raising money, you don't get unlimited bites at the cherry. An opportunity to make your case in person to a serious investor is not so easy to arrange. As with any other important presentation, you don't want to waste the opportunity. You want to go in prepared.

A presentation is a sales call. You are selling your company, your prospects, and, above all, you and your team. Think about it a moment. How much money are you asking for? Typical venture capital deals these days run to several million dollars. If you had a shot at making a multimillion-dollar sale of, say, some piece of electronic testing equipment, how would you handle it? Would you walk in to the appointment and wing it? Of course you wouldn't. You'd prepare and plan very carefully.

Developing Your Objectives

Your first step is to decide what you want to accomplish during the meeting. If it's a first meeting, getting the check is probably not a realistic objective. On the other hand, you should not settle for a vague, intangible response from the investor; "make a good impression'' is not a useful objective. You need to identify a specific response, a concrete action on the part of the investor, as the objective of your presentation.

What sort of commitments might you look for from a first meeting? Here are some possibilities:

Presentation Objectives

☐ Investor schedules further meetings or takes other action.
☐ Investor takes tangible step to begin due diligence—for instance, contacting your references.
☐ Investor requests that you provide specific further information.
☐ Investor opens discussion of deal terms.
☐ Investor states willingness to act as lead investor in the deal.
☐ Investor designates, and commits to contact, secondary investors.

You are probably not going to be able to get the investor to make a "firm" commitment to invest in your company at this first meeting. However, what you can accomplish, and what you should aim at accomplishing, is to induce the investor to take some real step toward doing the deal.

Objectives on the Other Side

To make any sale, you must understand the objectives of the customer. Having done your financier qualification, you should know a great deal about the firm you are presenting to and about what they are looking for in a deal. You should review this in preparation for your presentation.

You also want to profile your audience in personal terms. When venture firms make investments, individual people make the decisions. Venture firms are generally partnerships, some with many partners. You have gotten this far because at least one of them liked your business plan enough to set up the meeting. Remember: Nine out of ten business plans are rejected before this point. For the moment, you have an advocate in the firm.

You must identify not only the investor's objectives for the deal but his objectives for the presentation. The investor, just like you, wants to accomplish something with this meeting. You do not want to frustrate him. You want to know what he's looking for out of the meeting so that you can cooperate in making sure he gets it. What sorts of things do investors want to accomplish in an initial meeting? Here are some possibilities.

Investor Objectives

☐ Evaluate the credibility of the entrepreneurial team.
☐ Get an understanding of the key factors in the company's strategy.
☐ Clarify obscure points in the business plan.
☐ Find out if the entrepreneur has a realistic idea of possible deal terms.
☐ Check out personal qualities of the entrepreneur; for instance, is he articulate, composed, and organized?
☐ Determine the long-term vision and commitment of the entrepreneur.

Another factor that you should try to take into account is investor style. Some people are text-oriented; basically, they like to rely on written documents to understand things and make decisions. Others are very visual and tend to think in terms of images; graphics reach them much better than other media. Still others base their perceptions on personal contact; they don't trust written material and prefer to evaluate a deal by physically meeting the people involved. There are even some people who prefer to make evaluations by phone, perhaps because they find direct personal contact inhibiting. Of course, most investors are not "pure" types. When you do your financier qualification, you should be sensitive to how the individuals you will be dealing with like to operate, and adjust your presentation plans accordingly.

Features and Benefits

A key principle of effective selling is understanding the distinction between "features" and "benefits." Features are properties of your products; *benefits to the customer are what make the sale.* Features are effective in selling only to the extent that the customer can translate them into benefits.

The same principle applies to selling your company to investors. The features that are important to you, such as how innovative your product technology is, are, at best, of very limited interest to the investor. Your presentation should focus primarily on the benefits to the investor. You're ultimately making the sale not to a firm but to a person. Here are some things that motivate venture capitalists as they ponder whether to invest in a venture.

Obviously, you want to project that *this deal will be a winner.* The investor will get credit within the firm for having found and championed an investment that makes money.

You also want to cover the downside by projecting that *this deal will not be an embarrassing loser.* No venture capitalist is expected to be perfect. But if a deal goes in the tank because a partner was careless, reckless, or ignorant, a demerit will be handed out. So you want to present your venture as a plausible play—a risk, but a calculated risk.

This deal will not be troublesome. Repeatedly, venture capitalists emphasized to us that they like to deal with entrepreneurs who are reasonable people. They have enough troubles without pandering to prima donnas. We heard this commment: "We invested in this guy because he knew what he didn't know." And investors want people who will be helpful rather than annoying as the years go by. "Some entrepreneurs dodge our phone calls after they get the money. Not this guy—he gave us all the news like clockwork."

Keep in mind that the decision will be made by a person. Adapt your responses accordingly. For the senior partner who will be your "champion" within the firm, concentrate on the positive, but don't neglect the negative—that your venture is credible and will, even if it fails, be regarded as a "good try." For the other partners, emphasize the positives, the upside potential. As for the junior associates, apply some judicious flattery and compliment them on their shrewdness and expertise.

Although there is certainly a great deal of variation among

venture capitalists—and other types of investors may have different priorities—it's clear that what investors want to hear may not be the same things that interest you the most.

Once you've estimated the criteria that are most important to the investor, and the media that will be most effective in communicating, you are ready to develop the message you want to convey in your presentation.

Sending a Message

Your presentation should be aimed at conveying a *message* to the investor, key information that will persuade him to start the investment process. Your first step in developing the presentation is to define the message. Based on your knowledge of the investor and your preliminary interactions, you must decide what are the few critical things that you must say during this meeting. It is a mistake to try to tell the investor everything about your company, which is the natural instinct of the entrepreneur. It is also a mistake to be passive, to allow the investor to take the lead. And it is a mistake to fail to make a plan for pushing your message. An interview with an investor can be tense and stressful. After you've gone home, you don't want to find yourself saying, ''Damn! I forgot entirely to mention . . . .''
So identify the few key points—not more than five—that you definitely want to get across in your presentation. Have a checklist with you. Refer to it during the presentation to make sure you remember to cover each point.

Ask yourself: What are the key points we want to cover? What is the most effective way to convey each one? What order do we want to cover them in?

A good way to think of your presentation is that you want the investor to understand your venture well enough to be able to explain it to someone else.

As to content, the investor does not want a rehash of your business plan. But he will want to know the thinking behind the major aspects of the plan such as your market assumptions, your knowledge of the competition and competing technologies, and your product distribution strategy. Look at the presentation as the investor's "validity check" and do your preparation so that he will be convinced that you know your product, your market, and yourself. That's why preparation is so crucial; it forces you to do your homework.

Presentation Approach

Venture capitalists differ in how long they'll sit still for a presentation. However, the upper limit is probably half an hour or so. Most of them will start to squirm after only a few minutes. Very few investors will let you go through a formal presentation without interruption. So your best chance to get your points across in an organized manner is to keep your presentation as short as you possibly can.

The most common model for an initial meeting with investors is a short presentation—typically from fifteen to twenty minutes—followed by an hour or two of searching questions. Probably the meeting will not last less than a couple of hours unless you blow it and the investor decides to get rid of you quickly. On the other hand, the interrogation may be prolonged; you may be subjected to a sort of "stress interview" that lasts all day.

Presentation Formats

We found some variation among our venture capital interviewees on what they like to see in a presentation.

> "The presentation should not duplicate the plan. Review the business plan briefly, then go into more depth. We want to hear more focus on execution at this stage."

"We'll give you one or two hours for the first meeting. Be prepared to tell the story."

"We expect a formal presentation—but realize that it will be interactive. Usually it lasts about two hours."

"Walk through the plan, with an emphasis on your competition and your positioning in the market. Figure on fifteen minutes for your initial talk; then you should be ready to field questions. We feel that slides are helpful, but we don't insist you use them. Bring in the product to show us if possible."

"Always develop a formal presentation, even though you may not get a chance to give it. We expect the entrepreneurs to bring flip charts if it's a seed-money or early-state financing; if it's second-round, you should have slides. Bring backup material, including a list of six to ten references for each founder, a glossary of your dialect of technospeak, a page on each of your beta sites, and so on."

Your best approach is to *use your initial presentation to set up control of the ensuing discussion*. During this period you should assert your key messages. If they are accepted by the investor, you are off to an excellent start. If they are challenged, then at least you are arguing the topics on which you are prepared.

In general, investors tend to be put off by a presentation that is too "professional" in appearance. Just as a business plan prepared by a commercial plan-writing outfit is a negative, so is a slick presentation that betrays an obvious PR professional input. The key adjectives for your presentation are: short, to-the-point, and informal.

Incidentally, our informants are just about unanimous on the best way to ensure a very short meeting: Start out by asking: "How much money do we get and what do we have to give up?"

Building the Presentation

Many entrepreneurs have some experience giving presentations of one sort or another. Scientists and engineers, for instance, commonly have given talks at technical meetings. But a presentation for investors presents some unusual problems.

Most oral presentations have a fixed time span. Knowing that you have a certain amount of time, you naturally organize your talk so as to work up to a climax, presenting the most important results at the end so the audience will be left with maximum impact. Technical types especially are trained to present a logical chain of evidence, leading at the end to the key conclusions.

Unfortunately, following this model can get you into trouble at an investment presentation. The normal course of events for such a session starts with you giving your formal presentation. After a while you begin to be interrupted with questions, which rapidly become more frequent, until you find yourself under continuous inquisition. You can't predict in advance whether your audience will break in after five minutes or fifty, nor how much of your presentation will go unheard. What you *can* count on is that any topics you plan to take up toward the end of your talk will probably not get addressed.

This means that a logical structure is not appropriate for an investment presentation. Instead, you should plan your talk along the lines used for press releases. Start with your most crucial points—the items you really must get across—and proceed gradually to less important material. In practice, this typically means opening with your conclusions, then following up with supporting material.

The Rehearsal

If you have much experience at speaking, you probably are aware of the common tendency to underestimate the amount of time required to deliver a presentation. The only way to be sure that you can deliver your ten-minute talk in ten minutes is to rehearse it and time it. Unless you're an old hand, you'll find that it takes about twenty-five minutes. If you're an old hand, it will take about twenty minutes. So start cutting.

When you've got the time down to your objective, the next step is to clean up your presentation. Tape yourself—videotape if possible, but even an audiotape will help. You may be appalled. Most people, even experienced speakers who ought to know better, have at least one bad habit. You may find that you begin every sentence with "And, uh . . . ." Or that you have a distracting physical mannerism such as adjusting your tie (or your skirt) every thirty seconds. Practice on tape until you've overcome any bad habits.

Then work on content. Have some friends who are *not* familiar with your business plan listen to your presentation. Can they understand what you're talking about? Most presentations assume too much knowledge on the part of the audience. Also, did they get the information you wanted them to get? Most presentations overemphasize the product and underemphasize the more important subjects like team, market, and cash flow.

Finally, work on confidence. Do another rehearsal in front of three or four aggressive experts. See if you can get a friendly banker or accountant to participate (not your accountant—she'll be afraid to offend a client). If you can get a television reporter, that would be terrific. How about someone from the local university's debating team? Or a trial lawyer? You want people who can pick holes in you and won't be shy about doing it.

If you've chosen the right audience, this rehearsal will be painful. Make some notes on the most humiliating results—and repeat the rehearsal. Keep it up all day if you have to until you can handle yourself under fire. After a good workout of this sort, your meeting with the venture capitalists should be a piece of cake.

Opening Night

It's like a Broadway show. After all the preparation, the writing, the planning, the organizing, the rehearsals, there comes what you began to think you'd never see—opening night. Now you're on stage, and you've got a couple of hours to convince a very skeptical audience that your show merits a long run. What can you and your company do to disarm the critics?

The Costumes

Not to put too fine a point on it, your presentation is a business meeting and you should attend it in business dress. Readers in most of the country will no doubt take this for granted, but our fellow Californians sometimes need the admonition.

Obviously you should adapt your attire to the situation. If you're meeting investment bankers at the Trump Towers, you'll want to pull out your dark, pinstripe suit. If the prospect is a Texas cattle baron and he's invited you to his ranch, something a bit lighter is called for.

In general, you should aim to be at the same level of dress formality *or higher* than the investor. When you meet some deep-pockets angel in his home and find him in a sweat shirt and jeans, you may feel out of place in a tie. Don't. Wealthy people often have a double standard: *He* has it made and can dress as he pleases, but *you* had better be in uniform. Another consideration is that being a bit on the formal side makes it easier to adapt to conditions. You can become less formal, if it seems appropriate, by taking off your jacket or loosening your tie. If you show up in sports clothes and find the investor in full plate armor, you can't very well ask him to wait while you go home and change.

Finally, remember that you're there to communicate, and avoid distracting elements in your attire. Men who wear earrings or ponytails, women on the cutting edge of avant-garde fashion, divert attention from the message they are trying to convey. One venture capitalist told us:

> "We do a lot of high-tech deals and see plenty of scientists and engineers come in dressed a bit oddly. That doesn't bother us at all. But the guy who's going to run the company—*he* had better be wearing a suit. Once we had a CEO, who had a sales background, come in with gold chains around his neck.

We invested anyway—then had to fire him four months later. He was a terrible manager. Never again.''

Stage Fright

Judging by our experience at the Enterprise Forum, surprisingly few entrepreneurs are troubled by stage fright. Perhaps it's a matter of the well-known entrepreneurial ego. However, we occasionally encounter founders who are almost paralyzed with nervousness in front of an audience. If you find you have butterflies in your stomach before a presentation, here's a technique recommended by Los Angeles psychotherapist Nathaniel Branden: Just before you go ''on stage,'' stop somewhere private—your car, the restroom, whatever—close your eyes, and ''sink into'' your fear. Imagine the worst happening. Let yourself feel the panic rising until you're shaking with it. Then wake up, let yourself calm down for a moment, and go to your appointment. You'll find your nervousness gone, or at least much more manageable.

The Stage

Most commonly your first presentation will take place at the investor's office. The actual stage for your performance is likely to be a small conference room with a table and eight or ten chairs around it.

Be there early. This will give you time to check out the conditions for your presentation and to adapt to any unexpected problems without panic. It will also signal your investors that you value their time. One sure way to get your first presentation off on the wrong foot is to rush in late with an excuse about traffic.

If you're using slides, you'll have to take that constraint into account immediately. You will have to sit next to the screen, and so will any other member of your team who may have to use it. You'll also have to place one of your other people next to the projector. Simple and obvious? Sure, but it really is important to handle setup swiftly and efficiently. A group that can't organize a slide presentation does not inspire confidence in its ability to organize a growth company.

Give a moment's thought to seating arrangements in any case. All the members of your team should be able to see the presentation leader so that they can receive any necessary signals. The presentation leader should also be able to keep an eye on the audience.

> Of course, your careful planning may all go for nought. We have in mind one eminent venture capitalist who has a habit of moving around the room during discussions. Up, down, in his chair, then standing up, over to the other side, sitting on a credenza, then moving again . . . .

Your presentation will almost certainly be your first time in the room, so you'll have to adapt quickly to the surroundings.

It is possible that you will make the presentation on your own premises (if you have any), though this is more commonly the venue for a follow-up meeting. If you are fortunate enough to be operating on home ground, you should of course make sure that everything looks clean, efficient, and businesslike. Give the visitors a tour of the premises, but resist the temptation to show them everything, however trivial. Temper your urge to show off the product, the laboratory, and other manifestations of your technological genius. Instead, put as much emphasis as you can on the market. If you can arrange to have a customer or two on the premises, do it!

> "I like to go to the company for the first presentation. That way I can see the whole scene and get a better feel for the company. But most venture capitalists, including my part-ners, don't like to visit the company at such an early stage because it's so time-consuming. You can get two or three presentations in the office in the time it takes you to go out to visit a company."

Another possible meeting place is the office of an interme-diary. If you were introduced to the firm by your lawyer or some other middleman, your first meeting may take place on this neutral ground.

The first meeting may also be an informal encounter at a restaurant. In this case of course you will not be able to make a formal presentation with slides, and the show will be interrupted by the various distractions imposed by waiters. You will have to adjust your presentation—and your expectations—accordingly.

Props

Appropriate visual aids can be a tremendous help in communicating your message. Most venture capital firm conference rooms are equipped to handle slides or overheads, but you should use these expedients only with great caution. Flip charts may be preferable. If you have information—financial statements, tables of data, pictures, or whatever—that you want to present, you probably will do better to put it on paper, make several copies, and hand them out at the meeting. As for films or videotapes, forget it unless you have something essential that you can convey in no other way.

> American Rocket Corporation makes rockets—space-travel-type rockets. George Koopman, the CEO, developed a seven-minute videotape that explained his product's design and showcased its test firings at Vandenberg Air Force Base. It was quite effective. Here was a case of a product that couldn't be brought to the meeting, and a product that was spectacular and interesting to see in action. But George came to American Rocket with ten years of experience in making professional films and videos. Most people don't have that kind of skill.

If you choose to use an overhead projector, a general rule is to use no more than a dozen visuals. Viewgraphs are best as a guide to discussion, not to convey a lot of dense information. Remember: *Keep them simple*—one key idea or topic per visual explained by six or seven lines, with ten words or less per line. That requires discipline. The common tendency, especially among engineers, is to write a life history, transfer it verbatim to the visual medium, and then read it to the audience.

Speaking of which, *don't read your talk*. Even a well-written text, read from a TelePrompTer by a very experienced and polished speaker, is barely tolerable. Few people these days can memorize a long speech, so that's out too. The best procedure is to use short notes.

> I usually use a single sheet of paper, with numbered notes keyed to my slides. The slides themselves tell me what topic is next. The notes contain key points I want to add. I put everything on one sheet (rather than cards) to avoid any chance of confusion or disorder.

Avoid humiliating foul-ups. Double- and triple-check your slides; there is no excuse for lost slides or slides out of order. It helps to keep things simple. Don't use extensive, complex notes; all too often that leads to, "Wait a minute, I can't find the next part of my talk . . . ." Don't take a pile of paper with supporting facts to the lectern with you. You may want to be able to counter any objection with massive data, but your audience will get impatient as you shuffle through your sheets looking for the one you need. Instead, make copies of the backup data and hand them out. Then the investor can shuffle through paper looking things up. You should have an index, of course. And distribute as much supporting role as you can to the other members of your team. "The R&D budget? Dr. Nerdley, I believe, has the figures for that."

Use of "handouts" requires some care. Generally speaking, if you have copies of material that you want to give to your audience, distribute them *after* you complete your formal presentation. If you pass them out at the beginning, your audience will be flipping through the material while you talk, distracting them from your message; you will have lost control of the discussion. Keep in mind that a handout should be *supporting* material. It can provide more detailed information than you can supply in your talk. Or—and this can be very effective—it can be a magazine article, a market report, or some other document from an outside, objective source that validates your claims.

If your product is portable—*very* portable—you may want to bring it to demonstrate. Think twice before doing this; most entrepreneurs are far too obsessed with their products, and the last thing that investors are concerned with is the product. Under no circumstances bring to the investor's office equipment that requires any sort of setup or manipulation to make it work. Your audience does not want to sit around while you fiddle with it. Worse, it may be damaged in transport and not work at all! If you must demonstrate a computer or other gadget, bring the investors to your facility to see it.

The perils of product display are suggested by the following anecdote, which also demonstrates the need to be able to recover a fumble gracefully.

> A leading attorney specializing in venture deals was taken by an entrepreneur client to see an important venture capitalist. The widget was a device, for use with an Apple computer, to translate human speech into computer text. The founder set up the computer on the investor's desk and asked the attorney to speak into it. Nothing happened. A couple of adjustments. Still nothing. The inventor opened up the computer, pulled out a circuit board, and inspected it closely. The venture capitalist by this time was visibly impatient. And the entrepreneur said calmly, "Do you by any chance have a soldering iron?"
>
> The answer, of course, was no. But as it happened, a major aircraft firm was quartered in the same building. The inventor walked down the hall, borrowed a soldering iron from a laboratory, fixed a broken connection on the board right there on the venture capitalist's desk, and plugged it back in. Then he turned to his attorney and gestured. The lawyer spoke—and his words magically appeared on the screen.
>
> The company got the money. But unless you have sangfroid to the max, don't demonstrate your high-tech product at the investor's office.

The best props provide a simple and dramatic illustration of one of your key selling points.

> One of American Rocket Corporation's key selling points is the safety and environmental cleanliness of its fuel, which

is simply rubber "with some special herbs and spices."
George Koopman, the CEO, carries a piece of it to presentations; it's an effective prop.

The most common mistake with visual aids of any sort is
using them too freely and without consideration for why they
are needed. It's far more effective to use pictures or props to
deal with possible objections. If you expect to be challenged on
some point, consider whether there's a way to reinforce your
response with some sort of tangible evidence.

The Players

Investors want to meet with your team, at least the key members. Performing at such a session can be even more difficult
than doing the whole presentation by yourself. How many
members of your team should you take along? (If you're a lone
wolf, obviously you'll have to go by yourself.) There are two
factors to be taken into account.

First, who can make a contribution to the presentation?
Probably you don't want to have anyone else trying to be part
of the exposition phase; jumping from speaker to speaker is just
too much for such a short talk. But it can be very handy to have
your stable of experts—technical, marketing, and financial—
present to field tough questions.

On the other hand, you must take into account the person-
alities and capabilities of your co-founders. Some people just
aren't at their best in this kind of meeting. If you have a vice-
president with foot-in-mouth disease, or who for whatever reason is not likely to make a good first impression on the financier,
that might be a good person to leave at home.

But you must take into account the second consideration.
The investors are concerned above all else with the quality of
your team. A key objective of your presentation is to convince
them that your people are not just competent but impressive.

> "We want to see the whole team at the presentation. And
> we want to see them all participating."

Let's face it, the Broadway analogy holds here, too. Your show will be judged less on its script than on its stars. Plan your presentation so as to display the talents of your key people. Unless they're hopelessly unprepossessing, you should not only bring them along but showcase them.

The first principle of the team presentation is that one person must clearly be in charge. If your management team has not yet settled the lines of authority, do so before you go out for funding. If you're an idealistic bunch who believe in democratic management, forget it. Investors expect that some one person has ultimate authority and responsibility.

You must absolutely present a united front to the investors. If you and the other members of the management team haven't yet come to agreement on basic strategy, do so before you seek funding. Don't argue it out with one another in front of the investors.

> "It's amazing how often team members don't give consistent answers. And that's a definite red flag for investment."

Decide in advance the roles that the various members of your team will play during the presentation. You want to prevent those unedifying scenes in which you are all interrupting one another in your eagerness to answer. Plan and practice how the members of the team will "pass the ball" during discussion.

And establish a "shut up" signal. It not infrequently happens that one of your people gets rattled and puts her foot in it. Trying to recover, she keeps talking and just digs herself in deeper and deeper, as her colleagues squirm in their chairs. You want to be able to cut off such incidents quickly. A simple signal can be set up—for instance, the presentation leader taking off his glasses—which means "stop talking—now!" You may also want to set a signal for "let me in quickly," to be used when one of the team has an important point that must be made at once.

If you haven't filled all your key management positions yet, be sure to mention who *isn't* present. State your plans to recruit and how you're coping in the meantime. Don't pad your team with "ringers," who may have impressive credentials but who haven't participated in the business formation so far and are just "waiting in the wings" until you receive your financing. Investors should perceive not just you but all the members of your team as being fully committed to the venture.

The Audience

The size of your audience may vary from just one up to half a dozen or so. Commonly the investment firm will have two or three representatives, perhaps a general partner and a couple of junior people. The size of the audience isn't too important, but the composition is.

It is obviously of the first importance to have at least one of the firm's decision makers present. Unfortunately, this is a requirement over which you have very little influence. You can discreetly inquire, when the appointment is made, who will be present and what their function is in the firm. You probably will not be able to insist on the presence of any particular person. However, an investment firm will usually not waste the time even of a junior associate on a meeting purely for screening purposes. The norm is that, if they consider it worthwhile talking to you at all, at least one general partner or other responsible person will be present.

The participation of associates or assistants in the investment firm can be a negative from the entrepreneur's point of view. You should realize that the lot of the junior financier is not a happy one. Though competition for their jobs is fierce, they have no decision-making power to speak of and must spend most of their time doing due diligence scut work. The upgrade path to general partner is not easy to traverse. It's not surprising that many of these poor souls become a bit overaggressive as they try to show their chiefs how hardheaded and "realistic" they are. They're not going to get carried away by enthusiasm for a promising startup, no sirree! On the other hand, associates get promoted to partner by being associated with successful investments. Those who are always negative get nowhere.

If you were introduced to the firm by a leading venture lawyer or other intermediary, that person's presence is a definite plus. This is a person who has a stake in your success. If the deal goes through and is successful, she'll have enhanced her position with both you and the investor. If it doesn't, she's got a bit of egg on her face. So if she's present she'll be working to grease the wheels. Her help can be very valuable, since she knows both parties. An experienced attorney or accountant who has done hundreds of deals can be very suave indeed, smoothing out potential problems almost before you notice them. Keep an eye on her and let her help.

When the Curtain Rises

First impressions count. Many a deal has been ruined before the presentation even started. How you look, how you smell (watch out for that cologne), how you act will all affect that vital first impression. The moment you walk in the door you are "on," and a definite image is formed in less than five seconds.

Let the investor set the scale of formality or informality. Some are pretty stuffy; with such a case, you should be formal and very businesslike. Others quickly get down to their shirt sleeves and start twanging their yellow suspenders. With these guys you should be informal, friendly, and very businesslike.

It's easy to get distracted, when dealing with folksy types, from the essential business purpose of the meeting. You're not there to show what a nice guy or gal you are; you're there to demonstrate your ability to make a pile of money for the investor. Building a relationship is crucial, but it is a *business* relationship that you must build.

Starting the Show

Your initial description of the venture begins the meeting. Here's where it pays to be properly prepared and rehearsed so that you don't have to worry about your basic delivery. That will allow you to concentrate on other matters.

For one thing, you are quite likely to be interrupted. You must be able to field sudden questions—some of them difficult, or even embarrassing—without losing control of the presentation. A difficult balancing act is required. If you're not careful, the presentation will wander off into a fog of discussion. Eventually your time will be up and you'll find yourself leaving with key parts of your message unsaid. On the other hand, you can't bull ahead with too much "I'll get to that later" without risking the impression that you're evasive about tough issues.

You also need to be able to rapidly adapt your presentation to the audience. In spite of your prior research, you may find that the person to whom you're talking knows a great deal less— or more—about the technology or the market than you expected. You may need to expand or contract your presentation accordingly.

A crucially important skill is being sensitive to your audience. Most speakers talk to an audience as to a tape recorder. No, that's too generous; even when talking to a tape recorder, most people are aware of it at least to the extent of noticing when a cassette runs out. How often have we seen speakers who are so oblivious to the audience that they wouldn't notice if all of them stood up and walked out?

The purpose of speaking is to communicate and there's no point in continuing to talk if communication has broken down. You should look at your listeners rather than your notes. Even more valuable than your eyes are your ears. When an audience gets bored it starts to squirm, and in a quiet room you can often hear it even before you see it.

When you notice problems with your audience, you must respond in the correct direction. Most speakers tend to say *more* when they're not communicating; there's a tendency to feel that if you just explain things in more detail, the audience will understand better and become more interested. It's a much better policy to say *less*. As Tom Lehrer puts it, "I feel that if a person really can't communicate, the very least he can do is to shut up." If you're not keeping the interest of your audience, your best procedure is to zip through the prepared presentation and move quickly to the next phase. Invite questions.

Silence Is Golden, Even When You're Speaking

Many inexperienced speakers are terrified of silence. They feel that because they have the podium, it's their responsibility to ensure that there is not an instant of hush. They connect every sentence to its successor with "and, uh" to avoid even a split-second interruption in the cascade of sound.

All this is quite unnecessary. Train yourself to speak in complete sentences and to stop at the end of each one. If you feel you're off track, pause and regroup; a five- or ten-second period of silence is perfectly acceptable. In fact, if your audience is busy looking over a document or picture you've handed out, keeping your mouth shut for thirty seconds or even more, until they've digested the material and look up again, is not only acceptable but desirable.

One more thing: Train your team members too. Don't let them think they have to fill in the airtime every time you pause for breath.

One of the best things about the usual meeting format is that it lends itself naturally to *involving the audience.* Always remember that your primary objective is not to educate but to persuade. You want your listeners to get involved, to ask questions, to make suggestions, to develop the feeling that they want to be part of your venture. Again, you must build a relationship. You don't want to project the attitude, "I'll talk, you listen, and if you like what you hear get out your checkbook." You are instead *inviting the investor to join you.*

The Quiz Show

Most of your presentation will be occupied by the question-and-answer period. This is when you'll really be put to the test.

Getting Grilled: What to Expect

What questions will investors hit you with, and what do they expect of you in answering them?

Not surprisingly, they expect you to have the key facts about your venture at your fingertips.

> "If I ask an entrepreneur, 'When do your projections show the company reaching cash flow break-even?' and he replies, 'Duh, I dunno,'—forget it."

This applies not only to facts but to key decisions.

> "Never say you don't know which way to go on a major decision. Make a choice and be ready to defend it. You can always change your mind later."

Expect questions that test your commitment. The investor will want to know whether you have the determination and grit to carry through the venture. So inquiry into your motivations will definitely be on the agenda.

Finally, your ego will be probed.

> "We always ask, 'How do you feel about strengthening management?' "

This applies not just to the CEO but to the whole team. Questions are likely to be asked on such topics as "division of the spoils" that will test whether the members of management really are unified.

You must always have in mind the need to push for the close. You have set an objective for this meeting, and it probably won't accomplish itself. You must work to accomplish it. This means in practice that you must concentrate on achieving a positive satisfaction of investor queries. It's not enough just to have an answer; you must watch the response to your answers and follow up if it seems that your initial response was in any way disappointing.

Let's elaborate on this a bit. The natural tendency is to fear a searching, persistent cross-examination on one of the weak points of your venture. (And every venture has weak points, even yours!) When you're wriggling and writhing in torment, it's only natural to breathe a sigh of relief when the inquisitor gives up and goes on to some other area. But this is how sales are lost. OK, so the investor goes home and says, "Well, he sure managed to wiggle out of that one. I just couldn't pin him down." Did you win? No; you lost. You want the investor to be *satisfied*. When he bores in on a problem, you should put your whole attention on working to find a positive solution.

You need to listen—really listen—to your audience. If the

investor finds something to object to, that's not something to be quickly brushed aside and ignored as much as possible. The problem areas should receive, not the least attention, but the most attention.

One of the best ways to listen is not to talk too much. One of the reasons you should strive to cover all your key points in your initial presentation is that it will free you to concentrate on listening during the question-and-answer period. If you don't say what you need to say at the start, you'll feel a compulsion to go back to the neglected points during the interactive phase. Instead of concentrating on the investor's questions and answering them effectively, you'll be thinking about how you can sneak in a point that you neglected to make earlier, or maybe even change the subject.

As you are questioned, keep your answers short and to the point. Focus your attention on the investor and listen to the questions carefully.

If other members of your team are present, they too should be schooled to speak with discretion. You'll need to watch out for your technology guru. If a technological issue comes up, he'll instinctively want to explain the whole thing in detail, starting with a discussion of the First Law of Thermodynamics and of course clarifying all those subtle distinctions that laymen so often fail to appreciate. Be prepared to sit on him. Also beware of your sales VP, another potential conversational sand trap.

Finally, be sure you and the other members of your team keep your eye on the ball. Some investors take a relaxed, friendly attitude, and quietly watch how you behave when the situation seems informal. Never forget that you're on stage.

> I once attended a meeting that was held over dinner at a restaurant. One of the company's managers did not make a good impression. He gave the waitress a hard time, insisting on a combination that was not on the menu and sending her out for cigarettes and matches—and "thank you" apparently was not in his vocabulary. His attention to the discussion repeatedly faded as his eyes snapped to every attractive woman who crossed the room. The informal setting brought

out the worst in this person, to the evident discomfort of his partner—and the detriment of their company.

Skeletons in the Closet

An important part of the preparation for your presentation is anticipating potential problems. *Every business plan—and every venture—has its weak points.* The investor doesn't expect you or your plan to be perfect. But he does expect that you will be aware of the problems; that you will admit them; and that you will have ideas for dealing with them.

In preparing your presentation, you should try to anticipate the tough questions. Ask yourself, "What is the worst question they could throw at us?" What if they bring up that three-year blank period in the resumé of your marketing VP, when he was in the pen for wire fraud? What if they ask about that beta-test site that burned to the ground due to faulty wiring in your first model? Even if you think you've successfully swept all the dirt under the rug and locked all the skeletons in the closet, you may find that the investor has found out anyway. In that case, you'd better have your answers prepared. If you get caught by surprise and stand there stunned, if you stammer and snivel some incoherent excuse, you're dead meat for sure.

Grace Under Pressure

How do you field the tough ones? There are several things to keep in mind.

1. *Field them. Don't evade them.* Investors know that there is no such thing as a perfect deal or a venture with no drawbacks or risks. One of the things they want to find out from meeting with you is whether *you* know it. Are you realistic in your expectations? Are you capable of objectivity about your company? No matter how intelligent, how skilled, how experienced you are, if you can't control your enthusiasm, if you let yourself

lose touch with reality, you're doomed to failure. Investors are very sensitive to this hazard.

2. *Be candid.* Don't try to gloss over, minimize, or, worst of all, conceal the deficiencies in your plan or team. You don't have to go out of your way to emphasize the flaws. But once the subject comes up, it's better to immediately volunteer the disgraceful facts than to have them dragged out of you.

3. *Know what you don't know—and admit it.* Every business plan has gaps. When investors query you on subjects you haven't yet mastered, or ask for information you haven't yet assembled, don't try to bluff it out. Tell them you don't know— and then tell them what you're doing to find out.

4. *Avoid defensive responses.* There is a sort of automatic, jerky, reflexive, unthinking response that entrepreneurs tend to produce when their ventures are criticized. Anyone who's worked with them much can spot this sort of behavior immediately, and it's a dead giveaway of lack of objectivity.

It's a hard line to tread. You must be able to accept criticism and respond to it positively while sticking to your guns on the crucial issues. It's not automatically true that any disagreement means that you are right and the investors are wrong. Nor is it automatically true that they are right and you are wrong.

The best policy is to appeal to facts. When it comes down to "my judgment is better than your judgment," it's difficult to reach a satisfactory resolution. When a disagreement surfaces, you should take the attitude, "Well, let's get more facts and see who's right."

"And Then He Blew It"

Sometimes—not often, it turns out—an entrepreneur snatches defeat from the jaws of victory. An initial positive impression can be suddenly reversed. The examples we got from venture capitalists show that usually pretty egregious behavior is needed to blow it—but some entrepreneurs manage.

> "We had a term sheet signed at an agreed-on price. But the entrepreneur continued to negotiate with another group

and got them to offer him 50 percent more. He tried to reopen terms with us, but we wouldn't play. In fact, we dropped out— though we still ended up with 10 percent of the company as a result of the contract created by the original term sheet."

"We were doing our due diligence and we found out that the venture's proposed executive vice-president had lied on his resumé. We called up a company where he'd supposedly been a top executive and had a hard time finding anyone who'd heard of him. Finally we reached one of their people who said, 'Oh, yeah, he was a salesman here for a while.' I said to the entrepreneur, 'We're not going to do the deal if this guy's involved.' And he just came apart. He jumped up on top of the conference table and started screaming at us. Later he calmed down and wanted to continue, but we decided we really didn't need to do this deal."

"We were backing a company being put together by a fairly well-known personality. Everything was coming together nicely. Then one day while we were talking with her, out of the blue she says, "Oh, by the way . . ." and tells us she's decided to change the terms of the deal drastically. We declined to go forward."

"More than once we've had deals die because the entre-preneur had an incompetent lawyer. Some guy who doesn't have any experience with venture deals and doesn't know how things are done comes in here and tries to lay down the law to us."

The Interrogation

Most of the time spent in meetings with investors will be devoted to questions that explore the depth of your knowledge of the business, challenge your assumptions, and raise your stress level to see how well you function under fire. These questions will also form the basis for the investor's due diligence examination of you and your team. So you should have names of references who are acquainted with you, your past experience, and your business plans. Be sure to inform them in advance that they might be contacted.

You can anticipate some of the questions that investors will ask and you should be prepared with some of your own.

Commonly Asked Investor Questions

☐ What do you want from this business now, in five years, and beyond?

☐ How will you distribute the spoils? (This, of course, will be asked in front of your team, all of whom will be listening closely.)

☐ In what managerial areas do you think you are weak and how do you propose to fix them?

☐ How long has your team worked together?

☐ Are you thinking about your "next" product? Have you factored it into your planning, into your financial requirements?

☐ What is your *unique* competitive advantage?

☐ What is the basis for your sales forecasts and cash flow projections?

☐ How well do you know your customers; who are they; what are their key characteristics?

☐ What do you want from us besides money?

As a general rule, be prepared to address assumptions in your business plan that deviate significantly, up or down, from industry averages, for example, product pricing, net profit, average receivables collection time, inventory turns, sales per employee, or sales/working capital ratios. Your credibility will be even higher if you cover these up front in the presentation.

The investor expects you to ask questions during the meeting. The venture capitalists we interviewed all referred to the need to build a relationship between investors and entrepreneur as crucial to the success of the enterprise. You must demonstrate that you recognize this need in your questions.

Questions the Entrepreneur Should Ask

☐ Are you prepared to be the lead investor?

☐ How can you help us in areas where our plan is weak?

☐ Where will the next round of financing come from? (This shows a
    long-term perspective.)
☐ Do your credentials include operating experience?
☐ What are you prepared to bring to the enterprise besides money?

Developing Star Quality

How you answer questions is often more important than what
answer you give, for investors are primarily looking at you and
your team. They don't really care if your new computer product
runs at 10 megaFLOPS or 8 megaFLOPS; they want to know
whether you will be a flop.

Your entire presentation, formal and informal, should be
aimed at projecting the right image for your management team.
What traits do you want to project?

1. *Motivation.* Investors do not like to back entrepreneurs
who project a laid-back attitude. You should present yourself as
gung ho to the max. And keep in mind that fatalists are losers.
If you're the type who believes that factors beyond your control
will make the difference between success and failure, do your
damnedest to conceal it. The investor doesn't want any of this
fatalistic "Well, it was written" stuff. He wants another Law-
rence of Arabia: "Nothing is written until *I* write it!"

> "We want our entrepreneurs to have drive, energy, vision.
> You can't build a business by the numbers."

2. *Perseverance.* Starting and building a company is not, as
a general rule, easy. There's a lot of work involved. There are
difficulties, setbacks, and downright disasters. The situation is
frequently discouraging, not to say desperate. Investors like to
back entrepreneurs who don't give up easily—hardworking,
tireless, and jackass-stubborn people who just don't know when
to quit.

Lee had never beaten an adversary so soundly as he had

beaten this one in the course of the past two days [the battle of the Wilderness]. What it all boiled down to was that Grant was whipped, and soundly whipped, if he would only admit it by retreating: which in turn was only a way of saying that he had not been whipped at all.

—Shelby Foote,
The Civil War

3. *Integrity*. They hate it, they really hate it, but if they choose to back your venture, investors will have to trust you. Oh, they'll write all sorts of restrictions and covenants and protections into the deal documents. But they know, in the end, that if you want to swindle them you'll find a way. And they're not only worried that you'll clean out the corporate bank account and fly off to Paraguay. What if you turn out to be the defendant in the next big Defense Department procurement scam? What if your company is caught dumping carcinogens into the city reservoir? It won't exactly enhance the reputation of the people who backed you financially.

So be sure you project absolute integrity. You don't have to be a prig. But if you've ever done something to be ashamed of— be ashamed of it. Don't, even when discussing venial infractions, give 'em a wink and a nudge and say, "What the hell, everybody does it." That's just the sort of attitude that makes investors wonder if you might do it—to them.

4. *Objectivity*. Time and again, we heard from venture capitalists that one of the key things they look for in an entrepreneur is a *willingness to listen*. They expect, and they want, entrepreneurs to be enthusiastic, committed, and even obstinate. But when they encounter somebody with a mind closed to reason, who won't admit to unpleasant facts or listen to unwelcome advice—no deal.

Venture Capitalists on Objectivity

"Does he know what he doesn't know? Is he willing to listen to advice? Does he have a real zeal to build a company? Can he give a presentation and make himself clear? If he can't communicate with us, he can't communicate as a manager.

Can he keep his composure when we hit him with unfair questions?''

"We like entrepreneurs who listen and are responsive. A lot of people we see act like politicians; if you ask them a tough question, they change the subject or find some other way to evade it."

The Counterattack

While making your presentation, getting across your key points, and fielding everything the investors can throw at you, you must still be able to take the offensive and press them for information and a decision. You need some questions to throw back at them. By asking questions of your own, instead of remaining purely passive, you are able to project to the investor your valuable qualities.

To start with, let's consider some attitudes you *don't* want to project.

• *Passivity*. A question you should not ask is, "What do you want to know?" Be more aggressive than this.

• *Obsession with control*. Don't ask who will have control of the company. The investors will, or at least want to think they will. You don't want to sound as though you visualize the future of the company as a power struggle between you and the investors.

"A lot of entrepreneurs come in here with '51 percent' printed on their foreheads. As far as we're concerned, people who approach us with that kind of adversarial attitude are born to lose."

• *Obsession with money*. The "how much do I have to give up" question, as we've previously mentioned, is a real loser. The founder who's focused on the stock split rather than on building the company is unlikely to be a successful manager. And the venture capitalists can see themselves in endless conflict over the slicing of the pie. Save the issue for the negotiating period.

There are other attitudes you *do* want to project.

- *Realism.* You should ask such questions as, "Where do you see us getting future rounds of financing? Will you be involved at that stage?"
- *Positive partnership attitude.* Present yourself as ready to enter into a real partnership with the investor. The key question you want to ask is, "What will you bring to the company besides money? What areas or industries do you see your firm as being particularly expert in?"
- *Acceptance of investor exit.* As we've previously pointed out, investors aren't buying into your company because the stock certificates are so pretty. Before they even start, they're already thinking about their options when it comes time to cash in their chips. They want you to understand their needs and be prepared for the exit process. So ask, "How do you see yourself exiting from this investment? By acquisition, or by going public? How would you go about it?"
- *Strength.* You want (very subtly) to imply that you have, and are thinking about, alternatives to doing the deal with this firm. Ask: "What companies have you invested in? What have the results been? Would you feel comfortable taking the lead position in this investment? What other firms do you have in mind to participate? Have you worked with them before?"
- *Momentum.* "What is the decision-making process in your firm? What kind of schedule do you foresee? What can we do to facilitate your due diligence?"

Closing the Sale

Your meeting with the investor should terminate in some sort of specific, tangible step calculated to continue and advance the investment. You do not want the session to taper off with a vague, "Well, goodbye, thanks for coming by." Here are some ways you can try to get a commitment from the investor as you wind up the meeting.

"What do you see as the next step?" This is the logical question to close with. If things went well, the investor will respond with something like a request for references so that due diligence can get started. Or there may be a request for more information of some sort—additional financials, for instance. Or you may be asked to set up a meeting with another of the firm's partners or with representatives from another firm they'd like to bring into the syndicate. If you've accomplished this, the meeting was a definite success.

On the other hand, you may get a standard euphemism of the "let us think it over" class. In this case, you're probably never going to be financed by this firm. What you'd like to ask in this event is, "How did we blow it?" That, of course, is inadvisable. It's better to follow up on any difficulties that you encountered during the presentation. If, for instance, your sales projections were challenged, you might say, "We'd like to revise our projections to take into account the points you brought up. I think we could have them ready for you by next Thursday. Would that be satisfactory?" Offer to take some tangible step yourself, in a specific time frame. This may get the deal moving again. Even if it doesn't—and the odds are against you—it has a good chance of breaking loose the investor's real objections or at least eliciting a prompt and definite turndown so that you don't have to waste any more time.

Examples From the Enterprise Forum

Each meeting of the Enterprise Forum starts with a twenty-minute presentation by the entrepreneur to a live audience. We've been told by presenters that this provides them with an excellent dry run for the formal presentations they will later make to potential investors. The audience evaluates and comments on the presentation and on the prospects for success of the enterprise. We've reviewed some of the lowest- and highest-rated presentations and include some unexpurgated remarks made by the attendees.

Case 1

A company producing and marketing a variety of software and hardware for computer networks.

Audience Response:

"The presentation overwhelmed me because of the vast technical fields the presenter raced through with inadequate and incomprehensible explanation."

"Very complex. Hard to understand if you aren't an expert."

"Management team is heavy on the technical side but needs strengthening in business."

"Too many acronyms—technospeak."

"I liked the presenter's fielding of questions."

Comments:

This presenter got a low rating on his delivery and presentation content, but the management team was perceived as having the requirements to succeed. The company has received significant venture capital and has increased revenues twenty times since the presentation.

Case 2

An early-stage company developing a product based on space image processing.

Audience Response:

"Presenter was poorly prepared."

"I never figured out what the business was."

"Poor visuals." [There were last-minute alterations; the presenter admitted that some were incomprehensible.]

"Very vague, confusing and poorly prepared presentation. Seems focused on the technology rather than market need."

"Presentation was not tailored to allotted time." [It included a lengthy discourse on technology.]

"Company has a market analysis, but not products."

"Confused talking about a product with developing one. Pure hot air."

Comments:

The presenter was rated low on his presentation and the management team low in terms of technical and business depth. The company has since received some modest private funding that has allowed it to survive and is now negotiating funding from a large firm in an unrelated field that is seeking some diversification.

Case 3

A venture that has developed a unique microclimate control system for application principally in agriculture.

Audience Response:

"Too sketchy for fair evaluation; president poorly prepared to answer questions."

"Presentation was all technology. No treatment of competition, management, financial projections, etc."

"Presenter should have gotten that business plan to reviewers way ahead of time." [Some parts of the plan were given to the panel just before the presentation.]

"The presenter should read a book on business plans and follow some of the basic rules for presenting his plan."

"Excellent idea/product. Good visual presentation." [A short movie clip was used to show some currently installed systems.]

Comments:

The presentation was given moderately good ratings, but the management team was accorded a very low probability of achieving success. The company has since gone into bankruptcy but is still operating on a small scale.

Case 4

A company developing hardware and software products, based on organic molecular film technology, for the electronics industry.

Audience Response:

"An inspiring speaker, excellent presentation."

"Swell technology—what's the product? I was troubled by the presenter's lack of focus. Hearing that he intends to bring in a CEO does not cheer me up."

"Presenter did not ask for any particular help. It was just 'here I am, no problems.' "

"I predict that, a year from now, this enterprise will be nothing but a bad memory in the minds of its investors."

Comments:

Although there was some observer ambivalence, this presentation was not rated badly. However, the management's ability to drive the company to some success was rated very low. Two years later, the company was still going, however. There had been some management changes and the market focus had been shifted from electronic to medical applications.

Case 5

An enterprise developing a hybrid rocket system to launch small commercial satellite payloads.

Audience Response:

"Presentation was good, but lacked depth (too sales-oriented); no financials or organization details; technology rather than business orientation."

*"Excellent delivery." [It included a seven-minute movie clip
ending with a dramatic test firing of the rocket.]*

*"No business plan information in presentation. Stock market
crash affected funding prospects but was not covered."*

"The presenter had spirit."

Comments:
    The presentation was highly rated, and the management
team's rating was also high. The company has yet to receive
any orders and is continuing to survive via private bootstrap
financing. Meanwhile, several new competitors for smaller pay-
load launch services have emerged.

These cases illuminate several themes we have stressed in
our extended discussion of the venture presentation.

    1. The presentation definitely—and very strongly—affects
the way in which your management and leadership potential is
perceived. (Keep in mind, though, that most of the comments
given came from fellow entrepreneurs; investors generally are
less generous in their evaluations.)

    2. Insofar as your presentation conveys strong personal
qualities, such as confidence, motivation, capability, and candid-
ness, your venture will be judged to have a greater chance for
success. In the first case, the presenter's delivery was techni-
cally obscure; yet his management abilities were rated highly
due to his straightforward approach to questions and good grasp
of a complex technological marketplace. In the last case, positive personal qualities, particularly the CEO's indomitable
spirit, lifted the rating both of the presentation and of the
perceived success potential.

    3. Preparation is essential. In the third case, the company's
future potential was rated low because the business plan was
still in flux, the presentation did not cover the essentials, and, in
consequence, the CEO was poorly prepared to answer questions. An intriguing technology product demonstrated by good
visuals raised the ratings on the presentation, however, which

underscores the importance of the appropriate use of props to illustrate the attributes of your product.

Curtain Time

In the end, when the curtain goes up, you can only put on the best show you can. Break a leg.

Bibliography

Leech, Thomas. *How to Prepare, Stage, and Deliver Winning Presentations*. New York: AMACOM, 1982. An excellent, complete treatment of the business presentation. Includes an extensive bibliography of related material on presentations. A comprehensive source.

Molloy, John T. *Dress for Success*. New York: Warner, 1975.

———. *Molloy's Live for Success*. New York: Morrow, 1981.

———. *The Woman's Dress for Success Book*. Chicago: Follett, 1977. These three books provide a gold mine of solid, practical advice on dress, accessories, and business etiquette. If you're not absolutely sure of yourself, here's help.

7

Negotiating the Deal

Getting funded by professional investors is rather like taking a traditional sauna. When they tell you they're ready to go, that they are definitely going to finance your venture, you get that warm, comfortable glow. Then you have to negotiate the actual details of the deal. That's when they dump you in the snow and beat you with the birch switches.

As you go through the venture funding process, negotiation may start at any time. Even in the early contact stages, investors will sometimes start to "manage your expectations." They may, for instance, suggest that they are more likely to be interested in the deal if your ideas about deal valuation are "reasonable." This preliminary staking out of positions is a normal part of the financing minuet. However, the real negotiating process usually doesn't start until you've made a formal presentation and the investment firm's partners have caucused and decided to pursue the deal.

To the extent that the negotiation is adversarial—and *every* negotiation is adversarial to some extent—you are going to come out second best. Face it. You are up against the pros. They negotiate venture deals for a living. They know all the tricks, and they use them.

I once went to discuss a deal with a top-ranking venture capital outfit. The partner with whom I had an appointment was tied up on the freeway and called in on his car phone to ask me to wait for him. So I was shown into the conference room used for negotiations. The walls were covered with beautiful artwork: a stock certificate of the Montezuma Gold Mining Company of Costa Rica; an Imperial Chinese Railway bond; Confederate treasury bonds; and an assortment of other similar securities. Whether these decorations were intended to serve as a caution to the partners or as a softening-up mechanism for visiting entrepreneurs, I don't know. Maybe both.

Since you're going to be up against opposition of this caliber, what are your chances of coming out with a deal on satisfactory terms? Surprisingly good, if you can accomplish three things.

1. *Build a strong negotiating position.* If you approach investors as a supplicant, if you have no alternative to doing the deal on their terms, you can be sure that the terms will be distasteful.

2. *Learn at least the basic principles of negotiation.* As we'll see, just having a realistic understanding of the negotiation process, and a *plan* for conducting it, can give you a substantial boost.

3. *Aim for a positive-sum deal.* To the extent that your deal consists of you *versus* the investors, haggling over the slicing of a limited pie, you are going to lose. They're better bargainers than you are. If instead you become partners, working together to bake a pie so large that no conflict need arise, their superior negotiating skills become less relevant.

The Negotiating Process

A great deal has been written about negotiation—by business types, by psychologists, by politicians. You'll find some useful references in the Bibliography at the end of this chapter. In our own presentation of this topic we have tried to draw together the important theories and observations about negotiation and to organize them in a way that will provide you with a practical guide to applying the process to financing transactions.

We have rather arbitrarily divided the negotiation process into three phases.

1. *The Preparation Phase.* You (and presumably the other parties) define your positions and get ready for the negotiations.
2. *Resolution.* The negotiating parties interact in order to discover the obstacles to the deal and develop the information they need to find solutions.
3. *Settlement.* The problems between the parties are solved, their relationship is firmly defined, and the deal is finalized.

Please note that we assume that *there will be problems*. At the beginning of the negotiation it may appear that there are no major conflicts between the parties and that doing the deal merely requires cleaning up a few little details. Real-life negotiations are very seldom so smooth. You will be wise to expect major crises to occur as an inescapable part of the negotiating process. Be prepared to handle them.

Are You Ready to Negotiate?

Before you even begin to negotiate with investors, you'd better be sure you've finished negotiating with your co-founders.

Putting together a good management team can be tricky, and as you contend with three or four entrepreneurial egos you will be tempted to postpone those sticky little issues revolving around who gets what. The thinking goes like this: "We don't know what kind of deal we can get with investors. They might take 30 percent of the stock, or they might wind up with 70 percent. How can we decide how to split our share until we know how much we have available to divide? Better wait until we've got a deal with the venture capitalists; then we'll work out our individual percentages."

Plausible as it sounds, this is a recipe for disaster. What not infrequently happens is that just as the deal reaches a critical stage, the founders start brawling over how their pie will be sliced. The resulting dissension can fatally complicate closing with the investors.

We strongly recommend that you *settle all key issues among the founders before you get into negotiations with the financiers*. Even if, as is usual, you don't know how much stock will be available, you can decide on some formula for dividing it. At the same time, work out any issues that may still be open, including job descriptions, titles, board seats, and so on.

You'll also avoid some potential negotiating problems if you are wary of co-founders who reserve their commitment. If your CFO candidate is waiting until the deal is negotiated to decide whether she'll actually come on board, you'd better hope her decision, when it's finally made, is positive. A last-minute withdrawal, after you've introduced her to the venture capitalists, could blow the deal.

The Preparation Phase

Most of us handle the various negotiations that come up in our lives, whether it's buying a new car or developing a divorce settlement, pretty informally. We just go in and do it, getting it over with as quickly as possible, and generally expecting to be disappointed by the results. Professional negotiators have an entirely different approach. Whether it be a nuclear arms control treaty, a union contract, or a multigigabuck Wall Street take-over, the pros who are responsible for negotiating it will prepare carefully long before they sit down at the table. You should do the same.

The first step in your preparation is simply identifying your negotiating parameters. First, what are your objectives? What is your rock-bottom price? Don't limit your consideration just to the obvious monetary considerations. All sorts of issues may come up—personnel issues and management issues especially. If you're taken by surprise, you'll be caught at a disadvantage, required to decide on the spot what your needs are and what you must insist on. Sit down with your co-founders, if you haven't already, and thrash out a detailed list of your negotiating objectives.

The next step is to do exactly the same thing for the investors. During your investor qualification effort and the subsequent process of presentation and discussion, you should have learned a great deal about the investors and their objectives. Now is the time to pull together your vague impressions into a coherent model of their motives and requirements. You should try to figure out what is important to them, what is unimportant.

Then go beyond that analysis to consider the negotiating style of the investors. It's well worth the effort to call up some entrepreneurs who have previously dealt with the same firm. How did the investors behave? Did they just drop a "take it or leave it" proposal on the table? Or did they enjoy haggling like Persian rug dealers? Did they have any favorite ploys they liked to exercise? Half an hour of gossip with a previous investee can provide you with crucial information and allow you to avoid some disconcerting surprises.

You should take time to gather together and organize all the information you've developed about your venture, about the investors, and about any other factor that may influence the negotiations. You want to have access to it without delay when an issue arises during the talks. Pay particular attention to the history of your early discussions with the investor. Pull together all the letters and other documents, including your notes from meetings and phone conversations. It can be very useful to be able to say, "Well, we have a problem with that. On January 18 you told us that a two-year extension of the preemptive rights would be fine, so we planned on that basis. If you're changing your position now, we'll have to ask you to . . . ."

Your next step is to develop a detailed outline of the deal terms. Look at every issue that could possibly be negotiated and list them. These are the "negotiation variables." Make your list complete; *never simply assume that something is not negotiable*. Then go through them and mark off your positions. What are your minimum requirements? Where are you willing to make concessions? Where might you give way on one item in return for leeway on another? Once you have settled this, your detailed negotiating position, go through the list again. What issues do you feel that you and the investors are in essential agreement on? What issues are iffy? What issues are likely to pose major problems?

Be Prepared to Punt

The final step in your preparation is development of a fallback position. It can practically be guaranteed that if you have no viable alternatives to doing this specific deal, you will get screwed. Yes, you can try to bluff. But the odds that you will not be called are not good. We strongly recommend that you *not* negotiate with your back to the wall, even if you are desperate. It's not only that going into negotiations with a weak position will give you an unsatisfactory agreement. The real problem is that negotiations at the pistol point result in bad relationships. You'll never forget that you were hosed; the investor will never forget that he hosed you; and neither of you will ever be comfortable with the other.

It's a good exercise to sit down and imagine that negotiations fail. All the work is down the drain. You don't have any choice but to start over again. What would you do? Develop a short plan. You'd survive somehow, right? OK, there's your fallback plan. The author of *Getting to Yes* calls this your "BATNA"—Best Alternative To a Negotiated Agreement.[1] Now decide, would you really resort to your fallback plan if you couldn't get one of your "nonnegotiable" requirements? Would you *really?* Make these evaluations now, not in the middle of negotiations. The key principle here is to make decisions based on your BATNA rather than on comparison to your "bottom-line" position.

Negotiating a Venture Capital Deal

Let's go over the specific issues that you'll have to settle to negotiate a venture capital financing for your company.

1. R. Fisher, *Getting to Yes: Negotiating Agreement Without Giving In* (Boston: Houghton-Mifflin, 1981).

Valuation

The fundamental question, of course, is pricing. How much is your company worth? And, of at least equal importance, what will it be worth in the future?

The basic venture capital approach to deal pricing requires an estimate of future value. After a few years, the investors will want to liquidate their investment in your stock, usually by taking the company public. So, to determine pricing, they will make an estimate of your profits, say, five years down the road (which may or may not agree with your estimate). Using standard stock market price/earnings ratios, they can calculate what your company will be worth at that time. Working back from that figure, they then calculate what price they must buy stock at now in order to meet their investment objectives.

How a Venture Capitalist Thinks

"Let's see, these guys need $10 million. OK, figure we take Mutant Pomegranate Technologies Inc. public in five years and assume the stock market is valuing biotechnology companies at ten times earnings. Their projections show $50 million in sales five years out and 15 percent pretax, so earnings are $7.5 million and the theoretical valuation is ten times that, or $75 million. For us to make five times investment in five years we have to cash out for $50 million. So our $10 million investment has to buy two-thirds of the company. That is, if we believe their projections."

Obviously this procedure is full of uncertainties. The projected sales and profit numbers are extrapolations. Stock market experts can't predict what price/earnings ratios will be next month, let alone five years from now. Also, the venture will quite possibly need additional equity infusions before it goes public, which will result in dilution of the original investors. So at best, this type of estimate can give only a ballpark figure for your company's present value.

To improve the valuation of your company, you can argue from three positions: (1) its strong future value; (2) its strong present value; (3) its continuous or at least early liquidity. Let's take these in turn.

Can you convincingly argue that the future value of the company will be unusually high? You can of course try to inflate earnings estimates. This approach seldom works. You can also assert that the stock market will grant your company a higher than normal price/earnings ratio. For instance, you can modify the way you describe the company (or perhaps even modify the reality) to make it fit into an industry group with traditionally high valuations.

Another approach is to suggest that the company will not go public but will be sold or merged into a larger firm. In principle, this should produce a higher price than an IPO, because the buyer will pay a premium for control and perhaps a premium for your technology or market position. In reality, IPOs usually produce a better valuation because "the public" includes less sophisticated buyers. Nonetheless, venture capitalists are attracted to exiting by sale of the company. For one thing, they can get out completely and quickly. In an IPO, the underwriter will usually insist that the venture investors postpone the sale of their stock and then dribble it out slowly so as not to kill the market. Also, investors can't be sure that an IPO "window" will occur when they're ready to exit. Once an investment goes public, the venture capital investors are exposed to stockholder lawsuits and other hassles. Finally, sale to a large company can often be done much sooner, long before the venture is ready for an IPO. So your readiness to accept sale of your venture as an exit strategy can be a sizable plus.

Another line of argument stresses the present value of your company. If you are at the startup stage, of course, you have very little leverage along these lines. Your "book value" is simply any assets you may have, such as a patent. You can't very well claim much additional value unless you have an

ongoing business with some sort of track record. Then you can
try to assign a value to the business by any of several methods.

METHODS OF COMPANY VALUATION

The valuation of closely held companies is an art and a
science of no small difficulty. You probably will not have time
to master this discipline in your spare moments. However, it
may be helpful to be aware of the half dozen or so basic methods
for valuing a company.

Fair market value is just what it sounds like—the value
actually placed on the company when it is sold, or, in practice,
an estimate of the value that would be placed on it if it were
sold. This is the standard of value for tax assessment purposes
as well as, of course, for setting a purchase or investment value.

Fair value sounds almost the same but in fact is entirely
different. This is a legal term for the value set by arbitrary
formulas by court precedents in various states. These "fair
value" formulas are used to appraise a company when dissident
investors challenge, say, merger or buyout terms and claim
compensation. As you negotiate with investors, "fair value"
probably will not be relevant, but keep in mind that someday
you might be one of those dissident shareholders.

Investment value is a subjective term. It refers to the value
of the company to a specific investor. Each investor will assign
a different "investment value" to the company, depending on
the individual investor's situation. For instance, a pension fund,
which does not have to pay taxes, will value a dividend stream
differently from an individual investor, who does have to pay
taxes. The "investment value" is what venture capitalists and
other investors are trying to estimate for your company.

Intrinsic value or *fundamental value* is what stock market
analysts are always trying to calculate: what the price of the
company "ought" to be if the market were "rational."

Liquidation value is simply what the company would be
worth if it were shut down and the assets sold off. There are two
types of liquidation value: "orderly" and "forced." Liquidation
value can provide an ultimate downside number for the investor;
banks and other debt lenders often take it into account.

Book value is of course just the net worth of the company as shown on its balance sheet. Usually it has no practical economic significance. However, it can be a useful number for a very young company because the assets are still on the books at close to market value.

Rule-of-thumb value provides a first approximation or a simplified way of estimating discounted future earnings or discounted cash flow. Knowing typical financial ratios in a given industry, one can say that as a rule a radio station is worth ten times cash flow, or that a research services company is worth two times sales, or that a fine chemicals manufacturer is worth five times earnings. These rough approximations have more influence on actual negotiations than you might think. Because "everybody knows" this is the way companies in the industry should be valued, it can be hard for either buyer or seller to justify a major deviation from the rule.

Keep in mind that company valuation is very much future-oriented. Past performance is relevant only insofar as you can convince investors that it is evidence of future performance. You must make every effort to justify the plausibility and consistency of your financial projections.

Theoretical methods of valuing your company are generally hard to defend. The strongest argument that you can make for your company's price is its market value. If somebody else (not necessarily another venture capital firm) expresses an interest in buying your company at a higher valuation, that is very strong evidence as to its actual worth. If you can't get an alternative bid for your company, what about your competitors? Have any of them changed hands recently? If so, at what price?

The last approach to getting better valuation involves reducing the investor's risk premium. The basic venture capital argument is: "When the company goes public, the most we can cash out for is x. We're taking a tremendous risk that your company will crash and burn. Even if it survives and does fairly well, the odds are that it won't get big enough to go public and we'll be unable to get our money back out. So you have to sell stock to us at a very low price to give us a potential reward commensurate with our risk." Clearly, any argument you can make that the investment will be safer than usual gives you a chance to push for a better valuation.

You can deal with the risk factor either substantively or financially. On the one hand, you can argue that your business is planned so as to minimize risk. On the other, you can offer the investors financial instruments that will improve their liquidity, so that they will be able to exit the investment even if you don't reach the point where you can go public.

The liquidity factor is extremely important. A common rule of thumb states that going public will get you twice the valuation that you could get from private sources such as venture capital. Commonly this is ascribed to "the stupidity of the public." However, academic studies of "letter stock" values indicate that there is a significant discount—42 to 74 percent—associated simply with limited liquidity of a security.[2] So the higher valuation for public companies may well reflect this factor rather than the alleged lack of sophistication of IPO buyers. The moral: Stress your willingness to do everything possible to make your company's stock as liquid as possible, as quickly as possible.

There still remains the question: What can you reasonably expect in the valuation of your company?

OK, How Much Do You Have to Give Up?

What can you and your co-founders reasonably expect from a venture capital deal?

Very few companies make it all the way from the seed stage to going public with only one round of venture capital. Usually you have to go out for more money several times. Any particular one of these financings may be based on an unusually good, or

2. Shannon Pratt, *Valuing a Business: The Analysis and Appraisal of Closely Held Companies* (New York: Dow Jones-Irwin, 1981), pp. 238–262.

an unusually bad, valuation, but the results of the whole series of deals perhaps tend to average out.

For second-stage or "mezzanine" financings, valuations tend to be higher, of course, than for early-stage ventures. Yet we get the impression—we can't prove it—that venture capitalists actually pay a premium for early-stage deals. Are three or four bright guys with a plan, a prototype, and a patent *really* worth a couple of million dollars? Yet these deals get done.

Another interesting trend that emerged from our admittedly unscientific survey was the 50 percent factor. For seed and first-round deals, venture capitalists seem to take a position in the 50 percent range more often than could be expected on a chance basis.

We conjecture that despite all the talk of rational methods of business valuation, venture capitalists have an unwritten gut rule that goes something like this: Estimate how much money the company needs in this financing. If it's an early-stage company, demand 50 percent of the stock in return. If it's more advanced, demand 35 percent.

In Silicon Valley, for instance, a typical first-round financing is around $3 million. And, says one venture capitalist, if the company is three people and an idea, that will buy between half and two-thirds of the company. At the second round, the valuation can be double or triple what it was in the first round. For third-round or "mezzanine" financings, investors look to double or triple their money within eighteen months when the company goes public. Of course, these are elite, top-drawer ventures getting this kind of money.

It is likely that the most significant factor in deciding how much of your company you get to keep is not the terms of your first financing but *how many* financings you do. Here's what you might expect if you start with venture capital at the seed stage: The management team will end up with about 15 to 20 percent of the company by the time it goes public.

We must again stress that the best way to keep a large share of your company is to minimize outside equity capital in the first place. The more you can finance growth via customers, vendors, or other nonequity sources, the less venture capital you will need and the more stock you will own yourself.

Vesting

No, this is not a requirement that managers always wear three-piece suits. Would that it were.

Many entrepreneurs naturally assume that when they do a venture capital deal, the transaction involves only that portion of the stock that is sold to the investors. You may find it quite a shock to discover that *your* stock gets taken away from you as part of the transaction, albeit temporarily.

From the venture capitalist's point of view, some protection is needed to maintain your motivation. If a lot of money has just been put into the company, and you own a goodly chunk of it, what's to keep you from slacking off, or even taking early retirement? Of course, you may be bound by an employment agreement (which is discussed later in the chapter), but just to make sure, your stock will be given (or given back) to you only gradually. That's vesting.

The actual mechanics by which vesting is accomplished depend on the specifics of the deal. In seed-money financings, founder stock may simply not be issued at deal time but instead doled out later. For later-stage deals, where the corporation is already set up and management already owns stock, other methods must be used. For instance, the financiers may get an option to buy out a founder's stock at a low price if she leaves the company before a specified time. The contract will reduce the amount of stock subject to the option over several years.

There are many variations. Sometimes stock vests, wholly or partially, on milestones met by the company or individual founders rather than simply on time served. (Sophisticated systems have been developed for this approach; see the Bibliography to this chapter.) Investors differ in their attitudes toward this approach:

> "Investors often don't like milestone vesting provisions; they're too complex and difficult to negotiate."

> "We do vesting on time, but give the founders extra stock for meeting specific goals."

"For us, a complex structure is a turnoff."

You should consider asking for milestone-based vesting as a negotiating tactic, even if you don't expect (or want) to get it. When venture capitalists challenge your valuation because, they say, your projections are too optimistic, you can offer to tie your own stock percentages to meeting your goals. By putting your money where your mouth is in this way, you give yourself a very strong lever. Of course, you're also taking a hell of a chance!

Time-based vesting provisions are roughly comparable between venture capital firms:

"We do four-year vesting."

"Vesting provisions are negotiable. Normally we vest founder stock over a three- to five-year period."

"You should try to negotiate the vesting provision. A reasonable objective is to get 20 percent of your share of the stock up front and the rest over three years."

Performance Conditions

In addition to playing it close to their vests, the venture capitalists like to have another card up their sleeves: nonperformance forfeitures.

Entrepreneurs tend to be, shall we say, a bit obstinate. ("Stubborn as a jackass" is the way investors tend to regard it.) You may have a very clear idea of the best way to approach the market, which happens not to coincide with the way your customers feel is appropriate. As a result, your company fails to grow properly, but you refuse to change course. Sooner or later, you say, people will come around to your way of thinking.

From the venture capital point of view, this is a time when they want to whack you over the head with a two-by-four a few times just to get your attention. That's the idea of the performance clause.

The usual format for a nonperformance forfeiture is based on your business plan projections. If you fail to make projected sales or profits, the founder's share of the company's stock is reduced, according to some formula.

It is difficult to oppose this provision, because you sold the deal to the investors on the basis of your projections. You can't very well argue to them now that it's unfair to hold you to them. Your best ploy is to work the argument in the other direction. If you ought to lose stock for doing worse than projected, then you ought to gain stock for doing better. Taken to its logical conclusion, this results in a form of milestone-based vesting.

Stock Format

Your company may be as solid as the *Titanic;* but if it should hit an iceberg, who's first in line at the lifeboats? Forget the women and children; the venture capitalists want to hold reserved seats.

In the simplest deals, common stock is sold to the investors. Everyone is sharing the risk and the rewards of the venture on more or less even terms. If the company sinks, you all take a bath—founders and investors alike. If your ship comes in, you all live happily ever after. This is a good situation from your point of view, because it results in a community of interests between you and your investors. Since you're all in the same boat, as they look out for their own interests they will be looking out for yours, and vice versa.

However, the venture capitalists probably won't be unwilling to settle for more if they see the chance. Naturally they have a fiduciary responsibility to seek a deal in which as much of the risk as possible is pushed off on you.

One good way (from the investor's point of view) to establish a "heads we win, tails you lose" situation is to structure the investment with convertible bonds instead of stock. This gives them the best of both worlds. If the company starts to look shaky, their investment is a loan and they should be able to get back most or all of their money. If the company prospers, they convert the bonds to stock and cash in.

This is not such a good arrangement for you. There can be real problems if your company hits a bad spell. Instead of pitching in to help out, your investors may feel pressure to push you into liquidation and get their principal back.

That's not to say that you should never accept a deal of this sort. But first, look at the alternatives. Preferred stock, or warrants, or options to buy common stock under certain circumstances can provide additional protection for investors with less risk for you. In any case, if you agree to give the investors financial instruments other than common stock, you should explore the issues and ask for other concessions in return.

Be wary of any instrument that allows the investors to declare their investment "due and payable" at their option. ("Redemption at option" and "put" clauses have much the same effect.) This sort of provision greatly reduces the reserve buoyancy of your company. An unexpected setback, a couple of bad quarters, and you may find yourself involuntarily being liquidated. Before you sign, examine very carefully the conditions under which the venture capitalists can call in the money. They shouldn't be allowed to jump ship unless the situation is so ominous that survival is clearly impossible. Discuss in advance their commitment to the venture.

To the extent that investors get something safer than common stock, they should be expected to offer something in return. A good principle to use here is that *those who take the risk should make the decisions*. This is a general principle in investment. The captain may be expected to go down with the ship, but along with that obligation goes the authority to control the wheel. It's not fair for a passenger to insist on steering the vessel, and then run for the lifeboats if he rams an iceberg. So your concessions on stock risk should be balanced by investor concessions on control issues.

Antidilution Provisions

After your first venture capital financing, you and the investors will share ownership in the firm. Almost certainly, other rounds of financing will be necessary in the future. What happens to your ownership then?

Many entrepreneurs don't give much thought to the need for future financings and so pay little attention to antidilution provisions. As a result, they find themselves after a few years diluted down to a homeopathic dose of stock—effectively squeezed out of their own companies. These people tend to speak bitterly about greedy and unscrupulous venture capital, but they really have no one to blame but themselves. Venture capitalists simply are realistic about the need for future money and they plan accordingly. You should do the same.

The key question is this: How will the value of your company change over time? If all your projections are met and the company becomes increasingly valuable from financing to financing, there is no problem. Your *percentage,* and that of the investors, will of course decline each time new equity is brought in. However, the company's higher value will more than compensate, so that your *stock* and that of the investors will be worth more.

The problem arises in that inconceivable (but all too likely) case when your company gets into a little bit of a bind. If you then need to raise some more money, you may have to accept a lower valuation of the company than was used for your earlier round. In other words, on a per share basis, your stock and that of the investors will be worth less.

Your original investors don't like the consequences. They take the position that they are entitled to a sort of "most favored nation" clause. That is, no later investor should be allowed to buy in on more favorable terms than they got. They can't prevent new investment from coming in, because they'd rather get diluted than have the company fail. But they can insist retroactively on getting the same deal that the new investors get. And who pays for it? *You* do.

The venture capitalists may hand you a term sheet with a "full ratchet" provision for antidilution. (If so, hand it back to them.) Full ratchet works like this. The investors, let's say, have bonds that can be converted to stock at $100 per share. A couple of years later, the company has some problems and brings in new capital at only $50 per share. Under full ratchet, the bonds sold to the original investors automatically become convertible to stock at the new price—$50 per share. The founders get clobbered.

You should argue strongly for a "weighted ratchet" instead.

Here the new conversion price is determined by the weighted average price of all the stock. For example: If the first-round investors got 10,000 shares at a pricing of $100 per share, and management another 10,000 shares; and the second-round investors buy 5,000 shares at $50 per share, the new conversion price is:

$$(\$100 \times 20,000 + \$50 \times 5,000)/25,000 = \$90 \text{ per share}$$

Clearly a better situation, eh? As in so many parts of the transaction, attention to the fine print can be worth a lot of money to you in the future.

Employment Contracts

Perhaps the most crucial agreement in a venture capital investment is the employment contract. You as a founder should be very careful what you sign. All sorts of delicate issues will be settled in this document.

To start with, under what circumstances can you be terminated, or, not to mince words, fired? The investors have very much in mind that you may turn out to be incompetent; or you may go bonkers; or you may simply develop irreconcilable differences with the investors, or even with your co-founders. They want to be able to get rid of you if necessary. You, not unnaturally, want to be secure in your job. So your objective is an employment contract that specifically states that you can be fired only for cause; and what constitutes "cause" should be explicitly set out. The severance package, and provision for adequate notice, should also be negotiated up front.

On the other side of the coin, what if you want to quit? There are many reasons, some foreseeable and some not, why you might choose to leave before your time. But presumably you are a key person for the company, and the venture capitalists don't want you to walk out and leave them holding the bag. So you should expect to be contractually committed to the job for at least two or three years. It's probably unwise to sign on for a longer term.

Then there is the noncompete agreement. Regardless of

whether you jump overboard or are made to walk the plank, the investors will not want to find you coming back into the race on the crew of another boat. That's only sensible, but a strict noncompete provision can sentence you to slow starvation, particularly if you are a specialist. A reasonable noncompete will prohibit you from soliciting business from the firm's customers and from hiring its employees. But if you are required to get out of the industry entirely, better consider your alternatives before you sign. See to it also that there's a reasonable time limit—say, a couple of years—on the duration of the prohibition. Commonly you will be paid at some reasonable rate (less than full salary) during a noncompete period.

Related to these provisions is the question of technology ownership. If your venture is high-tech, then to a great extent your technology is what you are selling to investors, especially in an early-stage financing. Naturally, they want to own it. Situations in which the inventor retains the rights to the invention and licenses the company to use it do not attract venture capital. But what happens if your lifework is part of the deal and then the investors decide you're too difficult to work with and eject you? It's quite possible, if you're careless with your employment contract, to find yourself out on the street in a very nasty situation. Your invention is gone—the investors now own it. You have no stock in the company—it hasn't vested yet. You have no job—and no way to get one because of the noncompete.

Naturally your employment contract will specify salary and bonus arrangements. As we've pointed out before, venture capitalists won't remunerate you at a high level of munificence, especially if your previous employment was menial. This is no bad thing, as entrepreneurs should be focused on making money, not spending it. But you should carefully examine the provisions for sale of founder stock.

To see what a real-life employment contract in a venture deal looks like, refer to Appendix III. You may find it sobering.

Boards of Directors

As we've seen, control does not equal 51 percent of the stock. Neither does it consist of a majority on the board of directors.

However, you should carefully examine how the ultimate authority in the company will be exercised.

Before you sign, go over the proposed corporate bylaws with your attorney. There are all sorts of traps for the unwary.

The investors will no doubt insist on contractual provisions guaranteeing them one or more seats on the board, as well as other goodies. For instance, they will have a veto on decisions to merge the company, sell new stock, or enter into major transactions. You should try to pin down the same rights. You will not get equality, but you may get something. If one or more members of the founding team are going to serve on the board, their seats should be *guaranteed* by contract, just as the venture capital seats are. You'll want to try for a veto on decisions that could screw you, such as mergers; if you can't get a veto, at least insist on being notified well in advance.

Incidentally, the investors may start squabbling among themselves over seats on the board, and you can get caught in the cross fire. When several venture capital firms are participating, there may not be enough seats to go around without increasing the board to an unwieldy size. Directorships are status items for venture capitalists, so a game of musical chairs may result.

What about outside directors? They can be very valuable as mediators and as counselors. We'd suggest that big-name, big-company executives may not be ideal. Rather, you may wish to look for successful entrepreneurs.

The Resolution Phase

A major negotiation is a lot of just plain hard work. Once you start the resolution phase, you and the investors must labor together to build the deal—and to forge a relationship. Here are some key principles to guide you:

1. *Build a business relationship.* Your objective is to establish trust and confidence in a business context. If, over the years, you gradually become good buddies with the investors, that will be great. But too often entrepreneurs try to force intimacy where it is simply not appropriate. Don't be too pushy.

During the negotiating process you will be wise to avoid volunteering opinions on potentially controversial subjects. Your views on gun control, abortion, or the need for 50 percent of all management positions to be held by women simply aren't relevant. If the investor's views are opposed to yours, you probably will gain neither a convert nor the money. And even if the two of you are in agreement, you may still get into trouble by offending a third party.

> An entrepreneur at a meeting with investors found one of them a kindred soul. Happily these two discussed their mutual interest in antiwar activities and socially conscious investments. They were unaware that the other man present was strongly right-wing.

We recommend that you focus on business and confine small talk to the weather.

2. *Don't mix business with personal needs.* It sometimes happens that entrepreneurs unconsciously try to use the relationship with investors to satisfy emotional rather than business needs. For instance, if you, like many venture founders, are extremely competitive, you may find yourself being too aggressive, too focused on "beating" the investor instead of making a deal. Some people have a need for stroking or flattery that gets in the way of building a business relationship. Other entrepreneurs have a tendency to elevate the investor into a sort of father figure; striving for his approval, they melt down their own negotiating positions.

3. *Talk about your motives, not theirs.* This is an age of empathy, when everyone is telling you to put yourself in the other guy's shoes. It's easy to forget how very offensive it is to make assumptions about other people's motives.

Marriage counselors long ago learned that if people wish to communicate without conflict, they should never ascribe motives to the other party. When sentences start to begin with, "You're saying that because . . . ," the crockery soon starts flying.

Don't impute motives to the other side during negotiations,

even if those motives are innocuous or creditable. Explain your own motives, yes. *Ask* about their motives, yes. But don't tell them why they're doing what they're doing.

4. *Demonstrate trustworthiness in the little things.* You are asking investors to trust you with a large sum of money. They will have to rely not just on your honesty but on your industriousness and your determination. How can they tell whether you are really trustworthy?

Generally they look at your behavior in the little things. Do you keep your appointments? Are you on time? If you say you'll send them a document, do you send it? Does it arrive when you said it would? Are you reliable and conscientious, not just in dealing with them but with other people?

Some people say, "Well, I may be a bit careless with the little things, but when it's really important I always come through." Investors tend to look at it from an opposite perspective: "If he won't take the trouble to get to an appointment on time, what will he do when he *really* has to put himself out?"

Starting the Negotiation

Usually it's hard to sharply define when the initial exploration phase ends and the negotiation begins. But at some point you'll be sitting down with the investors and discussing terms.

Be sure you're working with the right people. You don't want to be talking to someone who doesn't have authority to sign the deal. They can draw you out, get you committed to terms, then tell you that their superiors have vetoed the agreement and that you must make further concessions.

Some types of investors, such as banks, use this method as routinely as auto dealers. Every loan must be approved by a shadowy and elusive committee; if you try to locate the real decision maker, you'll end up feeling like a character out of Kafka. This ploy is less commonly resorted to by venture capitalists, fortunately.

The first thing you want to accomplish is the development of a deal outline. In essence, this serves as the agenda for the negotiations. What is on the table? What is not on the table? If you let the other party take over the agenda, you've already lost. They'll set up the issues so that what's theirs is theirs; what's yours is what's up for negotiation. To counter this, you want to take the position: *First,* we talk about what we are going to talk about; *then,* we talk about it.

It's important to enforce both halves of this principle. Don't let the definition of the agenda be concurrent with the substantive negotiations; that allows the other party to suddenly whip out new issues to spring on you. At the same time, don't get into discussion of the issues *until* the agenda is settled; premature haggling can develop into an unnecessary deadlock.

The Deal Outline

- [ ] Valuation of the company
- [ ] Size of the investment
- [ ] Structure of the deal, including type of stock or security (common stock, preferred, convertibles, etc.)
- [ ] Vesting of founder stock
- [ ] Antidilution provisions
- [ ] Commitments for future investors
- [ ] Control issues, including composition of the board of directors, corporate bylaws, etc.
- [ ] Employment contracts for founders
- [ ] Ownership of technology
- [ ] Performance guarantees

Once you have the deal outline, you can start the real negotiating process. Most people think of negotiations as a tug-of-war between opposing objectives. We are inclined to see productive negotiation in terms of an *exchange of information.* The objective is not to "beat the enemy"; the objective is to get to a good deal, with which both sides will be happy. Of course, the two (or more) parties are not congruent in their goals, and inevitably there will have to be some give and take. The key to getting a good deal is for each party to *understand* the other party's needs; then they can figure out a deal that will maximize rewards for both sides.

We therefore recommend not being too secretive. Although you should conceal your quantitative, rock-bottom requirements, you should not try to hide what is important to you and what is not. Go ahead and tell them: "Our top priority is the stock percentages. To us, the composition of the board, and the wording of the preemptive rights clause, are less important."

At the same time, early disclosure allows you to "manage the expectations" of the investors. If you are up front with an asking price that is high but not out of line, you start in a good position.

Of course you want reciprocal frankness. The early stages of negotiation should focus on mutual interrogation rather than on attempts to settle issues. Find out what is important to the parties.

This allows you to use a well-known technique for conducting successful negotiations: Start with the easy points. The top of the agenda should consist of items on which the parties are already in agreement. Then go on to issues that are not of major importance to either party, and can thus be easily settled. In this way you develop a momentum of success that carries over into the more difficult issues.

> One popular adaptation of this general principle involves going down the agenda and asking for the other party's proposals. To each, you then say either, "I have no problem with that," or "Let's discuss that one later."

Negotiating Principles

Once the easy questions are out of the way, you can turn to resolution of the major disagreements. Even very difficult problems can be resolved if properly handled. In a productive negotiation, the parties adhere to certain principles of fairness and goodwill.

1. *Negotiators should regard tough issues as problems to be solved rather than as issues to be fought and "won."* Again,

you—and they—should focus on interests rather than positions. Your objective is to get what you want, not to prevent them from getting what they want. Negotiators should be looking for ways to meet the needs of both sides.

2. *No unilateral concessions should be expected by either side.* One party or the other may, at times, decide to give way on some point without asking anything in return, for instance, because the members concede that their position is unreasonable, or because they regard an issue as not worth defending. But as a general rule negotiators should expect to pay for concessions. This helps to preserve the cooperative nature of the proceedings. If the retreating party feels it is being coerced, it may entrench and resolve to hold its ground from now on at all costs. A small reciprocal concession for every retreat can prevent formation of a static battlefront.

3. *Both sides should renounce the use of "bargaining chips."* For negotiators to start insisting on things they don't really want, in order to have something to give away in return for substantive concessions, is not as clever as it sounds. The usual result is a series of complicated maneuvers leading to a major slowdown in the negotiating process, with no significant advantage achieved by either side. An investment deal is complicated enough without bringing in extraneous issues you don't really care about. Every demand made should have a reason behind it.

4. *The ultimate resort should be an appeal to fairness.* There's no point denying that the relative power positions of the two parties are going to influence the terms of the deal. But neither entrepreneurs nor investors can expect a good long-term relationship to develop out of a deal that is based solely on who holds the whip hand. When the two sides are stuck on an issue, it can be helpful to ask, "What do you think would be fair? Why?" Ask them to justify their position on the basis of some sort of objective standard of fairness. When the parties can agree on how to decide whether something is fair, they can usually agree on what's fair.

The Inevitable Problems

All sorts of problems can come up during negotiations. However, in general they can be classified into four types.

    1. Some problems occur because *one party does not understand the other party's objectives*. The negotiators are talking at cross-purposes. Party A makes increasingly painful concessions, trying to satisfy what he perceives to be Party B's desires, only to have them uniformly rejected. Naturally he begins to feel put upon; Party B is being unreasonable. Meanwhile, Party B is beginning to feel insulted; why does Party A keep trying to distract him with this side isssue instead of getting to the heart of the matter? Party A is not negotiating in good faith. The breakdown of communications can result in a breakdown of negotiations.

> An entrepreneur arranged to buy a small company with the idea of boosting its growth by implementing new production technology. He approached a larger, publicly traded high-tech company and proposed that this company put up part of the investment needed on a corporate partnering basis.
>
>   The high-tech people were very interested, and came back with a counteroffer: They'd simply buy the company and integrate it into their operations. At the same time, they'd put up some money to finance a separate, pure R&D company, which the entrepreneur could run.
>
>   To a classic inventor this offer could have been very attractive. But this entrepreneur was truly interested in the business side and found the proposition unattractive. In fact, he perceived the offer as almost offensive, thinking he was being told, "There, there, we'll buy you a nice lab to play in." Negotiations nearly broke down over this misunderstanding.

    An impasse of this sort can usually be avoided if you interrogate the other party carefully. As you work on the negotiation, don't be too prompt to assume that a stubborn indifference to your concessions is a negotiating ploy. Ask yourself if you're making concessions in the wrong area.

2. A related problem can arise when *one of the parties has failed to think out his own position.* Unfortunately, people are not always honest with themselves. You may be negotiating with someone who was attracted to the deal but doesn't really want to do it.

When you are negotiating with someone who doesn't really know his own mind, it's very difficult to get to yes. Here's where it pays to have the most complete possible knowledge of the other party, as well as a shrewd understanding of practical psychology.

3. A third problem is very simple and traditional: *Someone has gotten too greedy.* Usually this turns out, in a sense, to be a variant of the second problem. One party, without admitting it to himself, has a need to "win" that is overriding his practical need to do the deal.

One way to deal with this problem is hardball, tit-for-tat negotiation. In the end, the other party may, if pushed hard enough, subordinate the combative instinct to practical considerations. Another approach is judolike: Make an all-out, last-ditch stand on some issue you don't greatly care about, and let yourself be "beaten." What appears as excessive "greed" often has no real substance behind it; "winning" is the real issue for this person. The best way to deal with these cases is to start pleading, "Please don't throw me in that brier patch."

All these problems are "inside" problems in that they are problems within or between the actual negotiating parties.

4. A fourth type of problem occurs when *"outsiders" negatively affect the negotiating process.* In every major transaction, there are other people and organizations involved besides the principals. There are lawyers and accountants and consultants and hangers-on and relatives—all sorts of people who have their fingers in the deal for one reason or another and who may muck it up intentionally or unintentionally.

When venture capitalists make a major investment, they often like to see the company take on a Big Eight accounting firm. If the company has been using a smaller firm, their accountants, knowing that they're about to be displaced, may feel disinclined to put themselves out to provide extra financial statements or other assistance.

The "outside" problem, like the "inside" problem, is best dealt with preemptively. Unfortunately, when we plan for negotiations, we tend to focus exclusively on the investors, neglecting to consider the other people involved. If you think about this early and make an effort to identify peripheral issues that may come up, you can usually anticipate these bombshells and defuse them.

Greasing the Gears

"Outsiders" aren't always problems, of course. In fact, they can be a crucial part of the solution.

Once again we emphasize that *communication* is the key to successful negotiation. Any mechanism that will assist the parties in learning more about one another can help resolve conflicts and build a relationship. Someone who is disinterested—and, often, even someone who is not disinterested—can facilitate the negotiation by acting as a mediator.

Ideally, people would negotiate with perfect efficiency. The parties would simply tell each other what they needed to know to solve the problems raised by the deal. Real people don't communicate so well. They may fail to get across important information for any or all of a number of reasons:

- They may not themselves realize what they want or need.
- They may be ashamed or embarrassed to admit their objectives.
- They may have conflicts with other members of their own team.
- They may not recognize or understand the need for the information.
- They may not be able to express a need or demand for fear of losing face if it is refused.

A skilled mediator can act as an indirect conduit of information to prevent negotiations from stalling. You want someone who is experienced; who is good with people; who knows members of both sides; and who can be trusted. Trust is important; sometimes a mediator must solve a problem using confidential information from both sides.

A truly impartial mediator, who can meet these strict specifications, is not easy to find. Fortunately, true impartiality is not so important as all that. The primary need is for both sides to have confidence in the integrity of the mediator.

> How was Anne to set all these matters to rights? She could do little more than listen patiently, soften every grievance, and excuse each to the other; give them all hints of the forbearance necessary between such near neighbours, and make those hints broadest which were meant for her sister's benefit.
>
> —Jane Austen,
> *Persuasion*

Some Negotiating Tactics

All sorts of tactics may be used against you as you negotiate. We can't possibly describe every possible ploy, but let's discuss some of the more important ones.

• *Mutt-and-Jeff.* Also known as the "Good Cop, Bad Cop" routine, this involves pairing two members of the team to whipsaw you. A junior partner may be aggressive, even nasty, bringing out all the weak points of your proposal and putting you on the defensive. Then the senior partner steps in, tactfully setting aside your embarrassing problems, working to make you comfortable, perhaps even reprimanding his overly pugnacious associate. Naturally you feel like making things easy for this nice person.

• *The Gambit.* In chess, a gambit is the sacrifice of a small unit, usually a pawn, to gain the initiative. In negotiations, as in chess and many other games, a concession, even a small one, will almost always gain the initiative. Shrewd negotiators give up small points to give them momentum just before taking up more important subjects.

• *The Columbo Comeback.* After you think you have the key point settled, the other party suddenly says, "Oh, one more thing. . . ." This is why you want the agenda settled up front— and closed.

• *The Plain Old Ordinary Stall.* Chances are that you and the investor regard time from somewhat different perspectives. You may be gnashing your teeth over every delay, wondering whether your market window will close, whether the competition will catch up with your technology, whether you'll be able to make payroll Friday. . . . Meanwhile, the investor can afford to sit and wait. Oh, so very sympathetic, sorry about the delay, but "due diligence can take a lot of time, you know." There may be a gentle hint that action might be accelerated if you became more reasonable about the valuation of your company and other issues.

A good rule of thumb is never to negotiate with an investor while you have negative cash flow. Easier said than done, unfortunately! But at least you can try to get more than one investor lined up.

Some Negotiating Techniques

Here are a few techniques you may find helpful in negotiating your deal.

• *Take notes.* Every negotiating session should be preserved for posterity in a set of notes, as detailed as possible. Take notes on the spot during the session; don't wait until it's over and then try to reconstruct it from memory. Preserve in writing not just the final conclusions but all the give and take that led to them. And remember to keep notes of telephone talks too.

A record of this sort can be invaluable. That casual statement that one of the venture capitalists let fall may have crucial importance later in the negotiations. It pays to sit down and analyze the course of the talks just for the insight it can give you into the other side's thinking and behavior. And, finally, a good record of the proceedings can prevent those disastrous arguments that go: "But you said . . . ." "No, I didn't." "Yes, you did!"

• *Write up the results yourself.* Negotiations are almost entirely verbal, but what is agreed at them sooner or later finds its way onto paper. Diplomats long ago found out that if you let the other side write up the summary of what was agreed, you'll discover that you agreed to all sorts of things that you can't seem to recall. How strange! Much better to draft the agreement yourself.

• *Apply children's division.* Readers who have kids probably already know this one. But for those who don't, here's a good way to settle difficult splits. If a piece of cake must be divided, let one child cut it; the other then gets to choose which piece she wants. Leaves no room for argument. Variations on this method are useful in business negotiations.

> A company was set up by two partners. Foreseeing that someday one of them would probably want to leave the firm, they wrote a buy-back agreement. The problem was the price to be put on the stock. Who knew what it would be worth in a few years? So their agreement specified children's division: In the event of a split, one partner would set a value on the company's stock. The other would have the option to buy at that price or to require the first partner to sell at the same price. This method isn't always appropriate. In this case, the two partners had comparable personal financial resources. But if one is rich and the other poor, children's division becomes less practical.

• *Account for unaccountable numbers.* Negotiating positions based on "I want this because I want it" tend to produce deadlocks. Here's a very good question you can use to break through an impasse created by an unreasonable demand from the other side: "How did you arrive at that figure?" You may or may not agree with the way it was arrived at, but at least it elevates the argument to a new level where you can try to apply some sort of objective standard.

Of course this question may be used by investors too! Many entrepreneurs put arbitrary valuations on their ventures, picking a number that will allow them to get the investment they need without giving up "too much" stock. If a venture capitalist asks you, "How did you arrive at that figure?"—do you have a defensible answer?

• *Respond to an off-the-wall demand with silence.* When the other party comes out with a totally unreasonable requirement, you may feel like screaming. It can be more effective to say nothing. Just sit there. As the pause lengthens, they'll feel the pressure to say something. You'd be surprised at how often they'll say, "No? Well, would you accept . . .?"

The Settlement Phase

It is at the settlement phase of the negotiation that you and the investor finally *establish* your relationship. This is the decision point at which you have been aiming throughout the entire financing process. Like any important relationship, whether employer-employee, officer-military unit, or husband-wife, it has a definite beginning that is likely to be marked by some semblance of ceremony. The parties must make a *decision* to proceed, and take some overt action to implement that decision.

Persuading the investor to a settlement involves three factors:

1. *Motivation.* The investor must want to do the deal and must see a strong positive advantage in it. In addition to the intrinsic merits, you may gain a bonus in motivation if there has been a long, difficult financing and negotiation process. The investor has already made a big invest-

ment—of time and effort—and will naturally be reluctant to write it off.

2. *Confidence.* By this we mean that the investor will be reluctant to finally commit until convinced that he knows what makes you tick. As with any important relationship, each party wants to know that the other can be relied on.

3. *Respect.* All too many people enter negotiations with the idea that the objective is to make the other party fear you—or love you. Neither emotion will provide a foundation for a sound relationship. Your objective is to be respected.

These are the factors to keep in mind at the late stages of the negotiations. When it starts looking questionable whether the deal will jell or not, very likely the investor has a nagging doubt about one or another of these three areas.

Doing the Term Sheet

When you've settled the issues, the deal will be summarized in a "term sheet." This is an abbreviated summary of the final contract. (Appendix II contains an annotated sample.)

Most venture capital firms (and other professional investors) have a "template" for their deals. The numbers are plugged in, and some of the details are twiddled a bit, but the term sheets will have much the same structure from deal to deal for a given firm.

As we previously mentioned, though the term sheet is not, theoretically, "final," the reality is that *when you sign the term sheet the deal will be done on those terms.* You cannot make any significant changes later, so be sure there's nothing in it that you can't stand. Also, don't omit any major issues.

The deal agreement itself will be a *very* substantial legal document. For a typical venture capital deal, the final agreement, with its "exhibits" and other supporting documents, will run to something like a thousand pages and be bound into a huge book. Complex deals can run to several volumes.

The Follow-Up

You aren't finished with the financing process when the check is signed or even when it's deposited. After going to all this work to build a relationship with the investor, you now must work to *maintain* the relationship.

An unhappy investor is a tremendous negative for a business. Your chances of getting additional money in the future from the same source are of course ruined. What's more, word will get around, and financing from other sources will be much less available. An investor who wants to make trouble can exercise various legal rights in a way that will inconvenience you severely. Some members of your management team may be persuaded to side with the dissident financier, either openly or underground, and thus unleash a destructive civil war within the company. Even if you can handle all the practical threats presented, the battle will distract you from crucial management duties.

You need to worry about investor relationships from a very early stage. Investors, like anyone making a big purchase, are subject to buyer remorse.

> There is a story about the legendary General Doriot, the dean of American venture capital. It seems that after his firm, American Research and Development, put $70,000 into a 1958 startup that planned to make transistorized computers, Doriot on reflection was appalled by his recklessness and wished he could stop the check. As it happens, the startup was Digital Equipment Corporation, so it was fortunate that he could not.

It's inadvisable to ease off, even momentarily, after the financing is completed. You should already be thinking not only about how to spend the money but about how to keep the investors happy in the days and weeks and years to come.

Regardless of the investor type, the primary principle of investor relations is *no surprises*. Keep your investors informed of your progress on a regular schedule, and be frank with them. If you have a bad quarter, or even a bad year, few investors will jump on you. But when you have a bad quarter after telling them that things were going great, that's when they freak out like the Six Bunnie-Wunnies.

It is bad when investors get the impression that you are incompetent as a manager of the business they have financed. It is worse when they begin to feel that you are concealing things from them and they are left in the dark as to what's happening to the business. It is worst of all when they decide that you are intentionally deceiving them.

There's a great deal to be said for the idea that honesty is the best policy. If things go wrong, you can at least minimize damage with your investors by admitting it promptly and frankly. You'll get credit for your honesty. It also helps to take credit yourself, as CEO, for all failures. If one of your subordinates clearly bobbled it, that's *your* fault: You hired him. If customers display a perverse and irrational dislike for your water-soluble umbrellas, don't blame them, no matter how much they deserve your scorn. It's better to admit a mistake, because it encourages investors to believe that, knowing your error, you won't do it again.

In short, maintaining a relationship with the investor, like building it in the first place, is primarily a matter of *communication*. To the extent you allow your fear of criticism or hatred of interference to inhibit your frankness with the investor, you are likely to find yourself with problems. Investors will put up with a great deal—a great deal more than they should, in fact— from an entrepreneur who is honest with them.

Da Capo

Do you expect to go out of business? No? Then chances are you are going to need money again in the future. As your business grows and prospers, you'll need money for expansion. Or bad times will come and you'll need a bit extra to pull through. Or the market will change—markets do, nowadays more rapidly than ever—and you'll have to raise funds to change focus and take advantage of new opportunities.

So you should start planning now. It's not too early to start thinking about the next round of financing. The first step is to do your homework. . . .

Bibliography

Coffin, Royce A. *The Negotiator: A Manual for Winners*. New York: AMACOM, 1973.

Fisher, R. *Getting to Yes: Negotiating Agreement Without Giving In*. Boston: Houghton-Mifflin, 1981. An excellent guide to the negotiating process in general, full of useful advice and quite readable.

Hawver, D. A. "Plan Before Negotiating and Increase Your Power of Persuasion." *Management Review*, No. 73 (February 1984), p. 46.

Hoffman, H. M., and J. Blakey. "You Can Negotiate with Venture Capitalists." *Harvard Business Review*, No. 65 (March–April 1987), p. 16. This article provides a good listing of the issues involved in negotiating for venture capital and what you should try to obtain.

Jandt, Fred E., and Paul Gillette. *Win-Win Negotiating: Turning Conflict into Agreement*. New York: Wiley, 1985.

Kennedy, G. *Everything Is Negotiable: How to Get a Better Deal*. Englewood Cliffs, N.J.: Prentice-Hall, 1983. Another good text on negotiation. Kennedy tends more to the "hard" school of negotiation, in contrast to Fisher, who's more on the "soft" side. It's worth reading both.

Main, J. "How to Be a Better Negotiator." *Fortune*, No. 108 (September 19, 1983), p. 141.

Miles, Raymond C. *Basic Business Appraisal*. New York: Wiley-Interscience, 1984. Here's another textbook on business appraisal you may find useful.

Pratt, Shannon. *Valuing a Business: The Analysis and Appraisal of Closely Held Companies*. New York: Dow Jones-Irwin, 1981. Any ammunition you can get will help when you're arguing valuation with investors. If you're prepared to wade through some heavy financial analysis, this book can prove very useful.

Tyebjee, T. T., and A. V. Bruno. "Negotiating Venture Capital Financing." *California Management Review,* No. 29 (Fall 1986), p. 45. Here is a more analytical essay, discussing the overall negotiation process with particular attention to valuation of the venture. The article seems to be aimed primarily at high-tech entrepreneurs, but most of the material is applicable to other types of companies as well.

White, R. M. *The Entrepreneur's Manual.* New York: Chilton, 1977. Pages 113–126 discuss systems for vesting founder stock, including the author's complex and sophisticated milestone-based system.

Appendix I

About the Enterprise Forum

The CalTech/MIT Enterprise Forum operates on the CalTech campus in Pasadena, California. Organized by a group of entrepreneurs, investors, and other experts, the Forum has provided practical management counsel for dozens of small companies and startups. Our experience with this program and the people involved in it contributed greatly to this book.

The CalTech/MIT Enterprise Forum is a joint venture of the two schools, affiliated to a nationwide network. Since 1978, the Forum has served new and emerging companies with expert advice and access to an ever-expanding network of entrepreneurs, financiers, and business services. From its beginnings with a small group in Cambridge, the Forum has expanded to serve thirteen cities.

The Forum conducts case presentations of small ventures. The entrepreneur makes a formal presentation before a panel of experts, who also read the business plan. Their critique and suggestions are followed by feedback from the audience (commonly, from 100 to 300 people are present). The session lasts for one or two hours.

Each local unit operates independently, led by an Executive Committee. It selects the companies that make presentations. The presenter is assisted in preparing the plan and the presentation. The Executive Committee also selects the experts for the panels, which commonly include successful entrepreneurs, venture capitalists, prospective customers, and specialists in marketing and other areas.

Some local units concentrate primarily on technology companies. Others serve a broader clientele. In most cities, both startups and established (though young) companies are eligible as presenters, although some local units run them in separate programs.

Appendix II

Term Sheet for a Venture Capital Deal

When an initial agreement on a financing is reached, a "term sheet" is written up, which summarizes the basic outline of the deal. This document is not final; it is an "agreement to agree." However, once a term sheet has been agreed on, the investors are unlikely to accept any significant changes in the terms later. The final deal document will be much longer than the term sheet; commonly it is as thick as a large reference book. However, it will consist mostly of boiler plate; the real meat of the deal is settled on the term sheet. Entrepreneurs should therefore examine the term sheet carefully before they sign off on it. They should also get their attorney's opinion at this stage.

Following is an actual term sheet for a venture capital deal (with the names changed), which should give you an idea of what to expect. We've added some explanatory and advisory comments.

XYZ SYSTEMS INCORPORATED
SERIES A CONVERTIBLE PREFERRED STOCK
OFFERING

OFFERING:

80,906 shares at $6.18 aggregating $500,000 to ABC Ventures and Associates (the "Purchasers"). An additional

40,453 shares may be offered at this price to designees of
the Company subject to Purchasers' approval, which will
not unreasonably be withheld.

*[ABC Ventures is the lead investor. As can be seen, in
this case convertible preferred stock is being used. Room is
being left to raise another $250,000 if the company can
round up some more venture capitalists.]*

RIGHTS, PREFERENCES, PRIVILEGES, AND RESTRICTIONS:

Dividends: Quarterly dividends of $.1236 per share,
except that the first year's dividends may be deferred for
payment in three equal installments at the end of the
second, third, and fourth year from closing.

Liquidation Preference: In the event of any liquidation
or winding up, the Series A will receive as a preference to
the Common an amount equal to the sum of: (i) $6.18 per
share of Series A plus (ii) all accrued but unpaid dividends
on such shares (the "Preferential Amount"). After the payment of the Preferential Amount to the Series A, the Common shall be entitled to receive an amount equal to the
book value per share of the Common Stock on an as-
converted basis (but not to exceed $6.18 per share). After
the payment of the aforesaid amounts, the remaining assets
or property distributed upon such liquidation shall be divided pro rata among the Common and Series A on an as-
converted basis.

Merger, Consolidation: In the event of a merger, corporate reorganization, sale, or any transaction in which all
or substantially all of the assets of the Company are sold
(other than a merger into a wholly owned subsidiary), the
Series A shall be entitled to receive in cash or securities the
amount they would have received on a liquidation.

*[In other words, if the company goes bust the investors
are at the head of the line to get anything that can be
salvaged.]*

Conversion: The holders of Series A shall have the right to convert at any time into shares of Common. The initial conversion rate shall be 1:1 (conversion price of $6.18), subject to adjustment in accordance with the antidilution provisions.

Automatic Conversion: The Series A shall be automatically converted into Common, at the then applicable conversion rate, upon the closing of a firm underwritten primary public offering of shares of Common of the Company at a per share price not less than $8 per share and for a total offering of not less than $5,000,000 (after deduction of underwriter commissions and expenses). If the price is less than $12.36, however, the conversion will be effective only if the offering is made after a stock split for which the pre-split price is at least $12.36.

[Assuming all goes well and the company goes public (subject to certain minimum standards), the venture capital investors must convert their stock to common, which can be sold after the initial public offering. The underwriters will want to get rid of the preferred, so the public investors who buy the common won't feel like second-class citizens.]

Antidilution Provisions: Full antidilution protection shall be provided for stock splits, stock dividends, etc. In the case of stock offerings made at less than the conversion price, except under the Employee Stock Option Plan, additional shares will be issued to the Purchaser so that: (i) if made within 24 months of closing, effective price to the Purchasers will be equal to the subsequent offering price or (ii) if thereafter, effective price to the Purchasers will be the weighted average purchase price of the Series A shares plus the subsequent shares.

[Here we have a compromise provision on what happens if the valuation of the company goes down. If they have to finance again within two years, the investors get full ratchet; after that, they get partial ratchet.]

Redemption: After the fourth anniversary of the closing date, Purchasers may require the Company to repurchase all or any portion of the shares at an amount per share equal to the Preferential Amount, plus interest at the rate of 8 percent per year.

> [*Now we see that the preferred is actually a two-way convertible. If the company takes off, the preferred gets converted to common. If it becomes one of the walking dead, the above clause effectively turns the preferred stock into a loan payable on demand after four years. They get you coming and going.*]

Voting Rights: Each share of Series A will carry a number of votes equal to the number of shares of Common Stock then issuable upon its conversion. The Series A will vote together with Common and not as a separate class except as specifically provided herein or as otherwise required by law.

Board Representation: As long as more than 50 percent of the shares of the Series A is outstanding, its holders shall have the right to nominate and elect one director.

Protective Provisions: Consent of the holders of at least 66 percent of the Series A shall be required for any action which (i) alters or changes the rights, preferences, or privileges of the Series A, (ii) increases or decreases the authorized number of shares of Series A, (iii) creates (by reclassification or otherwise) any new class or series of shares having rights, preferences, or privileges senior to or on a parity with the Series A, (iv) results in the redemption of any share of Common (other than pursuant to employee agreements), (v) results in any merger, other corporate reorganization, sale of control, or any transaction in which all or substantially all of the assets of the Company are sold, or (vi) amends or waives any provisions of the Articles relative to the Series A.

> [*This is a later-round financing, and a rather small one, so the investors don't get control. However, they get a seat on the board, protection against diddling with their stock, and a veto on really major decisions like mergers.*]

INFORMATION RIGHTS:

So long as the Purchasers continue to hold shares of Series A or Common issued upon conversion of the Series A, the Company shall deliver to the Purchaser all information that is prepared for the Company's Board of Directors, as well as audited annual and un-audited quarterly financial statements, and the Purchasers shall be entitled to the same inspection and visitation rights as the directors. Other than with respect to the delivery of audited annual and un-audited quarterly financial statements and rights generally provided to shareholders by law, these provisions shall terminate upon an underwritten public offering as described under Automatic Conversion.

REGISTRATION RIGHTS:

Demand Registrations: Twice on Form S-1 upon request of holders of 20 percent or more of the Series A, provided no demand can be made until after the Company's initial public offering. Unlimited demand registrations on Forms S-2 or S-3.

Piggyback Registration: Unlimited with respect to all registrations of the Company or on any demand registrations of any other investors, subject to the right, however, of the Company on request of its underwriters to reduce the number of shares proposed to be registered pro rata in view of market conditions. No shareholder of the company shall be granted piggyback registration rights relative to the demand and piggyback rights contained herein which would reduce the number of shares includable by the holders of the registrable securities in such registration without the consent of 70 percent of the registrable securities.

Expenses: The Company shall bear the registration expenses (exclusive of underwriting discounts and commissions) of all such demand and piggyback registrations (excluding the expense of any special counsel to the Purchaser).

Transfer of Rights: The registration rights may be

transferred provided the Company is given written notice thereof.

Standoff Provision: No Purchaser holding more than one percent of the Company's shares will sell shares within 120 days of the effective date of the Company's initial public offering if all officers, directors, and other one percent shareholders are similarly bound.

.Other Provisions: Other provisions shall be contained in the Purchase Agreement with respect to registration rights as are reasonable, including cross-indemnification, the period of time in which the Registration Statement shall be kept effective, and underwriting arrangements.

[*Stripped of all the jargon: When and if the company goes public, the investors want their stock to be registered so it can be freely sold and they can liquidate their investment. Various cheapos that can be used to screw minority stockholders are explicitly ruled out.*]

RIGHTS OF REFUSAL:

Each Purchaser shall have a right of first refusal to purchase its pro rata share of offerings of new securities and a pro rata right of second refusal (after the Company) on the purchase of management shares. These rights may be transferred, provided the Company is given written notice thereof.

[*If the company issues more stock, or if the founder sells his, the investors get first crack at it before it can be offered to new investors. Fair enough, but the purchase agreement should have a clause setting a time limit for the investors to make up their minds whether or not they'll buy.*]

BOARD OF DIRECTORS:

The Bylaws shall provide for five directors. After the closing of this financing, the Board shall be comprised of two nominees of management, one nominee of the Purchasers, and two additional seats to be filled as directed by the resultant Board of three.

PURCHASE AGREEMENT:

The investment shall be made pursuant to a Stock Purchase Agreement reasonably acceptable to the Company and the Purchasers, which Agreement shall contain, among other things, appropriate representations and warranties of the Company, and covenants of the Company reflecting the provisions set forth herein. The Stock Purchase Agreement shall require as a condition of closing that the Purchaser receive an appropriate opinion from K, L, & M, counsel to the Company. The Stock Purchase Agreement shall further provide that it may only be amended and any waivers thereunder shall only be made with the approval of the holders of 50 percent of the Series A (or Common issued upon conversion thereof or combination of such Common and Series A but excluding shares previously sold to the public).

EMPLOYEE STOCK:

Employee Pool: There are currently 1,052,514 employee shares outstanding. Under the Company's Stock Option Plan, options to purchase 19,500 shares have been granted, and options to purchase an additional 91,000 shares remain available for future grants.

Stock Vesting: All stock for employees will be subject to vesting as follows: (i) Original founder Mr. P—owns 985,000 shares which, as of closing, will be 100 percent vested; (ii) current employees—option holdings and vesting provisions to be reviewed for possible revisions satisfactory to the Purchasers; (iii) new management and employee hires—five-year vesting; (iv) a repurchase option shall provide that upon termination of employment of the shareholder, with or without cause, the Company retains the option to repurchase at cost any unvested shares held by such shareholder.

*[The founder gets immediate vesting—nice work if you
can get it! Usually you can't. Pity the poor "current employees" who are subject to retroactive "revisions" of their
stockholdings.]*

PUT OPTION:

If (i) the Company has not closed an underwritten
public offering as described under Automatic Conversion
prior to January 1, 1994, and (ii) the Company's stockholders' equity as shown on its consolidated financial statements for fiscal year ending in 1993, or any subsequent
fiscal year, exceeds twice the stockholders' equity shown
on its consolidated financial statements for the fiscal year
ending March 31, 1989, each Purchaser shall have the
option to sell the Company all or any portion of its shares
at twice the original purchase price. Payment may be 25
percent cash plus a three-year note for the balance payable
in annual installments of 25 percent plus accrued interest
at the rate of 8 percent. Purchase of shares is subject to the
restrictions of Chapter 5 of the California General Corporation Law.

*[What if the company is successful but management
decides it doesn't want to go public? The venture capitalists
would be locked in and unable to liquidate their investment.
This clause protects them by allowing them to force the
company to buy them out at a price comparable to what
they'd get in the IPO.]*

DIRECTOR INDEMNIFICATION:

The Articles and Bylaws will be amended, and an in-
demnification agreement will be provided, to accord the
Purchasers' director-nominee protection from personal liability to the full extent authorized by the California Corporations Code.

SHAREHOLDER AGREEMENT:

Mr. P will enter into an agreement with the Purchasers
whereby: (i) <u>Co-Sale</u>. Mr. P shall not sell his shares to a

third party without arranging for the third party to offer to purchase each of the Purchasers' shares pro rata on the same terms; (ii) Put Option. To the extent that the Company is not able to purchase shares pursuant to the put option above specified, Mr. P shall purchase such shares on the same terms.

> [*The investors have to protect themselves not only from the company (the corporation), but from the founder.*]

OTHER MATTERS:

Finders: The Company and the Purchasers shall each indemnify the other for any finder's fees for which either is responsible.

Legal Fees and Expenses: The Company shall reimburse the Purchasers for their legal fees and expenses in an amount not exceeding $17,500.

> [*This is the only truly substantive clause in the term sheet. The Company is committed to pay the venture capitalists $17,500 for their trouble.*]

Appendix III

Entrepreneur's Employment Contract for a Venture Capital Deal

The employment contract for the entrepreneur is a crucial document. Consider it carefully and get advice from an attorney—*your* attorney.

You should be thinking about its terms at an early stage in the deal negotiations. If you leave it to the end and then find that unfavorable terms are proposed, your position can be awkward. If, at this late stage, you balk at the employment agreement, the whole deal may unravel; the investors can act indignant, and your co-founders may strangle you.

Here is an actual employment agreement for an entrepreneur in a venture capital deal (names and certain other details have been omitted to protect the guilty). We've annotated the text with some explanatory and advisory comments. This is a fairly typical contract, but keep in mind that the terms negotiated generally depend on the bargaining powers of the parties; your mileage may differ.

EMPLOYMENT AGREEMENT

THIS EMPLOYMENT AGREEMENT (the "Agreement") is made and entered into as of the ___ day of _____ ,19___ by

257

and between _____, a California corporation (the "Company"), and _____
("Employee").

1. EMPLOYMENT AND DUTIES

1.1 <u>Primary Position</u>. Employee is initially employed
to perform services for the Company in the capacity of
_____ (the "Executive Position") pur-
suant to which Employee will have such duties and responsibilities as are customary for the position and as may be
specified from time to time by the Board of Directors (the
"Board"). While employed in the capacity of Executive Position, Employee shall devote his full inventive faculties related to the business of the Company and his full business
time and energy to the interests and affairs of the Company.
Employee agrees to perform, to Company satisfaction, all
tasks and services Company may direct or request.

*[CEO and sometimes other "executive positions"
make you an officer of the corporation. Officers often have
specific duties and responsibilities, defined in the corporate
bylaws, so look into this question.*

*Note that the entrepreneur has to put full-time effort
into the venture. Also, any inventions relevant to the company's business go to the company; bright ideas in other
areas may be reserved by the entrepreneur. However, he
can't start another firm to develop a separate invention.]*

1.2 <u>Advisor Capacity</u>. Employee's employment capacity may, pursuant to Section 4 below, be changed to that of
Advisor, pursuant to which he will have such duties and
perform such services as may be specified from time to
time by the Board. While employed in the capacity of Advisor, Employee shall not be required to devote his full business time to his duties but shall devote up to twelve hours
per month as may be directed or requested by the Board.

*[If things don't work out, the entrepreneur can be
retained on a consulting basis.]*

2. TERM

2.1 <u>One-Year Term</u>. This Agreement shall expire one year from the date hereof, or one year from the anniversary date hereof should an extension be effected pursuant to Section 2.2 below, or one year from the date of written notice to Employee of a change in employment status to that of Advisor pursuant to Sections 1.2 and 4 of this Agreement.

[Note that if the entrepreneur is dropped to advisor status, it lasts for a maximum of one year.]

2.2 <u>Company's Option to Extend</u>. The Company shall have the option to extend the term of this Agreement for one year from the expiration date of the initial one-year term or for one year from the expiration date of an extension of the initial term. Not less than 60 days prior to the expiration date of this Agreement, the Company shall give written notice to the Employee stating whether or not Company will exercise its option to extend the term of this Agreement. If the Company fails to give written notice pursuant to this Section 2.2, the Company shall be deemed to have exercised its option, and the term of this Agreement will be extended for one year from the anniversary date hereof. In no event shall the term of this Agreement be extended more than four times.

3. COMPENSATION AND BENEFITS

3.1 <u>Compensation</u>. While employed in the capacity of the Executive Position, Employee shall initially be compensated at the annual rate of $_____, which shall be payable in equal monthly or more frequent installments as is the policy of the Company. If the term of this Agreement is extended pursuant to Section 2.2 above, Employee's compensation shall be reviewed in connection with such extension. While employed in the capacity of Advisor, Employee shall be compensated at the annual rate of $6,000, or at such higher rate as the Board may determine in its sole and absolute discretion (the "Advisor Rate"), which shall be payable as set forth above, plus reasonable out-of-pocket expenses.

> *[If the entrepreneur gets dropped to advisor, his consulting fees are set at $42 per hour, which is pretty miserable.*
>
> *There's no mention of what happens with regard to stock vesting if the entrepreneur moves to advisor status. Presumably the main deal agreement takes care of this issue. However, it is very likely that once the employee becomes an advisor, there will be no further vesting of his shares.]*

3.2 Benefits. While employed in the capacity of the Executive Position, Employee may participate in such stock option and other compensation plans and insurance and other benefit plans (for which he is eligible) which are now in effect or may in the future be established. Should Employee's employment capacity be changed to Advisor, he shall no longer have the right to receive any of the benefits described in the preceding sentence, and such change of employment capacity shall for all purposes related to such compensation and benefit plans be treated as if Employee had been terminated.

> *[There are a couple of zingers here. Since (as we'll see in Section 4) the Company can drop this poor chap to advisor status* without notice, *he'll have to be fast on his feet if he wants to maintain health insurance coverage. An instantaneous cutoff of benefits could cause him some problems.*
>
> *The other point to question involves bonuses. If a bonus is promised for meeting some specific goal (such as completing development of an invention or achieving some level of sales), the company ought not to be allowed to escape paying it by suddenly dropping the employee to advisor status.]*

4. CHANGE IN EMPLOYMENT CAPACITY

4.1 Company's Option to Change. The Company shall have the right to change the employment capacity of Employee from Executive Position to Advisor without notice at any time with or without cause, provided, however, that if the Company changes the employment capacity of Employee without cause, the Company shall pay Employee one month's compensation based on Employee's compensation while employed in the capacity of Executive Position. As used in this Agreement, "cause" shall mean: (i) the conviction of Employee of any felony; (ii) theft; (iii) embezzlement; (iv) a material breach of this Agreement; (v) habitual neglect of Employee's employment duties; (vi) failure to follow the directions of the Board; (vii) failure or demonstrated inability to perform his employment duties in accordance with the standards expected from the general population of Employee's professional or technical peers; or (viii) voluntary resignation from Employee's employment in the capacity of Executive Position. From the effective date of a change in employment capacity, Employee shall be compensated at the Advisor Rate.

> [*Here (and in the corresponding clause in Section 8) we have the very heart of the agreement. What protection does the entrepreneur have against getting dumped? In this contract, as is commonly the case in early-stage venture capital deals, essentially none. The founder can be ejected "with or without cause" at any time. He isn't even guaranteed the courtesy of getting notice; he can come in one morning and find a new lock on his office and his belongings in a cardboard box.*
>
> *Obviously, you would like to negotiate an employment agreement that specifies that you can be fired or downgraded only for cause. Unfortunately, that tends to fall into the "nice work if you can get it" category. And—be reasonable now!—you as a boss want your subordinates to be employed "at will," so you're not in a very good position to complain.*
>
> *Still, you might want to fight for some guarantee of notice at least—for instance, a clause stating you may not be fired without a month's notice except for cause. And, as noted above, you've some reason to challenge a contract*

that permits the company to filch your hard-earned bonus or your almost-vested stock by a carefully timed firing. However, as a practical matter your best protection against being ripped off is to make yourself indispensable.]

5. EMPLOYEE'S REPRESENTATIONS AND WARRANTIES

5.1 <u>Qualifications</u>. Employee represents that he is fully qualified, without the benefit of any further training or experience, to perform the duties of the Executive Position.

5.2 <u>Notification of Other Post-Employment Obligations</u>. Employee represents and warrants that, except as expressly stated in writing to the Company prior to entering into this Agreement, Employee is subject to no restraints of any kind which would have any effect on Employee's employment with the Company and which result from any prior business relationship of Employee with any other person or entity. Such restraints include, but are not limited to, confidentiality obligations and covenants not to compete. In addition to other remedies which the Company might have for the breach of this Agreement, Employee agrees to indemnify and hold the Company harmless from any breach of this Section 5.2. A material breach of, or a material misstatement in, these representations and warranties shall be deemed a material breach of this Agreement and cause for change in employment capacity under Section 4 hereof or termination under Section 8 hereof.

[Techies are commonly prone to be a little careless about intellectual property rights. If you had a bright idea one day while you were working at Mobytronic Industries and did a few tests in the lab there to see if it would work, Mobytronic almost certainly owns the rights. It may even own the rights (depending on your employment contract with them) to ideas you had at home and never told them about. When you start (or join) a venture, the investors want to be sure that the inventions or ideas you bring along aren't owned by anyone else. Hence Section 5.2.

That "hold harmless" language is very rough stuff, so

be damned sure you have clear title to any inventions you're contributing to the venture and that you're squeaky clean on confidentiality agreements and such.]

6.   EMPLOYEE LOYALTY DURING TERM

6.1   <u>Employee's Efforts</u>. During the term of this Agreement, Employee shall devote his full energies, interests, abilities, and productive time to the performance of this Agreement, and shall not, without the Company's prior written consent, render to others services of any kind for compensation, or engage in any other business activity that would materially interfere with the performance of Employee's duties under this Agreement.

[In short, the Company wants his full attention. Fair enough, but the language is a bit ambiguous.

As this section is written, it appears to prohibit him from doing anything to earn money outside his employment. Suppose, for instance, that he gets an opportunity to write a magazine article that will help to promote the Company's products. If he gets paid for the article, it seems that he's violated this employment agreement. Perhaps a comma between "activity" and "that" would be appropriate.

Argue over a comma? This is a matter that could be of some tangible importance. Suppose you and the investors aren't getting along so well and you're beginning to suspect that they may decide at the next Board meeting to dump you in the street—exercising their option to do so without cause or notice. You might just want, in this situation, to get started on a little something else on the side that could protect you from financial disaster.]

6.2   <u>Non-Interference With Company</u>. During the term of this Agreement, Employee shall not: (i) either directly or indirectly, carry on, engage in, or have any interest in any business that competes with the Company, or (ii) without the express written consent of the Company, accept employment with, or in any other manner agree to provide, for compensation, services for any other person or entity that competes, directly or indirectly, with the Company, or (iii) materially disrupt, damage, impair, or interfere with the business of the Company, whether by way of interfering with or soliciting its employees, disrupting its relationships with customers, agents, representatives, or vendors, or otherwise.

> [*No matter how upset he gets with the firm, he's not allowed to sabotage it. But this is a generous noncompete clause. The entrepreneur is completely free as soon as his employment terminates. No attempt is made to restrict his activities after he leaves (although he is bound while serving as an advisor). Court decisions in California (and some other states) have made it very difficult to enforce postemployment noncompete contracts.*]

6.3 Loyalty Under Advisor Status. In the event that Employee's employment capacity is changed to Advisor pursuant to Section 1.2 above, Employee shall not be prohibited from seeking other employment, consistent with the provisions of Section 6.2 above, and shall use Employee's best efforts promptly to obtain such employment. Prior to accepting such employment, Employee shall deliver a notice to the Company setting forth the name of the person or entity for which Employee intends to work and the nature of the services Employee intends to perform. Whether or not Employee seeks or accepts other employment, Employee shall remain obligated as an Advisor under the terms of this Agreement until the Agreement expires or is terminated under Section 8 below.

> [*Now it comes out very clearly that demotion to advisor status is just a face-saving way to get rid of the entrepreneur. He's not only allowed, but required, to seek another job. But he has to give advance notice before accepting another job so that the Company can make sure he will not be with a competitor or otherwise threaten their trade secrets.*]

7. COMPANY'S REMEDIES FOR BREACH

7.1 Company's Right to Sue. Employee acknowledges and agrees: (i) because his employment duties will provide him access to and/or possession of trade secrets and other confidential and proprietary information of the Company and its business and products and/or services and (ii) because of his intimate knowledge of the Company and his particular experience, that his services to the Company, either in the capacity of Executive Position or Advisor, are of a special, unique, unusual, and extraordinary nature and, therefore, any activities or employment on his part which would constitute a breach of Section 6 above will cause irreparable harm to the Company and money damages would be inadequate to compensate the Company completely for its loss resulting from such breach. Employee therefore agrees that the Company, in addition to all other rights, shall have the right to file a lawsuit, in any court of competent jurisdiction, to enjoin Employee from engaging in such activities and to seek any other equitable relief that may be appropriate.

[*Very pretty! This guy, who—unlike the janitor, probably—can be fired without notice or cause, now turns out to be providing services of such a "special, unique, unusual, and extraordinary nature" that the Company needs to be able to nuke him with an injunction if they think he's getting out of line. But the full beauty won't be apparent until we get to Section 9.*]

8.   TERMINATION

8.1   <u>Circumstances for Termination</u>. This Agreement may be terminated: (i) by the written consent of both parties, (ii) by death of Employee, (iii) at the option of the Company, in the event of permanent or temporary disability (whether partial or complete) of Employee, or (iv) at the option of the Company with or without cause, provided, however, that if the Company terminates this Agreement without cause, the Company shall pay Employee one month's compensation based on the Employee's compensation while employed in the capacity of Executive Position.

[*The Company can fire the entrepreneur if he gets a cold, or, as in Section 4, just for the hell of it. He might at least ask for a clause releasing him from his obligations if the company goes bankrupt.]*

9. EMPLOYEE'S REMEDIES FOR BREACH

9.1 <u>Arbitration</u>. Any claim that Employee may have arising out of or relating to this Agreement, or the breach thereof, or Employee's employment by the Company, or the termination of Employee's employment by the Company, shall be settled by binding arbitration in accordance with the Commercial Arbitration Rules of the American Arbitration Association, and judgment upon the award entered by the arbitrator(s) may be entered in any court having jurisdiction thereof. Neither the Company's right to file a lawsuit seeking an injunction nor the Company's right to injunctive relief is subject to arbitration or to the provisions of this Section 9.1.

[Arbitration clauses are great; every contract should have one, in our opinion. But this one seems a bit imbalanced, to say the least. "We can sue you, but you can't sue us." Hang on, it gets better yet.]

9.2 <u>Liquidated Damages</u>. Because Employee's damages resulting from a breach by the Company of this Agreement would be difficult to fix in an actual amount, and because the parties hereto recognize that the business of the Company and the employment of the Employee are inherently risky undertakings and the parties hereto wish to maximize the Company's flexibility and reduce the Company's risks to the maximum extent possible, the liquidated amount of damage presumed to be sustained from any material breach of this Agreement by the Company will be _____ months' compensation based on the Employee's compensation while employed in the capacity of Executive Position, or an amount equal to compensation for the period remaining until expiration of this Agreement, whichever is less. That sum is agreed on as compensation for the injury that may be suffered by Employee and not as a penalty.

[This is a classic. No matter how serious the Company's violation of the contract, the employee can never recover more than a few months salary.

As a general rule, a contract clause beginning with a preamble explaining why it's needed is a tip-off that someone's getting a raw deal. In this case the preamble is needed so that the damage-limitation clause will have a chance of being upheld in court.

Now that poor Mr. Entrepreneur is bound and gagged, there remains only some standard boiler plate to get through.]

10. ASSIGNMENT AND SUCCESSION

10.1   Rights and duties of the parties under this Agreement shall not be assignable by either party except that this Agreement and all the rights hereunder may be assigned by the Company to any corporation or other business entity which succeeds to all or substantially all of the business of the Company through merger, consolidation, corporate reorganization or by acquisition of all or substantially all of the assets of the Company and which assumes the Company's obligations under this Agreement.

[If the company is sold, merged, or whatever, the entrepreneur's new boss inherits all rights.]

11. MISCELLANEOUS

11.1   Amendments or Alterations. This Agreement may be altered or amended only by a written instrument signed by both parties.

11.2   Integration. This Agreement constitutes the complete and exclusive statement of the agreement between the parties and supersedes all prior and concurrent proposals, understandings, and agreements, whether oral or written, and all other communications between the parties, relating to the subject matter of this Agreement. No person has any authority to make any representation or promise on behalf of either party not set forth in the

Agreement, and this Agreement has not been executed in reliance upon any representation or promise except as contained herein.

> *[If the investors made any promises—even in writing— to the entrepreneur beyond what's in the contract, this section makes it clear that they are legally entitled to welsh on them. This is an important point. While you're negotiating, a venture capitalist may say something like "We won't clutter up the contract with it, but I give you my personal assurance that we'll boost your salary once we get to positive cash flow." You'd better have checked out this person, because if the personal assurance is no good, you have no recourse.]*

11.3 Severability. The provisions of this Agreement are severable. The parties to this Agreement expressly agree and contract that it is their intention not to violate any public policy, any statute, any rule or regulation, or the common law. Should any valid federal or state law or formal determination of any administrative agency of competent jurisdiction affect any provision of this Agreement, the provision or provisions so affected shall be automatically conformed to the law and otherwise this Agreement shall continue in full force and effect. Should any one or more provisions be determined to be legally unenforceable, the remaining provisions shall nevertheless be binding and enforceable. To the extent that any one or more provisions may be determined to be legally unenforceable in any state or states, or county or counties, in which the Company transacts its business, such provisions shall not be affected with respect to any other state or county.

11.4 Notices. Any and all notices or other communications by or between the parties required or permitted by this Agreement shall be in writing and may be personally served or sent by United States registered or certified mail with first-class postage prepaid.

As employment contracts go in venture financings, this one is not particularly onerous. Clearly there are a number of points where you should try to get a better deal. But don't be surprised if you have to accept something comparable to what we've shown.

Reading a contract like this might turn you off to venture capital. That's not our intention. Once again we must stress that *your relationship with the investor is crucial.* As long as entrepreneur and investor are working together on the same team, issues can be settled amicably by mutual agreement, and they'll generally be settled on satisfactory terms. You and the venture capitalist can function as equals on a basis of mutual respect. But if the relationship breaks down, your interaction with the investor will default to the legal terms agreed on. You'll each get what you have by contract and nothing more. And look at that contract. You won't be an equal, you'll be a serf.

So the message is, *Know* your investors. Do you like them? Do you trust them? Are you sure they are fair and decent people? They'd better be, or you're in big trouble!

And *don't* rely on your impression that these are nice guys. Investigate them. Look into their pasts. Get the facts. It's a lot of work, of course. Any time you feel your energy flagging, reread this contract and ask yourself whether you feel comfortable yet trusting the investor with that much power over you.

Glossary

Terminology, Buzzwords, and Just Plain Slang You May Encounter in the Money-Raising Process

beta test   Initial customer testing of a new product, especially a high-technology product. In-house testing is called an "alpha test." Then selected customers ("beta-test sites") are given the product so that bugs can be found in actual use.

Big Eight   Traditional term for the largest accounting firms. Currently being reduced by mergers to the Big Five—or maybe fewer.

blind pool   Back when stock companies had just been invented, there was an Olde English offering for "a Company to Carry Out an Undertaking of Great Advantage, but Nobody to Know what It Is." That was the first blind pool. Today, such offerings normally appear in such places as the Denver Stock Exchange. The promoters raise money by a public stock offering, then attempt to find a profitable investment for it, such as merging with an operating company. In essence, a blind pool is the deliberate creation of a public shell (qv).

blue sky laws   Laws regulating the sale of stock or other securities. Each state has different requirements, and there are also federal laws on the subject.

book   Venture capitalist slang for "business plan."

bridge loan   A loan made during the negotiation of a financing to keep the company operating effectively until the permanent funding is secured.

burn rate   Negative cash flow, in dollars per month.

corporate partnering   Umbrella term for close cooperative arrangement between companies, often involving purchase of equity or founding a joint venture.

deal flow   The series of investment opportunities presented to a financier.

dilution   Reduction in the equity of a stockholder that occurs when additional stock is sold at a lower valuation to somebody else.

due diligence   An investor's investigation of a proposed deal and of the principals offering it conducted before the transaction is finalized.

exit strategy   An investor's plan for cashing in an investment if it succeeds or if it fails.

fiduciary responsibility   The responsibility of someone who invests or manages money to the people whose assets he is handling.

finder (or **five-percenter**)   Someone who offers to locate investors in return for a cut of the money invested.

first-round financing   The money needed to actually get a company into business, that is, to start sales. This follows seed funding (qv), which is used to get the company organized and up to the verge of entering the market.

haircut   When investors calculate how much a venture is worth, they take the pro formas in the business plan and lower the sales, profit, and cash flow projections to obtain more realistic numbers. This is known as "giving the projections a haircut" or "haircutting" them.

hockey stick   Financial projections commonly show the company's sales and profits at a moderate level initially, then suddenly making tremendous jumps a couple of years out. This type of graph is called a "hockey stick" in the trade.

initial public offering (IPO)   The first sale of securities (almost always stock) in a corporation under the regulations governing a public company (qv).

leveraged buyout (LBO)   Purchase of a company using a very small amount of equity and a large proportion of debt. Commonly the debt is paid down either by sale of some of the assets of the company or by milking the company's operation to maximize cash flow. LBOs are often conducted by the management of the company.

limited partnership   A partnership in which some of the partners have limited liability in that they are not liable for more than their investment no matter what the losses of the company. These "limited partners" are not allowed to participate in the management of the company and are treated in many ways like corporate stockholders. There must be at least one "general partner" who is responsible for management of the company and whose liability is *not* limited.

line of credit An agreement (usually by a bank) to lend money on request up to a certain limit.

liquidity The ability to turn an asset into cash.

mezzanine financing Generally refers to the final round of nonpublic financing. When a company has been highly successful, a mezzanine financing allows it to expand operations sufficiently to qualify for an IPO (qv).

offering memorandum A description of an offering of securities, which is required to disclose all the material factors a prospective investor would need in order to make a rational decision.

pro formas Short for "pro forma statements," that is, financial statements produced as a matter of form, to show what the performance of a company should be in the future given certain assumptions; also called financial projections.

public company A corporation that is allowed to sell securities to large numbers of people without having to investigate or qualify its investors.

public shell A public corporation that no longer functions as an operating company but still retains legal existence. It may contain cash that was obtained by the sale of assets and not distributed to the stockholders; or it may retain tax-loss carry-forwards that can be used to reduce taxes for another profitable company. A private company can become public by merging with a public shell.

put The right to require somebody to buy a security such as stock at a specified price. A put may be a part of a venture capital deal as a means of guaranteeing that the investors can exit from their investment.

ratchet A reduction in the effective price of a company's stock held by early investors, given them when later investors buy in at a reduced valuation.

reconstruction When investors buy into a privately held company, they need realistic financial data in order to do a valuation. Commonly the owner will have used various legal but nonstandard accounting techniques to reduce reported profits and thus taxes. Also, all sorts of expenses (such as company cars) may have been put in as perks to the owner. It's therefore necessary to "reconstruct" the financial statements of the company to figure out what its performance really is.

Regulation D The basic federal law governing private offerings of securities.

second-round financing In general, the money raised and used for the expansion of a company that has demonstrated a basic viability in the market.

securities Stocks, bonds, promissory notes, and other financial obligations of a company.

security (for loan) Collateral or similar protection for a lender.

seed money The earliest investment in a company, usually before it is even organized as a company; commonly used to investigate the market or develop product technology.

term sheet A summary of the important terms of an investment agreement (usually venture capital).

vesting The release of a company founder's stock over time.

warrant An option to buy stock in a corporation.

Index